Hello! 365 Meat Appetizer Recipes

(Meat Appetizer Recipes - Volume 1)

Best Meat Appetizer Cookbook Ever For Beginners

Mr. Appetizer

Content

CHAPTER 3: JERKY RECIPES.................51

CHAPTER 4: TURKEY RECIPES.............65

CHAPTER 6: CHICKEN RECIPES 138

Introduction

***

Hi all,

Welcome to MrandMsCooking.com—a website created by a community of cooking enthusiasts with the goal of providing books for novice cooks featuring the best recipes, at the most affordable prices, and valuable gifts.

Thank you for choosing "Hello! 365 Meat Appetizer Recipes" as your next stop for your infinite love of appetizers. The 3 parts of a perfect meal is composed of an appetizer, the main dish and lastly, dessert. I always anticipate the first in the list and it is my favorite, the appetizer. It is usually enjoyed for about 10 to 15 minutes in order to stimulate your appetite for the main dish and not to make you feel full. Appetizers are often presented in such a way that it is not boring while waiting for the next part of the meal and often consumed slowly so diners can talk and enjoy each other's company. The quality of an appetizer is very important because it would also affect the quality of the next dishes of the meal.

I have written this series because of my endless passion for appetizers. The books in this series is not only a collection of recipes of appetizers, you can expect to read some of my experiences and precious lessons that I learned along the way. I hope my experiences will also be useful to you while preparing delicious dishes. So what are you waiting for? Impress your family, friends and even yourself by preparing a perfect meal starting with an awesome appetizer. I'm sure it will make a huge difference to your home-cooked meal.

These are the following topics in this series:

- Bruschetta
- Dips And Spreads Recipes
- Wraps And Rolls Recipes
- ...

Enjoy preparing your appetizers every day!

I really appreciate that you have selected "Hello! 365 Meat Appetizer Recipes" and for reading to the end. I anticipate that this book shall give you the source of strength during the times that you are really exhausted, as well as be your best friend in the comforts of your own home. Please also give me some love by sharing your own exciting cooking time in the comments segment below.

List of Abbreviations

LIST OF ABBREVIATIONS	
tbsp(s).	tablespoon(s)
tsp(s).	teaspoon(s)
c.	cup(s)
oz.	ounce(s)
lb(s).	pound(s)

Chapter 1: Pork Recipes

***

1. Anne's Hot Ham And Swiss Dip

"Hot and easy!"
Serving: 8 | Prep: 10m | Ready in: 2h10m

Ingredients

- 1 lb. thinly sliced deli ham, sliced into thin strips
- 1 (8 oz.) package cream cheese, cut into cubes
- 1 (10.75 oz.) can condensed cream of mushroom soup, undiluted
- 1 (10.75 oz.) can condensed cream of celery soup, undiluted
- 2 cups shredded Swiss cheese
- 2 (1 lb.) loaves cocktail rye bread

Direction

- Mix cream of celery soup, cream of mushroom soup, cream cheese and ham in a slow cooker; mix in Swiss cheese. Cover; cook for approximately 2 hours till cheese is melted on Low while occasionally mixing. Serve over cocktail rye slices.

Nutrition Information

- Calories: 483 calories;
- Total Carbohydrate: 11.6 g
- Cholesterol: 123 mg
- Total Fat: 35.6 g
- Protein: 29.1 g
- Sodium: 1476 mg

2. Arkansas Sin

"A yummy spread with ham, Cheddar and cream cheese. Add another jalapeno pepper for spice."
Serving: 10 | Prep: 15m | Ready in: 55m

Ingredients

- 1 (8 oz.) package cream cheese, softened
- 4 cups shredded Cheddar cheese
- 8 oz. diced cooked ham
- 1 small onion, chopped
- 1 jalapeno pepper, seeded and chopped
- 1 (1 lb.) loaf round sourdough bread
- 1 cup buttery crackers

Direction

- Preheat the oven to 175°C or 350°F.
- Mix jalapeno peppers, onions, ham, Cheddar cheese and cream cheese together in a medium bowl. On top of the bread, cut out a circle and take out the middle, leave a bread shell with 1-inch thickness. Add cheese mixture to fill the bread.
- Bake in the preheated oven for 35-40 minutes to heat through the dip. Serve the dip with crackers.

Nutrition Information

- Calories: 483 calories;
- Total Carbohydrate: 32.1 g
- Cholesterol: 85 mg
- Total Fat: 29 g
- Protein: 23 g
- Sodium: 1001 mg

3. Artichoke, Mushroom And Parma Ham Tart

"“Serve this dish at room temperature or warm. Use as a side dish with the meal or an appetizer if the turkey is taking longer to roast than you imagined.”"
Serving: 6

Ingredients

- 1 3/4 cups sifted all-purpose flour
- 2 oz. grated Parmesan cheese
- 2/3 cup butter, diced
- 1 egg, beaten
- 1 tbsp. olive oil
- 8 oz. fresh mushrooms, sliced
- 3 oz. Parma ham
- 1/2 (14 oz.) can artichoke hearts, drained
- 7/8 cup creme fraiche
- 4 eggs
- 1 tsp. chopped flat leaf parsley
- 1/3 cup milk
- salt to taste
- ground black pepper to taste

Direction

- Put a pinch salt, butter, Parmesan cheese, and flour in a food processor and briefly process. Put in the 1 tbsp. oil and egg through feeder tube, adding extra oil if needed; you should be able to bring the dough together in your hands. Use plastic to wrap it, and refrigerate for 1 hour.
- Roll out to fit a 9-inch quiche pan with a loose bottom. Prick all over. Refrigerate for at least 2 hours, ideally overnight.
- Use foil to line pastry, and cover the bottom with uncooked beans. Bake for 15 minutes at 375°F (190°C). Take off the beans and foil, then cook for 5 minutes longer. Remove and cool.
- Sauté mushrooms in 1 tbsp. olive oil for 10 minutes. Strain and cool.
- Put ham over the pastry base, and place artichokes and mushrooms on top. Whisk milk, parsley, eggs, and creme fraiche. Add black pepper and salt to season; pour the mixture over the vegetables and ham. Bake until golden, 40 minutes. Serve cold or warm.

Nutrition Information

- Calories: 615 calories;
- Total Carbohydrate: 35.1 g
- Cholesterol: 279 mg
- Total Fat: 45.1 g
- Protein: 20.6 g
- Sodium: 839 mg

4. Big Game Dip

"Everyone will go crazy for this."
Serving: 20 | Prep: 10m | Ready in: 2h20m

Ingredients

- 1 (2 lb.) loaf processed cheese (such as Velveeta®), cubed
- 1 lb. bulk spicy pork sausage
- 1 (24 oz.) jar hot salsa
- 1/2 cup hot pepper sauce (such as Frank's RedHot®)
- 3 large jalapeno peppers, chopped (optional)

Direction

- In a slow cooker, melt the processed cheese on Low. Cook and stir the pork sausage over medium heat in a large skillet for about 10 minutes, or until crumbly and browned; strain the excess grease. Next, in the cooker, mix the sausage into the processed cheese, stir in jalapeno peppers, hot sauce, and salsa. Cook for 2 hours; immediately serve when it's hot.

Nutrition Information

- Calories: 211 calories;
- Total Carbohydrate: 6.1 g
- Cholesterol: 49 mg
- Total Fat: 15.5 g
- Protein: 12.1 g
- Sodium: 1068 mg

5. Blue's Lumpia

"These lumpia taste great, meat mixture isn't cooked before rolling and can be made ahead of time."
Serving: 50 | Prep: 1h30m | Ready in: 2h

Ingredients

- 1 lb. ground beef
- 1 lb. ground pork
- 1 small onion, finely diced
- 1 cup shredded carrots
- 1 (8 oz.) can water chestnuts, chopped
- 2 tbsps. minced garlic
- 1 egg
- 1/2 cup oyster sauce
- salt and ground black pepper to taste
- 100 lumpia wrappers (egg roll wrappers)
- 1 egg, beaten
- 1 quart vegetable oil for frying

Direction

- In a big bowl, combine black pepper, salt, oyster sauce, 1 egg, garlic, water chestnuts, carrots, onion, pork and beef till well incorporated.
- On egg roll wrapper with a corner towards you, put a tbsp. pf beef-pork mixture. Fold the corner nearest to you on top of filling; fold 2 corners on side going to the middle and keep rolling wrapper securely surrounding the meat. Brush a bit of beaten egg on the surface corner and press to enclose. Redo with the rest of the wrappers and filling. Keep rolls in container with cover.
- In a big saucepan or deep-fryer, heat the oil to 175 °C or 350 °F.
- Working in batches, fry the rolls for 7 minutes till golden brown. Allow to drain on plate lined with paper towel. Serve right away.

Nutrition Information

- Calories: 122 calories;
- Total Carbohydrate: 10.4 g
- Cholesterol: 23 mg
- Total Fat: 6.5 g
- Protein: 5 g
- Sodium: 125 mg

6. C And L's Stuffed Black Olives

"A delicious family snack or a really tasty appetizer for a party."
Serving: 8 | Prep: 25m | Ready in: 35m

Ingredients

- 4 oz. ground pork
- 4 oz. ground beef
- 1 1/2 tsps. Italian seasoning
- 1 tsp. garlic powder
- 1/2 small onion, shredded
- 1 tbsp. dried parsley
- 1/4 cup grated Parmesan cheese
- salt and pepper to taste
- 1 (15 oz.) can black olives, drained
- 2 eggs
- 2 cups Italian-style dried bread crumbs
- 2 cups vegetable oil

Direction

- Cook the ground pork and ground beef in a large skillet on medium-high heat until they are browned evenly.
- Let the meats drain. Combine in pepper, salt, Parmesan cheese, parsley flakes, onion, garlic powder, and Italian seasoning. Carry on cooking on moderately high heat until they are combined thoroughly, for 1-2 minutes.
- In a small bowl, whisk the eggs. In a small bowl, arrange the Italian-style dried breadcrumbs. Fill the meat mixture into the olives. Plunge the filled olives into the eggs and then into the breadcrumb mixture. On a flat surface, arrange the coated olives and allow them to sit for 10 minutes.
- In a large, heavy saucepan or the deep fryer, heat the vegetable oil to 190°C (375°F). Repeat

the steps of plunging each olive into the egg and the bread mixture.

- Fry the olives in small batches until they turn golden brown, or for 1-2 minutes. Put on the paper towels to drain.

Nutrition Information

- Calories: 778 calories;
- Total Carbohydrate: 25 g
- Cholesterol: 72 mg
- Total Fat: 71.2 g
- Protein: 12.4 g
- Sodium: 1069 mg

7. Cha Gio Vietnamese Egg Rolls

""Making a double batch of this recipe is a must cause' these egg rolls freeze really well. Add some shredded cabbage or taro (julienned) for a change. You can also add a minced crab for an added savory."

Serving: 12 | Prep: 45m | Ready in: 1h5m

Ingredients

- 1 cup uncooked bean threads (cellophane noodles)
- 1 large dried shiitake mushroom
- 1 lb. ground pork
- 1/2 lb. shrimp, chopped
- 1 large carrot, peeled and grated
- 1 small shallot, minced
- 2 1/4 tsps. Vietnamese fish sauce
- 1 1/4 tsps. white sugar
- 1 1/4 tsps. salt
- 1 1/4 tsps. ground black pepper
- 24 egg roll wrappers
- 1 egg, beaten
- oil for deep frying

Direction

- Soak the shiitake mushroom and vermicelli in warm water for about 15 minutes until pliable; drain thoroughly and mince the mushrooms.
- Combine shiitake, carrot, shrimp, shallot, sugar, fish sauce, pepper, salt, pork and vermicelli in a big bowl. Toss them well to pull apart the pork and equally distribute the ingredients for the filling.
- Diagonally lay 1 piece of egg roll wrapper on a flat surface. Spread a little 2 tbsps. of filling across the middle of the wrapper. Fold the bottom corner over the filling, then fold in the corners to secure the filling. Brush the top corner of wrapper with egg and continue to roll to secure. Make more egg rolls using the same method.
- In a deep-fryer, large saucepan or wok, heat the oil to 350°F (175°C), or test a drop of water if it sizzle on the surface.
- Fry the egg rolls for 5 to 8 minutes until it turns golden brown. Place the rolls on paper towels to drain, or you may also use paper bags.

Nutrition Information

- Calories: 227 calories;
- Total Carbohydrate: 13.8 g
- Cholesterol: 68 mg
- Total Fat: 13.5 g
- Protein: 12 g
- Sodium: 464 mg

8. Chorizo Bites

""This delectable appetizer is gone in a matter of seconds once served! They are so delicious that one serving is just not enough!""

Serving: 35 | Prep: 15m | Ready in: 25m

Ingredients

- toothpicks
- 4 cooked chorizo links, cut into 1/2-inch slices
- 5 cloves garlic, slivered, or to taste
- 35 dates, sliced open and pitted

Direction

- Preheat the oven to 400°F (200°C).
- Fill each date with several slivers of garlic and a piece of chorizo. Use a toothpick to secure

- the fillings inside each date. Place the stuffed dates on a baking sheet.
- Put in preheated oven and bake for 10 minutes until well-heated.

Nutrition Information

- Calories: 112 calories;
- Total Carbohydrate: 21.5 g
- Cholesterol: 6 mg
- Total Fat: 2.7 g
- Protein: 2.4 g
- Sodium: 85 mg

9. Cocktail Beer Balls

"A very simple recipe to create a tasty appetizer to enjoy on any occasions with your family."

Serving: 8 | Prep: 15m | Ready in: 4h15m

Ingredients

- 3 cups ketchup
- 1 (12 oz.) bottle light beer
- 2 tsps. salt, divided
- 2 tsps. ground black pepper, divided
- 2 lbs. ground beef
- 1/2 lb. ground pork
- 1/4 cup bread crumbs
- 1 egg
- 2 tbsps. grated Parmesan cheese
- 1/2 tsp. onion powder
- 1/2 tsp. garlic powder

Direction

- In a pot, stir together with a tsp. of pepper, a tsp. of salt, beer, and ketchup on medium-low heat. Allow to simmer.
- In a bowl, combine together garlic powder, onion powder, a tsp. of pepper, a tsp. of salt, Parmesan cheese, egg, breadcrumbs, ground pork, and ground beef. Roll to form the mixture into cocktail-sized meatballs. Arrange the meatballs in the sauce and bring to a simmer for 4-6 hours until the meatballs are cooked thoroughly and the flavors combine.

Nutrition Information

- Calories: 428 calories;
- Total Carbohydrate: 26.5 g
- Cholesterol: 112 mg
- Total Fat: 23.2 g
- Protein: 27.2 g
- Sodium: 1719 mg

10. Crispy Pork Belly

"A dish that will make people no longer hate eating fat."

Serving: 6 | Prep: 10m | Ready in: 14h15m

Ingredients

- 1/2 lb. whole pork belly, skin removed
- 1/2 tsp. smoked paprika, or to taste
- kosher salt and ground black pepper to taste
- 1 tbsp. olive oil, or to taste

Direction

- Set an oven to 95°C (200°F) and start preheating.
- Season the pork belly all over with black pepper, salt, and smoked paprika. Use parchment paper to wrap the pork; use aluminum foil to wrap a second time, and use another sheet of aluminum foil for the third time. In a baking dish, arrange the pork packet.
- In the prepared oven, roast for 6 hours until tender. Allow to cool to room temperature in the wrappings; put the cooled packet in the fridge and let chill for 8 hours or overnight.
- Remove the wrap off the chilled meat. Reserve any rendered fat that falls away when removing the wrap.
- Divide evenly the meat into 6 portions. Use 1/8-inch slashes to slice 1/8-inch into the fat-side of the pork. Flavor with salt.
- In a skillet, heat 2 tbsps. of retained pork fat on medium heat. Arrange the pork belly with the fat side down in heated fat; cook it for 5-10 minutes until heated thoroughly and all sides

are well-browned. Place the pork belly into a plate, pour olive oil over and flavor with pepper.

Nutrition Information

- Calories: 87 calories;
- Total Carbohydrate: 0.3 g
- Cholesterol: 14 mg
- Total Fat: 7.4 g
- Protein: 4.6 g
- Sodium: 352 mg

11. Crispy Wontons

"Simple but appetizing wontons with the unique flavors from the pork filling."
Serving: 10

Ingredients

- 3/4 lb. ground pork
- 8 canned water chestnuts, finely chopped
- 1/4 cup finely chopped green onions
- 1 tbsp. Kikkoman Soy Sauce
- 1 tsp. cornstarch
- 1/2 tsp. salt
- 1/2 tsp. grated fresh ginger root
- 1 (16 oz.) package wonton skins
- Vegetable oil for deep-frying
- Tomato ketchup and hot mustard or Kikkoman Sweet & Sour Sauce

Direction

- In a medium bowl, blend ginger, salt, cornstarch, soy sauce, green onions, water chestnuts, and pork; combine thoroughly. Fill the center of each wonton skin with 1/2 teaspoonful of the pork mixture. Shape into a triangle by folding the wonton skin over the filling. Bend the top of the triangle down to meet the fold. Turn it over; add water to one corner to moisten. Put the opposite corner overlapping the moistened corner; press firmly together.
- In a large saucepan or a wok, heat the oil on medium-high heat to 375°F. Deep-fry a few wontons at a time until they are crispy and brown, or for 2-3 minutes. Place on the paper towels to drain. Serve them warm together with sour and sweet sauce or mustard (as desired) and ketchup.

12. Deep-fried Creamy Chicken Gravy

"Creamier chicken croquettes."
Serving: 16 | Prep: 25m | Ready in: 2h45m

Ingredients

- 1/2 cup unsalted butter
- 1/2 yellow onion, finely chopped
- 1/2 cup all-purpose flour
- 1/4 tsp. freshly ground black pepper
- 1 pinch freshly grated nutmeg
- 1 pinch cayenne pepper
- 2 1/2 cups whole milk
- 1 tsp. salt, plus more to taste
- 2 cups finely chopped, cooked chicken meat
- 1/2 cup finely chopped ham
- 2 tbsps. freshly chopped Italian parsley
- Breading:
- 1 cup all-purpose flour, or as needed for dredging
- 2 eggs, beaten
- 2 cups bread crumbs
- 2 cups vegetable oil for frying

Direction

- In pan, liquify butter over moderate heat. Put the onions; cook and mix for 5 minutes till onions start to turn clear. Mix in half cup of flour and cook for 3 or 4 minutes till flour no longer tastes raw. Put cayenne pepper, nutmeg and black pepper; mix. Take off heat.
- Into the butter-onion mixture, add the milk to create bechamel sauce. Mix till blended. Bring pan back to moderately-high heat and keep mixing for 1 or 2 minutes till mixture is thick;

keep cooking and mixing for 3 or 4 minutes. Take off heat and mix in salt.

- In bowl, put parsley, ham and chopped chicken. Put the bechamel sauce and stir well. Cool mixture to room temperature; place plastic wrap to cover and chill for 2 or 3 hours till set.
- In big saucepan or deep fryer, heat the oil to 175 °C or 350 °F.
- In 3 individual shallow bowls, put bread crumbs, beaten eggs and a cup flour.
- Spoon out refrigerated mixture into equally-sized parts, approximately golf ball-size, to make croquettes. Turn balls initially in flour, then dip in beaten eggs, and then roll in bread crumbs.
- Working in batches, let croquettes fry for 4 minutes till crispy. Allow to drain on paper towels and remove to rack.

Nutrition Information

- Calories: 248 calories;
- Total Carbohydrate: 20.8 g
- Cholesterol: 58 mg
- Total Fat: 13.3 g
- Protein: 10.7 g
- Sodium: 335 mg

13. Deviled Eggs With Dill And Prosciutto

"These deviled eggs are great to enjoy as appetizers. They have a lot of Dijon mustard and dill and also a prosciutto layer."

Serving: 24 | Prep: 20m | Ready in: 1h20m

Ingredients

- 12 eggs
- 3/4 cup chopped fresh dill
- 1/2 cup mayonnaise
- 1/4 cup Dijon mustard
- 2 thin slices prosciutto, or as needed
- ground black pepper to taste
- 24 slices cucumber
- 1 pinch paprika, or as desired

Direction

- In a saucepan, put eggs and cover with water. Boil it, take away from heat, and let the eggs stay in hot water for 15 minutes. Take the eggs out of the hot water, put under cold running water to cool down, and remove the shells.
- Slice the eggs into two lengthwise; put the egg yolks in a bowl. Use a fork to crush the yolks, mix in Dijon mustard, mayonnaise, and dill.
- On a serving dish, put the egg whites with the cut side turning up. Slice each prosciutto slice into 6 pieces and use 1 piece to put into each egg white half. Stuff the yolk mixture into each egg white, use black pepper to drizzle, put 1 slice of cucumber on top, and use paprika to drizzle. Chill with a cover for 30 minutes until eating.

Nutrition Information

- Calories: 77 calories;
- Total Carbohydrate: 1.7 g
- Cholesterol: 95 mg
- Total Fat: 6.4 g
- Protein: 3.5 g
- Sodium: 136 mg

14. Drunken Sailors

"This easy-to-make appetizer is perfect any occasions."

Serving: 6 | Prep: 15m | Ready in: 6h15m

Ingredients

- 1 (14 oz.) bottle ketchup
- 1 (12 oz.) bottle barbeque sauce
- 1/2 cup brown sugar
- 1/2 cup whiskey
- 1 (16 oz.) package kielbasa sausage, sliced into 1/2 inch pieces
- 1 box toothpicks

Direction

- Pour the barbecue sauce and ketchup into a slow cooker. Then stir in the sausage, whiskey, and brown sugar. Cook for about 6 hours on Low. Serve hot using toothpicks.

Nutrition Information

- Calories: 499 calories;
- Total Carbohydrate: 57.1 g
- Cholesterol: 50 mg
- Total Fat: 21 g
- Protein: 10.4 g
- Sodium: 2054 mg

15. Feta Cheese Stuffed Meatballs

"This will fill you up."
Serving: 8 | Prep: 15m | Ready in: 40m

Ingredients

- cooking spray
- 1 lb. ground beef
- 1 lb. ground pork
- 1/4 cup Italian-seasoned bread crumbs
- 1 (1 oz.) package onion soup mix
- 1 egg
- 1 tbsp. ground black pepper
- 1 tbsp. Italian seasoning
- 1 tbsp. minced garlic
- 1/2 cup crumbled feta cheese

Direction

- Set the oven at 220°C (425°F) to preheat. Use cooking spray to lightly spray a baking sheet.
- In a bowl, mix garlic, Italian seasoning, pepper, egg, onion soup mix, bread crumbs, ground pork, and ground beef together. Form a 2 to 3-inch meatball around 1 1/2 tsps. feta cheese. Put the stuffed meatballs on the greased baking sheet.
- In the preheated oven, bake for 10 minutes. Flip the meatballs and continue to bake for 10-20 minutes more, until browned and cooked through. Check by inserting an instant-read thermometer into the center and it should state at least 70°C (160°F). Remove the meatballs from the oven, transfer to a separate pan and use aluminum foil to cover for 3-5 minutes.

Nutrition Information

- Calories: 309 calories;
- Total Carbohydrate: 6.7 g
- Cholesterol: 109 mg
- Total Fat: 20.6 g
- Protein: 23.5 g
- Sodium: 621 mg

16. Fig-proscuitto Crostini

"This recipe makes a simple but still elegant appetizer"
Serving: 24 | Prep: 15m | Ready in: 15m

Ingredients

- 24 French bread slices, 1/2 inch thick
- 2/3 cup fig jam
- 1/4 cup chopped toasted walnuts
- 1/4 lb. prosciutto, cut into 24 pieces
- 1 1/2 cups KRAFT Shredded Triple Cheddar Cheese with a TOUCH OF PHILADELPHIA
- 1 tbsp. chopped fresh rosemary

Direction

- Turn on the broiler and start heating.
- Arrange bread slices in a single layer on baking sheet; spread jam on top of each slice.
- Put remaining ingredients on top.
- Place bread slices 4 inches from the heat source and broil for 3 minutes or until cheese is melted.

Nutrition Information

- Calories: 81 calories;
- Total Carbohydrate: 5.8 g
- Cholesterol: 12 mg
- Total Fat: 5 g
- Protein: 3.7 g

- Sodium: 198 mg

17. Game Day Sausage Snacks

"These cheese and sausage snacks are tasty and great for parties or any other occasions."
Serving: 15 | Prep: 15m | Ready in: 20m

Ingredients

- 12 oz. ground pork sausage
- 12 oz. spicy ground pork sausage
- 1 (16 oz.) jar processed cheese sauce
- 1 (1 lb.) loaf sliced pumpernickel party bread

Direction

- Start preheating the broiler.
- Cook spicy ground pork sausage and ground pork sausage in a big, deep frying pan over medium-high heat until evenly brown. Strain the sausage. Toss in processed cheese sauce. Put 1 layer of pumpernickel party bread slices on a medium-sized cookie sheet. Use an equal amount of the sausage mixture to put on each slice.
- Put in the preheated broiler and broil until toasted, about 3-5 minutes, checking regularly.

Nutrition Information

- Calories: 351 calories;
- Total Carbohydrate: 18.3 g
- Cholesterol: 53 mg
- Total Fat: 25.3 g
- Protein: 12 g
- Sodium: 971 mg

18. Goi Cuon (vietnamese Spring Roll With Pork And Prawns)

"Spring roll, fresh roll, salad roll. Vietnamese roll. Whatever everybody calls it, it's a healthy, delicious and a classic snack. Best served with a Vietnamese dipping sauce called nuoc cham or serve with hoisin dipping sauce."
Serving: 6 | Prep: 45m | Ready in: 55m

Ingredients

- 1/2 lb. pork tenderloin, cut into thin strips
- 1/2 lb. prawns, peeled and deveined
- 1/4 lb. rice vermicelli noodles
- 1 (12 oz.) package rice wrappers (such as Blue Dragon®)
- 1 bunch fresh cilantro, leaves picked from stems
- 5 spring onions, cut in half
- 1/4 cup fresh mint leaves, or more to taste
- 1/4 head romaine lettuce, cut into bite-size pieces

Direction

- Place a skillet and heat over medium heat; once hot, add the pork, cook and stir for about 5 to 7 minutes until cooked well.
- Fill a pot with water and bring to a boil; stir in prawns and cook until the meat turns pink. Drain water and cut the prawns in half lengthwise.
- In big pot, add water with light salt and bring to a rolling boil. Mix in vermicelli and return to a boil. Cook the vermicelli for 2 to 4 minutes until soft yet firm to the bite. Drain.
- Put warm water in a big shallow bowl.
- Submerge the rice wrapper into the bowl of warm water for about 3 to 5 seconds until softened. Put the rice wrapper on your work surface. Allow the rice paper to soften for about half minute. Assemble the roll and place the pork, followed by a prawn half, then the vermicelli noodles, mint leaves, spring onions, cilantro and finish the layer with romaine lettuce, placing on the bottom third of the wrapper; roll it up halfway. Fold in each side

and finish rolling the rest of the wrapper. Repeat with the rest of the ingredients.

Nutrition Information

- Calories: 328 calories;
- Total Carbohydrate: 56.6 g
- Cholesterol: 74 mg
- Total Fat: 2 g
- Protein: 19.6 g
- Sodium: 88 mg

19. Ham And Pineapple Pinwheels

"This sweet version of a pinwheel is a great combination of crushed pineapple, cream cheese, and sliced ham."
Serving: 32 | Prep: 15m | Ready in: 2h15m

Ingredients

- 1 (8 oz.) package whipped pineapple cream cheese
- 1 1/2 cups crushed pineapple in juice, well drained
- 6 (8 inch) flour tortillas
- 6 oz. sliced fully cooked deli ham

Direction

- In a bowl, combine together pineapple and cream cheese until evenly combined. On a clean working surface, position the tortillas. Spread the cream cheese mixture onto 2/3 of each tortilla, then put a slice of ham over the cream cheese. Roll up each tortilla towards its uncovered edge. Use a dollop of cream cheese to seal the edge, if necessary. Use plastic wrap to wrap each tortilla roll then seal tightly. Chill for a minimum of 2 hours; unwrap and cut into 1/2" wide pieces.

Nutrition Information

- Calories: 61 calories;
- Total Carbohydrate: 7.1 g
- Cholesterol: 8 mg
- Total Fat: 3.1 g
- Protein: 1.4 g
- Sodium: 65 mg

20. Ham And Swiss Sliders

"Simple amazing."
Serving: 12 | Prep: 15m | Ready in: 37m

Ingredients

- 1 tbsp. olive oil
- 1 large red onion, sliced
- 12 dinner rolls, split
- 3/4 cup honey mustard dressing (such as Ken's Steak House®)
- 3/4 lb. honey ham, thinly sliced
- 2 cups shredded Swiss cheese
- 2 tbsps. butter, melted
- 1/2 tsp. Worcestershire sauce

Direction

- Preheat an oven to 175°C/350°F.
- In a skillet, heat olive oil on medium heat then add sliced onion; mix and cook for about 10 minutes till soft. Take off the heat.
- Spread bottom and top half of each roll with honey mustard dressing; line bottom halves of rolls on bottom of a 9x13-in. baking dish. Layer ham, cooked onion and Swiss cheese over bottom halves of rolls; use top halves of rolls to cover.
- Mix Worcestershire sauce and melted butter in a small bowl; evenly brush over tops of rolls. Use aluminum foil to cover baking dish.
- In the preheated oven, bake for 12-15 minutes till cheese melts and lightly browned.

Nutrition Information

- Calories: 227 calories;
- Total Carbohydrate: 7.3 g
- Cholesterol: 40 mg
- Total Fat: 18 g
- Protein: 9.7 g
- Sodium: 501 mg

21. Ham Pate

"Perfect for finger sandwiches or crackers."
Serving: 4 | Prep: 15m | Ready in: 15m

Ingredients

- 4 oz. cubed cooked ham
- 2 tbsps. ranch salad dressing (such as Hidden Valley® Original Ranch®)
- 1 tbsp. capers with juice
- 2 tsps. prepared mustard
- 2 tsps. finely chopped onion
- 1 pinch minced garlic

Direction

- Get a food processor and put in the garlic, onion, mustard, capers, ranch dressing and ham; blend well until you reach the consistency you want.

Nutrition Information

- Calories: 109 calories;
- Total Carbohydrate: 0.8 g
- Cholesterol: 18 mg
- Total Fat: 9.2 g
- Protein: 5.5 g
- Sodium: 524 mg

22. Hamballs

"A super easy and delicious recipe."
Serving: 6 | Prep: 15m | Ready in: 1h

Ingredients

- 1 lb. ground beef
- 1 lb. ground pork
- 1 egg, beaten
- 1 (18 oz.) bottle barbeque sauce (such as Sweet Baby Ray's®)
- 1 (10.75 oz.) can tomato soup
- 1/2 cup milk
- 1 tsp. vinegar

Direction

- Set the oven at 175°C (350°F) to preheat. Then grease a 13x9-inch baking dish.
- In a large bowl, mix egg, ground pork, and ground beef; roll into small balls. Place in the greased baking dish.
- In a separate bowl, stir vinegar, milk, tomato soup, and barbeque sauce.
- In the preheated oven, bake the meatballs for half an hour, until the juices run clear. Drain the fat from baking dish and pour over the meatballs with the sauce. Continue to bake for 15 minutes more, until the sauce is hot.

Nutrition Information

- Calories: 474 calories;
- Total Carbohydrate: 38.2 g
- Cholesterol: 129 mg
- Total Fat: 22.2 g
- Protein: 28.7 g
- Sodium: 1323 mg

23. Hawaiian Ham And Cheese Sliders

"“Excellent for potlucks!”"
Serving: 12 | Prep: 15m | Ready in: 50m

Ingredients

- cooking spray (such as Crisco®)
- 1/2 cup butter
- 1 onion, minced
- 3 tbsps. Dijon mustard
- 1 tbsp. poppy seeds
- 2 tsps. Worcestershire sauce, or more to taste
- 1 (12 count) package Hawaiian sweet rolls, split, or more as needed
- 1 lb. sliced deli ham, or more as needed
- 8 slices Swiss cheese, or more as needed

Direction

- Prepare the oven by preheating to 350°F (175°C). Use cooking spray to coat a 9x13-inch baking dish.
- In a saucepan set on medium-low heat, dissolve butter; stir and cook the onion for 5-10 minutes until it is softened. Add Worcestershire sauce, poppy seeds, and mustard; stir and cook for 5 minutes.
- In the prepared baking dish, place the bottoms of every roll. Scoop 2/3 of onion mixture on the roll bottoms. Place Swiss cheese and ham to every roll. Place tops roll on the Swiss cheese layer. Then brush the rest of 1/3 onion mixture on tops of rolls. Use aluminum foil to cover the dish.
- Place in preheated oven and bake for 15 minutes. Take off the aluminum foil then bake for 5-10 minutes until tops of rolls browned lightly.

Nutrition Information

- Calories: 484 calories;
- Total Carbohydrate: 46.5 g
- Cholesterol: 99 mg
- Total Fat: 16.5 g
- Protein: 25.7 g
- Sodium: 899 mg

24. Hawaiian Ham And Pineapple Salsa

""Be ready for party with this Hawaiian Ham and Pineapple Salsa. A fruity salsa of mango nectar, jalapeno, and pineapple is the best base for salty chunks of cooked canned ham flavored with Grill Mates® Baja Citrus Marinade. Place it inside hollowed out pineapple bowls for a delicious salsa.""

Serving: 32 | Prep: 15m | Ready in: 20m

Ingredients

- 1 (1 oz.) package McCormick® Grill Mates® Baja Citrus Marinade
- 1/2 cup mango nectar or orange juice
- 2 tbsps. honey
- 2 tbsps. lime juice
- 1 (12 oz.) can canned ham, such as Spam® Classic, cut into small cubes
- 4 cups finely chopped fresh pineapple
- 1/2 cup finely chopped red onion
- 1 jalapeño pepper, finely chopped
- 1/2 cup chopped macadamia nuts

Direction

- In a big bowl, combine lime juice, honey, mango nectar, and Marinade Mix. Take 1/4 cup of marinade mixture; reserve.
- In a big skillet set on medium heat, cook 1/4 cup of leftover marinade mixture and cubed canned ham until browned lightly. Separate from heat.
- Mix jalapeno, onion, and pineapple in the rest of the marinade mixture in a big bowl until well combined. Place ham mixture on top. Dust with nuts. Then serve dip with some tortilla chips.

Nutrition Information

- Calories: 68 calories;
- Total Carbohydrate: 5.6 g
- Cholesterol: 7 mg
- Total Fat: 4.5 g
- Protein: 1.7 g
- Sodium: 224 mg

25. Holiday Cheese Spread

"This is an ideal cheese spread to make for any holidays."

Serving: 48 | Prep: 15m | Ready in: 15m

Ingredients

- 3 (8 oz.) packages cream cheese, softened
- 2 (4.5 oz.) cans deviled ham spread
- 1 lb. Colby cheese, shredded
- 1/4 cup chopped green olives
- 2 tbsps. prepared mustard

- 1/2 tsp. dry mustard
- 1 1/2 tsps. chopped fresh chives
- 1/2 tsp. celery salt
- 1/2 tsp. cayenne pepper
- 1/2 tsp. garlic salt

Direction

- Combine together prepared mustard, green olives, Colby cheese, deviled ham and cream cheese in a big bowl. Season with garlic salt, cayenne pepper, celery salt, chopped fresh chives and dry mustard, then cover and chill until ready to serve.

Nutrition Information

- Calories: 102 calories;
- Total Carbohydrate: 0.8 g
- Cholesterol: 27 mg
- Total Fat: 9.3 g
- Protein: 4.1 g
- Sodium: 194 mg

26. Homemade Spinach Pizza Rolls

"Tasty, bite-size pinwheels."
Serving: 8 | Prep: 20m | Ready in: 45m

Ingredients

- Reynolds Wrap® Non Stick Aluminum Foil
- 1 tbsp. cornmeal
- 8 oz. bulk Italian sausage
- 1 (13.8 oz.) package refrigerated pizza dough
- 1 cup shredded mozzarella cheese, divided
- 1 cup fresh baby spinach
- 1/4 cup grated Parmesan cheese
- 1 egg, lightly beaten
- 1 (8 oz.) can pizza sauce, warmed

Direction

- Preheat an oven to 375 °F. Line Reynolds Wrap(R) Non-Stick Aluminum Foil on a big baking sheet; scatter cornmeal over. Reserve.
- In big skillet, brown the sausage on medium-high heat. Let drain and reserve.
- Onto prepped baking sheet, roll pizza dough out. Cautiously expand or roll the dough into a rectangle, 13x10-inch in size. Place sausage on dough to within half-inch of edges. Scatter half cup mozzarella over. Lay spinach over cheese. Put the leftover half cup of mozzarella and Parmesan on top. Beginning from a lengthy side, roll dough up to create a 13-inch long loaf. Pinch seam and ends together to enclose.
- On the prepped baking sheet, put the loaf, seam side facing down. Brush with the egg. Slice 4 2-inch cuts in top with a sharp knife for vent.
- Allow to bake till golden brown for 20 to 25 minutes. If needed, place cover on the final 5 minutes of baking to avoid excessive browning. Take out of oven and cut into circles to serve along with pizza sauce.

Nutrition Information

- Calories: 310 calories;
- Total Carbohydrate: 39.1 g
- Cholesterol: 45 mg
- Total Fat: 9.9 g
- Protein: 14.8 g
- Sodium: 788 mg

27. Italian Nachos Restaurant-style

"Cheesy nachos with pepperoni and sausage."
Serving: 8 | Prep: 15m | Ready in: 25m

Ingredients

- 1 lb. bulk Italian sausage
- 1 (7-1/2 oz.) bag tortilla chips
- 1 (2 oz.) package sliced pepperoni
- 1/2 lb. shredded mozzarella cheese
- 1/2 cup banana peppers, drained
- 1 1/4 cups pizza sauce

Direction

- Preheat the broiler.
- Place a large skillet over medium heat, cook crumbled sausage, stirring, until it is not pink anymore. Drain.
- On a baking sheet, arrange the tortilla chips. Top chips with banana peppers, mozzarella cheese, pepperoni, and the crumbled cooked sausage. Place under the broiler and broil for 5 to 8 minutes, or until the cheese has melted. Serve nachos with a pizza sauce as a dip.

Nutrition Information

- Calories: 453 calories;
- Total Carbohydrate: 22.5 g
- Cholesterol: 69 mg
- Total Fat: 31.7 g
- Protein: 19.3 g
- Sodium: 1133 mg

28. Keto Pork Belly Cracklins

"A keto-friendly cracklin snack."
Serving: 12 | Prep: 10m | Ready in: 1h35m

Ingredients

- 3 lbs. skin-on pork belly
- water
- 4 tbsps. Cajun seasoning, divided

Direction

- Put the pork belly in the freezer for about 45 minutes, until partially frozen. This will make the cubing easier.
- Slice the pork belly into 3/4-inch cubes.
- Fill a 5-quart cast iron pot with water, 1/4 of the way. Add 1 tsp of Cajun seasoning. Then bring the water to a roaring boil. And pork belly cubes and let it cook for about 20 minutes, until the fat renders from the pork and all of the water evaporates. Once the fat starts to pop and sizzle, cover the pot. Let it cook and stir for about 15 minutes, until the cracklins become crisp and golden brown.
- On paper towels, drain the cracklins and season it with remaining Cajun seasoning.

Nutrition Information

- Calories: 209 calories;
- Total Carbohydrate: 1.7 g
- Cholesterol: 41 mg
- Total Fat: 15.8 g
- Protein: 14.1 g
- Sodium: 1340 mg

29. Kim's Armadillo Eggs

"These jalapeno sausage biscuits definitely please the crowd's appetizing."
Serving: 16 | Prep: 20m | Ready in: 1h20m

Ingredients

- 1 (16 oz.) jar whole jalapeno peppers, drained
- 2 cups shredded Cheddar cheese
- 1 lb. ground pork sausage
- 2 (10 oz.) cans refrigerated biscuit dough

Direction

- Set an oven to 175°C (350°F) and start preheating.
- Cut the jalapenos along the length to remove the seeds. Fill Cheddar cheese in the jalapenos.
- Split the ground pork sausage into small balls. Press the sausage balls to form into thin strips. Arrange a filled jalapeno onto each strip of sausage. Roll jalapenos in the sausage and press firmly.
- On a medium baking sheet, place the wrapped jalapenos. In the prepared oven, bake until the sausage turns brown evenly for 40-50 minutes. Take away from the heat and let cool for about 10 minutes.
- On a medium baking sheet, place the refrigerated biscuit dough. Use each piece of dough to wrap jalapeno roll and 1 sausage.

- In the prepared oven, bake until golden brown, or for 10-12 minutes.

Nutrition Information

- Calories: 288 calories;
- Total Carbohydrate: 15.7 g
- Cholesterol: 34 mg
- Total Fat: 20.9 g
- Protein: 9.2 g
- Sodium: 643 mg

30. Loaded Pulled Pork Totchos

" "Perfect for every party!" "
Serving: 8 | Prep: 25m | Ready in: 52m

Ingredients

- 1 (28 oz.) package frozen bite-size potato nuggets (such as Tater Tots®)
- salt to taste
- 2 1/2 cups cooked pulled pork
- 1 cup barbeque sauce
- 1/4 cup sour cream
- 1/2 tsp. smoked paprika
- White Cheddar Cheese Sauce:
- 2 tbsps. unsalted butter
- 1 1/2 tbsps. all-purpose flour
- 2 1/2 cups milk
- 5 oz. shredded white Cheddar cheese
- salt and ground black pepper to taste
- 1 cup canned pinto beans, drained
- 1/2 cup chopped roasted red bell peppers
- 1 tbsp. thinly sliced green onion (optional)
- 1 tsp. minced thyme (optional)

Direction

- Heat oven to 220°C (425°F) beforehand. On a baking sheet, spread potato nuggets in a single layer.
- Allow to bake for 20-25 minutes in the preheated oven till crispy and browned. Remove to a large bowl; use salt to season lightly.
- In a bowl, mix together barbeque sauce and pulled pork till pork gets coated evenly.
- In a small bowl, whisk together smoked paprika and sour cream.
- In a saucepan, melt butter over medium heat. Whisk in flour for 2-3 minutes till it forms a paste. Whisk in milk till no lumps left. Cook while stirring for approximately 5 minutes till sauce thickens enough to cover the back of a spoon. Remove from heat; whisk in Cheddar cheese till melted. Use pepper and salt to season sauce.
- Drizzle potato nuggets with Cheddar cheese sauce. Pour pulled pork mixture over, then put dollops of sour cream on top. Finish off with thyme, green onion, toasted peppers, and pinto beans.

Nutrition Information

- Calories: 537 calories;
- Total Carbohydrate: 52.7 g
- Cholesterol: 88 mg
- Total Fat: 25.7 g
- Protein: 28 g
- Sodium: 1620 mg

31. Lumpia (shanghai Version)

" "Filipino proud recipe that I know of! Lumpia (shanghai type) is a type of egg roll, except it's normally packed with meat. You could apply beef or pork broth! It's a delicious recipe and excellent to present as finger food. I enjoy to use both pork and beef but you can alternate one for the other. SUPER SIMPLE!" "
Serving: 20 | Prep: 1h | Ready in: 1h20m

Ingredients

- 1 lb. ground pork
- 1 lb. ground beef
- 1 medium onion, finely chopped
- 1 carrot, grated
- 1/4 cup soy sauce
- 2 1/2 tsps. black pepper
- 1 1/2 tbsps. garlic powder

- 2 tbsps. salt
- 1 (16 oz.) package spring roll wrappers
- 1 1/2 quarts oil for frying

Direction

- Mix carrot, onion, and ground beef and pork in a large bowl. Make sure to fully blend everything. I recommend using your hands, getting down and dirty. Massage the meat in the bowl if you must. Slowly mix in the salt, garlic powder, black pepper, and soy sauce until everything are equally distributed.
- On a flat surface, lay out a few wrappers at a time, and put about 2 tbsps. of the filling in a line down the middle of the wrapper. Be sure the filling is not thicken than your thumb, or the wrapper will cook faster than the meat. Fold the bottom and top edges of the wrapper towards the center Grab the right and left sides, then fold them towards the middle. Dampen the last edge of the wrapper to enclose. Now continue with the rest of the wrappers, and have the children or hubby to help you out.
- In a heavy skillet or deep fryer, add oil to heat to 375°F (190°C). Cook lumpia, 3 or 4 at a time. Then fry for approximately 3 or 4 minutes, flipping once. Once the lumpia floats, they are cooked, and the wrapper turns golden brown. Slice in half, or serve as is paired with dipping sauce. We like banana ketchup, soy sauce with lemon, or sweet and sour sauce.

Nutrition Information

- Calories: 261 calories;
- Total Carbohydrate: 14.6 g
- Cholesterol: 38 mg
- Total Fat: 17.8 g
- Protein: 10.2 g
- Sodium: 1037 mg

32. Memphis Wontons

"A recipe that guides you to cook the best meats."
Serving: 8 | Prep: 20m | Ready in: 25m

Ingredients

- 8 oz. cooked pulled pork, chopped
- 1/2 white onion, minced
- 1 (12 oz.) package wonton wrappers
- 2 quarts canola oil
- 1 cup barbeque sauce

Direction

- In a bowl, mix together the onion and pulled pork.
- Top the center of each wonton wrapper with about a tsp. of the pork mixture. Add water to 2 of 4 sides of each wrapper to moisten, fold the wrapper over the filling to shape into a triangle. Seal by pressing.
- In a large saucepan or a deep fryer, heat the oil to 325°F (165°C) or until nearly smoking.
- Fry wontons in batches in the heated oil for a minute until they turn golden brown. Place the cooked wontons onto the crumpled paper towels. Serve together with the barbeque sauce right away.

Nutrition Information

- Calories: 410 calories;
- Total Carbohydrate: 38.3 g
- Cholesterol: 21 mg
- Total Fat: 24.1 g
- Protein: 9.6 g
- Sodium: 769 mg

33. Miami Cuban Dip

"A Miami Cuban Dip contains all of the sabor you love from a Cuban sandwich. Stuff a bread bowl with real-deal ingredients then bring it home with Pork Gravy for a long lasting taste of Little Havana."

Serving: 22 | Prep: 15m | Ready in: 32m

Ingredients

- 1 (16 oz.) loaf Italian bread
- 1 cup milk
- 1 package McCormick® Pork Gravy Mix
- 1 1/2 cups shredded Swiss cheese, divided
- 5 tbsps. dill pickles, coarsely chopped, divided
- 1/4 cup mayonnaise
- 1 tbsp. prepared yellow mustard
- 1/2 cup cubed ham
- 1 cup deli-sliced roast pork cut into bite-size pieces

Direction

- Preheat oven to 350°F.
- Put bread on baking sheet. Make an oval on top of bread and take out the center to make space for the dip. Split removed bread center and bread top into bite-size pieces. Put aside to serve.
- In a medium saucepan, slowly whisk milk into gravy mix. Cook on medium heat, stir frequently till gravy boils. Lower heat to simmer. Mix in mustard, mayonnaise, 4 tbsp. of the pickles and 1 1/4 cups of cheese. Cook till cheese melts, for 2-3 minutes. Mix in ham and pork.
- Scoop dip into bread. Drizzle with leftover 1/4 cup of cheese.
- Bake till bread is warm and cheese melts, for 10 minutes. Drizzle dip with leftover 1 tbsp. of chopped pickles. Together with bread pieces, serve.

Nutrition Information

- Calories: 126 calories;
- Total Carbohydrate: 12.3 g
- Cholesterol: 15 mg
- Total Fat: 5.5 g
- Protein: 6.4 g
- Sodium: 291 mg

34. Minced Pork And Watermelon Lettuce Wraps

"It's a nice and easy meal for you kids."

Serving: 4 | Prep: 30m | Ready in: 50m

Ingredients

- 1 tbsp. vegetable oil
- 1 tbsp. minced garlic
- 1 tbsp. minced fresh ginger root
- 1 onion, finely chopped
- 1 lb. lean ground pork
- 1 carrot, finely chopped
- 2 stalks celery, finely chopped
- 1 tsp. soy sauce
- 1/2 cup chopped green onion
- 1/2 cup hoisin sauce
- 3/4 cup pine nuts
- 2 cups diced (1/2-inch) watermelon
- 12 iceberg lettuce leaves

Direction

- In a heavy, nonstick skillet, heat the vegetable oil on high heat. Cook and mix onion, ginger and garlic in the hot oil for a minute, until tangy. Put in ground pork and cook for 7-10 minutes, until browned thoroughly; drain any excess liquid from the skillet.
- Lower the heat to medium, then put celery and carrot into the pork mixture. Cook and stir for 2-3 minutes, until celery and carrot start to soften. Stir green onions and soy sauce into the mixture. Take away from the heat and put in pine nuts as well as hoisin sauce. Stir the mixture until evenly blended, then fold watermelon into the mixture.
- Scoop into the middle of the lettuce leaves with the pork mixture, then wrap the lettuce around the filling to serve.

Nutrition Information

- Calories: 535 calories;
- Total Carbohydrate: 31.3 g
- Cholesterol: 75 mg
- Total Fat: 34 g
- Protein: 29.2 g
- Sodium: 681 mg

35. Minnesota Hot Dish Dip

"Warm dips for cold days! In a bowl, whisk McCormick® Original Country Gravy Mix and milk together. Add frozen vegetables, shredded Cheddar cheese and cooked sausage. Then bake for ten minutes until melty and warm. You can have this along with potato tot dippers."

Serving: 16 | Prep: 5m | Ready in: 27m

Ingredients

- 2 cups milk
- 1 package McCormick® Original Country Gravy Mix
- 1/2 lb. ground breakfast sausage
- 1 cup frozen mixed vegetables
- 1/2 cup shredded Cheddar cheese

Direction

- Preheat the oven to 350 degrees F. Slowly mix the milk into gravy mix with whisk in a medium bowl. Reserve.
- Over medium heat, brown the sausage in a large skillet for around five minutes. Drain the fat. Place the sausage back into the skillet. Mix in the gravy mixture and veggies. Heat to boil over medium heat while stirring regularly. Decrease the heat and let to simmer for two minutes. Transfer to 9-inch glass pie plate and top with cheese on top.
- Bake for about ten minutes or until the cheese has melted. You can serve together with potato tots.

Nutrition Information

- Calories: 93 calories;
- Total Carbohydrate: 5.5 g
- Cholesterol: 14 mg
- Total Fat: 5.9 g
- Protein: 4.1 g
- Sodium: 295 mg

36. Mr. Kirk's Won Tons

"Delicious won tons stuffed with bamboo shoots, bok choy, pork, and other amazing ingredients will be a wonderful dish for a party."

Serving: 12 | Prep: 1h | Ready in: 2h

Ingredients

- 1/2 lb. ground pork, finely chopped
- 1/2 tsp. salt
- 1 tbsp. soy sauce
- 1/2 (8 oz.) can water chestnuts, drained and finely chopped
- 1/4 cup bamboo shoots, drained and finely chopped
- 1/4 cup green onions, finely chopped
- 1/2 cup bean sprouts, finely chopped
- 1/2 egg, beaten
- 2 leaves bok choy, finely chopped
- 1 tbsp. cooking sherry
- 1 (14 oz.) package wonton wrappers
- 2 quarts oil for frying

Direction

- Combine sherry, bok choy, egg, bean sprouts, green onions, bamboo shoots, water chestnuts, soy sauce, salt, and pork in a large bowl.
- Fill the center of each wonton wrapper with a tsp. of the pork mixture. Fold to the center of the wrappers to shape a triangle. Use your moistened fingers to press gently the edges together. Fold in half again along the length, then fold it back and gather the corners together. Press together the 2 corners.
- Heat oil on high heat in a heavy wok or skillet. Deep fry for 2 minutes per wonton. Take out and put on paper towels to drain.

Nutrition Information

- Calories: 285 calories;
- Total Carbohydrate: 22.6 g
- Cholesterol: 24 mg
- Total Fat: 18.2 g
- Protein: 7.9 g
- Sodium: 391 mg

37. Mum's Aussie Sausage Rolls

"These are surely the most tasty sausage rolls you ever eat."

Serving: 24 | Prep: 20m | Ready in: 40m

Ingredients

- 1 (16 oz.) package roll sausage (such as Jimmy Dean®)
- 1/2 cup Italian-seasoned bread crumbs
- 2 tbsps. dried minced onion
- 1/2 tsp. paprika
- 1/2 tsp. garlic powder
- 4 slices white bread, crusts removed
- 2 tbsps. warm water, or more as needed
- 1 sheet puff pastry, thawed
- 1 egg yolk, beaten
- 1 tbsp. water

Direction

- Set the oven at 175° C (350° F) to preheat. Use aluminum foil to line a baking sheet.
- In a bowl, mix sausage, garlic powder, paprika, onion, and bread crumbs.
- Shred the bread slices into pieces and put in a bowl; moisten by adding 2 tbsps. warm water. Put into the sausage mixture; stir until well blended.
- Open the puff pastry sheet; roll out to make a 12x16-inch rectangle. Cut the sheet into 3 equal parts lengthways. Mix 1 tbsp. water and egg yolk together then glaze the edges of the pastry.
- Next, split the sausage mixture into 3 equal parts. In the middle of each pastry strip, spread 1 part. After that, roll the pastry edges up and gather by pinching them to form 3 long pastry-covered sausages. Flip the rolls and glaze with the egg mixture. Then cut each roll into 1 1/4-inch pieces and place on the prepared baking sheet.
- Bake for around 20 minutes in the preheated oven, or until these rolls turn golden brown.

Nutrition Information

- Calories: 135 calories;
- Total Carbohydrate: 8.6 g
- Cholesterol: 19 mg
- Total Fat: 9.6 g
- Protein: 3.3 g
- Sodium: 161 mg

38. Perfect Pot Stickers

""These homemade dumplings are one of a kind and you can even modify these to your taste and preference. Ground pork, ginger, cabbage, and green onions make up these delectable treats!""

Serving: 6 | Prep: 25m | Ready in: 1h

Ingredients

- Filling:
- 1 lb. ground pork
- 4 cloves minced garlic
- 1/2 cup finely chopped green onions
- 3 tbsps. very finely minced fresh ginger
- 2 tbsps. soy sauce
- 1 tsp. soy sauce
- 1 tsp. sesame oil
- 1 pinch cayenne pepper
- 1 1/2 cups finely chopped green cabbage
- Dough:
- 2 1/2 cups all-purpose flour
- 3/4 tsp. kosher salt
- 1 cup hot water, about 130 -150 F (55-65 C)
- Dipping Sauce:
- 1/4 cup seasoned rice vinegar
- 1/4 cup soy sauce
- For Frying:

- 6 tbsps. vegetable oil for frying, or as needed - divided
- 8 tbsps. water for steaming, divided

Direction

- In a mixing bowl, combine the ground pork, ginger, garlic, green onions, sesame oil, 2 tbsps. + 1 tsp. soy sauce, and cayenne then top this with chopped green cabbage. Using a fork, mix all of them together until well blended. Lightly press together then cover it with plastic. Keep it refrigerated for about 1 hour until it has chilled.
- In a mixing bowl, combine the kosher salt and flour then gradually add hot water. Using a wooden spoon, stir together until the mixture has formed a rough dough. Cover your hands with flour and then move the dough to a work surface. Knead the dough for about 3-5 minutes until it's become smooth and pliable. Just drizzle with a little flour if the dough gets a bit sticky. Using a plastic wrap, wrap the dough and leave it for 30 minutes to rest.
- Divide the dough into 4 equal parts when it has rested. Use a dishcloth to cover the 3 parts while you are working on the first part of dough. Roll each dough into a small log about 3/4 inch, around the thickness of a thumb. Each log should be divided into 6 equal parts then each part should be formed into pot sticker wrappers by rolling each into about 3 1/2-inch thin circle on a surface that's been lightly floured. Do this to all the remaining dough pieces.
- Wet your finger to lightly moisten a wrapper's edges. Scoop a small part of the ground pork mixture and place it onto a wrapper's center. Fold the 2 sides of the wrapper up and pinch it together in the center. Create pleats along one side of the wrapper by pinching together the remaining edges. Flatten the bottom of the pot sticker by lightly tapping it on the work surface and make a slight curve in the sticker to make sure it stands upright in the pan. Move the pot sticker to a plate that's been well-floured and repeat the process with the rest of the dough and filling.
- Combine the soy sauce and seasoned rice vinegar in a small mixing bowl. This will be the dipping sauce for the dumplings.
- Place a cooking pan over medium-high heat and heat the oil in the pan. Put around 6-7 potstickers in the oil with its flat side down. Cook the potstickers for about 2 minutes, until the bottoms are golden brown. Sprinkle with some water and cover the pan immediately then leave it to steam for 3 minutes. Uncover the pan and lower the heat to medium. Cook for 1-2 minutes more, until the bottoms of the stickers are already brown and crunchy and the water has evaporated. Move the pot stickers to a warm serving bowl or plate. Do the same with the remaining dumplings then serve together with the sauce for dipping.

Nutrition Information

- Calories: 438 calories;
- Total Carbohydrate: 46.2 g
- Cholesterol: 54 mg
- Total Fat: 18.8 g
- Protein: 19.8 g
- Sodium: 1453 mg

39. Polish Mistakes

"A great appetizer loved by all."
Serving: 15 | Prep: 10m | Ready in: 20m

Ingredients

- 1 lb. lean ground beef
- 1 lb. sausage
- 1 tsp. minced onion
- 1 lb. processed cheese food, cubed
- 1 tsp. dried oregano
- 1 1/2 tbsps. Worcestershire sauce
- 1 (1 lb.) loaf cocktail rye bread

Direction

- Preheat the broiler.
- In a large, deep skillet, put onion, sausage, and ground beef. Cook over medium-high heat

until the onions are softened and the meat is evenly brown. Strain the liquid.

- Mix in Worcestershire sauce, oregano, and processed cheese food. Continuously stir until the cheese is melted.
- Cut the bread into thin slices if it is not sliced yet. Scoop onto each slice about 1 tbsp. of the mixture. On a baking pan, put the slices in a single layer.
- Broil the slices until the bread is toasted and the cheese is slightly browned, for 10 minutes.

Nutrition Information

- Calories: 308 calories;
- Total Carbohydrate: 3.3 g
- Cholesterol: 63 mg
- Total Fat: 25.9 g
- Protein: 14.9 g
- Sodium: 532 mg

40.Prosciutto Parmesan And Pine Nut Bruschetta

"A lightly toasted French baguette slices spread with a diced prosciutto and Parmesan cheese blend."
Serving: 12 | Prep: 20m | Ready in: 30m

Ingredients

- 1 cup butter, softened
- 1 cup diced prosciutto
- 1 cup grated Parmesan cheese
- ground black pepper to taste
- 2 French baguettes, cut into 1/2 inch slices
- 1 cup toasted pine nuts

Direction

- Preheat the oven to 175 °C or 350 °F.
- Cream the butter in a medium bowl. Mix in ground black pepper, Parmesan cheese and prosciutto.
- On a medium baking sheet, put the baguettes. In the preheated oven, heat for 10 minutes till toasted lightly.
- Scatter butter mixture on baguette slices. Set on a big serving plate. Scatter pine nuts over.

Nutrition Information

- Calories: 496 calories;
- Total Carbohydrate: 44.7 g
- Cholesterol: 58 mg
- Total Fat: 28.5 g
- Protein: 17.2 g
- Sodium: 949 mg

41. Rye Bread Party Pizzas

"Great for making ahead of time then freezing."
Serving: 15 | Prep: 30m | Ready in: 45m

Ingredients

- 1 lb. ground beef
- 1 lb. ground pork sausage
- 1 lb. processed cheese food
- 1 tsp. Worcestershire sauce
- 1 tbsp. ketchup
- 1 (1 lb.) loaf cocktail rye bread

Direction

- Preheat the oven to 175 degrees C/350 degrees F. Line aluminum foil on a medium baking sheet.
- In a big, deep skillet, put ground pork sausage and ground beef. Cook on medium high heat until browned evenly. Drain. Put aside.
- In a big, microwave safe bowl, put processed cheese food. Microwave for 3-4 minutes on high until processed cheese food melts.
- Mix in ketchup and Worcestershire sauce in the bowl of melted processed cheese food. Blend thoroughly. Mix in pork and beef.
- On every cocktail rye bread slice, put about 2 tbsp. of mixture.
- In 1 layer on the prepped baking sheet, put cocktail rye bread slices. Bake for 10-15 minutes in preheated oven until crisp and lightly browned.

Nutrition Information

- Calories: 291 calories;
- Total Carbohydrate: 3 g
- Cholesterol: 63 mg
- Total Fat: 24.5 g
- Protein: 14.1 g
- Sodium: 618 mg

42. Sausage Balls

"A really easy but delicious recipe that you have to try!"
Serving: 24

Ingredients

- 2 cups buttermilk baking mix
- 1 lb. pork sausage
- 1 (11 oz.) can condensed cream of Cheddar cheese soup

Direction

- Preheat the oven to 350°F (175°C).
- Mix the sausage, cheddar cheese soup and baking mix together in a large bowl. Mix everything together thoroughly and form the mixture into balls that are 1 inch in size.
- Put it in the preheated oven and let it bake for 15-20 minutes until the balls turn golden brown in color or a toothpick poked in the middle comes out clean.

Nutrition Information

- Calories: 128 calories;
- Total Carbohydrate: 8.5 g
- Cholesterol: 16 mg
- Total Fat: 8.8 g
- Protein: 3.6 g
- Sodium: 416 mg

43. Sausage Balls II

"A simple and appetizing dish for any party."
Serving: 12 | Prep: 10m | Ready in: 25m

Ingredients

- 1 1/2 cups biscuit mix
- 1 cup shredded Cheddar cheese
- 1 lb. fresh, ground pork sausage

Direction

- Set an oven to 175°C (350°F) and start preheating.
- Combine the sausage, Cheddar cheese, and biscuit mix together in a large bowl. Roll to form the mixture into walnut-size balls, then place them on an ungreased cookie sheet.
- Bake at 175°C (350°F) until browned and cooked completely, or for 5-15 minutes. Drain on paper towels and allow to cool.

Nutrition Information

- Calories: 260 calories;
- Total Carbohydrate: 10 g
- Cholesterol: 36 mg
- Total Fat: 20.7 g
- Protein: 8 g
- Sodium: 502 mg

44. Sausage Stuffing Balls

"This recipe came from my cousin. This baked sausage ball are meant as appetizers, but you can also recreate them for a perfect meatballs."
Serving: 20 | Prep: 20m | Ready in: 1h

Ingredients

- 1/2 cup herb-seasoned dry bread stuffing mix
- 3/4 cup hot water
- 1 lb. ground pork sausage
- 1/2 cup finely chopped onion
- 1/2 cup finely chopped celery
- 1 egg, beaten

- 1/2 tsp. baking powder

Direction

- Set the oven for preheating to 325°F (165°C).
- Mix the hot water to the herb-seasoned dry bread stuffing mix in a medium bowl. Add the pork little by little and mix until incorporated with the stuffing mix. Mix in the celery, onion, baking powder and egg.
- Form the mixture into an inch balls. Arrange the balls on a big baking sheet, cover using a foil and let it bake inside the preheated oven for roughly 15 minutes.
- Take the foil off. Increase the oven temperature to 350°F (175°C). Continuously bake for 25 minutes until it turns golden brown.

Nutrition Information

- Calories: 120 calories;
- Total Carbohydrate: 4.6 g
- Cholesterol: 25 mg
- Total Fat: 9.6 g
- Protein: 3.6 g
- Sodium: 246 mg

45. Sausage-stuffed Piquillo Peppers

"These delicious stuffed piquillo peppers can be paired with anything under the sun."
Serving: 12 | Prep: 15m | Ready in: 45m

Ingredients

- 8 tsps. olive oil, or as needed, divided
- 4 oz. chorizo sausage, casings removed and meat crumbled
- 1/2 cup diced green onion
- salt and ground black pepper to taste
- 1/2 cup cooked long-grain white rice
- 2 oz. goat cheese
- 1 large egg
- 3 tbsps. chopped fresh parsley, divided
- 2 cloves garlic, crushed
- 1 tsp. ground cumin
- 1 blood orange, zested and juiced
- 1 pinch cayenne pepper, or more to taste
- 12 piquillo peppers
- 2 tbsps. chopped almonds

Direction

- Preheat the oven to 200°C or 400°F. Grease a baking pan with a tbsp. of olive oil.
- On medium-high heat, heat a tbsp. of olive oil in a pan; add sausage, green onion and a pinch of salt. Sauté in heated oil for 5-7 minutes until the onion is translucent and the meat is crumbly and brown. Take off heat and let it cool for 10 minutes.
- In a bowl, combine rice, cayenne pepper, goat cheese, a tsp. blood orange zest, egg, cumin, 2 tbsp. parsley, and garlic; scoop rice mixture into peppers. Arrange stuffed peppers on a single layer in the greased baking pan. Sprinkle almonds and a tsp. of olive oil on top; season with salt.
- Bake in the 400°F or 200°C oven for 15-20 minutes until the stuffing is hot and the peppers are heated through. Drizzle the remaining tsp. of olive oil, a tbsp. blood orange juice, and leftover parsley on top.

Nutrition Information

- Calories: 128 calories;
- Total Carbohydrate: 6.8 g
- Cholesterol: 28 mg
- Total Fat: 9.4 g
- Protein: 5 g
- Sodium: 928 mg

46. Savory Oregano Salami

"This dish is perfect for lunchtime."
Serving: 8 | Prep: 10m | Ready in: 20m

Ingredients

- 1 lb. salami, cut into bite-size pieces

- 1 tbsp. extra-virgin olive oil
- 1 1/2 tsps. salt
- 1 tsp. ground black pepper
- 1/3 cup grated Parmesan cheese, or more to taste
- 1 1/2 tsps. chopped oregano
- 4 sprigs parsley

Direction

- In a frying pan or a grill pan, put salami over medium-high heat. Drizzle olive oil over and use pepper and salt to season. Cook for 5-7 minutes until forming grill marks. Turn the salami over and cook the second side for 5-7 minutes until turning brown.
- In a small bowl, put the salami, stir in oregano and Parmesan cheese. Use parsley to garnish.

Nutrition Information

- Calories: 244 calories;
- Total Carbohydrate: 3.4 g
- Cholesterol: 60 mg
- Total Fat: 18.7 g
- Protein: 14.9 g
- Sodium: 1636 mg

47. Scrumptious Sausage And Raisin Appetizer Balls

"An easy, hearty, and warm dish."
Serving: 10 | Prep: 15m | Ready in: 40m

Ingredients

- 1 lb. bulk pork sausage
- 1/2 cup golden raisins
- 1/2 tsp. dried basil
- 1 pinch paprika, or as needed

Direction

- Set the oven at 190°C (375°F) to preheat.
- In a bowl, mix basil, raisins, and sausage together; form into walnut-size balls. Place these balls on a jelly roll pan with sides or baking sheet; dust with paprika.
- In the preheated oven, bake for 15 minutes. Remove the sheet from the oven, drain off fat; if needed, re-roll the balls and dust with more paprika. Continue to bake for 10-15 minutes more, or until cooked through. Check by inserting an instant-read thermometer into the center and it should state at least 70°C (160°F). Drain.

Nutrition Information

- Calories: 138 calories;
- Total Carbohydrate: 6.2 g
- Cholesterol: 26 mg
- Total Fat: 9.8 g
- Protein: 6.4 g
- Sodium: 406 mg

48. Shrimp Nicholas

"A tasty dish."
Serving: 10 | Prep: 20m | Ready in: 30m

Ingredients

- 24 medium shrimp, peeled and butterflied
- 4 oz. fresh mozzarella cheese, cut into strips
- 12 thin slices prosciutto
- 1 jarred roasted red pepper, drained and cut into strips
- 1/2 cup all-purpose flour
- 1 egg
- 2 tbsps. water
- 1 pinch salt
- 1 cup panko bread crumbs
- vegetable oil for deep-frying

Direction

- On a clean surface, lay the shrimp out so the 2 halves are spread open like a book. Put in the center with a strip of mozzarella cheese, followed by a strip of roasted pepper. Close the shrimp and wrap each with a slice of prosciutto.

- In a small dish, put the flour. Use a fork to whisk the egg, salt, and water in a separate dish. In the third dish, put the panko crumbs. In a large skillet, heat the oil over medium to medium-high heat, or until it reaches 190°C (375°F). To coat the wrapped shrimp, dip them in flour, then continue to dip in the egg mixture. Then roll in the panko crumbs until coated evenly.
- In the hot oil, fry the shrimp for about 1 minute each side, or until the cheese is melting and the shrimp is golden brown. Use a slotted spoon to remove and drain on paper towels before serving.

Nutrition Information

- Calories: 198 calories;
- Total Carbohydrate: 13.3 g
- Cholesterol: 57 mg
- Total Fat: 12.9 g
- Protein: 9.1 g
- Sodium: 303 mg

49.Spicy Ham And Cheese Squares

"Delicious spicy cheese and ham squares that are baked excellently."

Serving: 12 | Prep: 20m | Ready in: 50m

Ingredients

- olive oil cooking spray (such as PAM®)
- 1 (8 oz.) package refrigerated crescent rolls
- 1/4 lb. deli ham
- 1/4 lb. sliced pepperoni
- 1/4 lb. sliced salami
- 1/4 lb. Swiss cheese
- 1/4 lb. provolone cheese
- 3 eggs, beaten
- 1 (8 oz.) package refrigerated crescent rolls

Direction

- Preheat the oven to 175 degrees C/350 degrees F.
- Spray cooking spray on a 9x13-in. baking dish.
- In prepped baking dish, press 1 package of crescent rolls. Push seams together.
- On top of crescent rolls, layer ham, pepperoni, salami, Swiss cheese and provolone cheese.
- Put beaten eggs on cheese and meat layers. Keep about 1 tbsp. egg.
- On the cheese and meat filling, layer 2nd package of crescent rolls. Brush on reserved egg.
- Bake in preheated oven until crescent rolls brown and cheese melts.
- Cut to squares. Serve.

Nutrition Information

- Calories: 340 calories;
- Total Carbohydrate: 15.8 g
- Cholesterol: 86 mg
- Total Fat: 23.1 g
- Protein: 15.3 g
- Sodium: 880 mg

50.Spicy Kielbasa Dip

"This dip is very easy to control the heat by removing the seeds and ribs. For a very spicy dip, leave all the seeds and ribs intact. Serve greatly with sliced sourdough baguettes."

Serving: 8 | Prep: 15m | Ready in: 30m

Ingredients

- 1 (3 oz.) package cream cheese, softened
- 1 cup mayonnaise
- 7 oz. fully cooked kielbasa sausage, diced
- 4 green onions, chopped
- 1/2 cup shredded Italian 6-cheese blend (such as Sargento® Chef Blends®)
- 1 jalapeno pepper, seeded and minced
- 1/2 tsp. garlic powder

Direction

- Set the oven to 190°C or 375°F.
- In a bowl, fold together garlic powder, jalapeno pepper, Italian cheese blend, green onions, sausage, mayonnaise and cream cheese until blended evenly, then turn to a small baking dish.
- Bake in preheated oven for 15 to 20 minutes, until bubbling and hot.

Nutrition Information

- Calories: 340 calories;
- Total Carbohydrate: 2.9 g
- Cholesterol: 44 mg
- Total Fat: 34.3 g
- Protein: 5.9 g
- Sodium: 474 mg

51. Spicy Rye Rounds

"This perfect recipe for holidays can be prepared in advance and frozen until serve"
Serving: 8 | Prep: 10m | Ready in: 17m

Ingredients

- 1 lb. lean ground beef
- 1 lb. spicy Italian sausage
- 1 lb. processed cheese food, cubed
- 1 (1 lb.) loaf cocktail rye bread

Direction

- Set oven to 325°F (165°C) and start preheating.
- Cook sausage and ground beef in a big skillet until browned. After sausage and beef are browned, add cheese and mix frequently. When all ingredients are well combined, spoon on each piece of rye bread with 1 tbsp. of the beef and sausage mixture. Place bread with toppings on a baking sheet.
- Bake for 5 to 7 minutes.

Nutrition Information

- Calories: 676 calories;
- Total Carbohydrate: 31.7 g
- Cholesterol: 122 mg
- Total Fat: 45.2 g
- Protein: 34.6 g
- Sodium: 1375 mg

52. Spring Rolls

"Serve your favorite sauce with these delicious spring rolls that are full of pork, seafood, and veggies! Instead of ground pork, you can use ground turkey in this recipe."
Serving: 20 | Prep: 1h30m | Ready in: 1h50m

Ingredients

- 2 oz. dry soy vermicelli
- 4 eggs, beaten
- 1 onion, finely chopped
- 2 oz. mushrooms, drained and chopped
- 3/4 (4 oz.) can small shrimp, drained and chopped
- 1 lb. lean ground pork
- 2 tbsps. vegetable oil
- 1 carrot, shredded
- 2 oz. crabmeat
- 3 oz. bean sprouts
- 2 pinches ground black pepper
- 1 tbsp. soy sauce
- 3 tbsps. fish sauce
- 1 clove garlic, chopped
- 20 rice wrappers (6.5 inch diameter)
- 1 quart oil for deep frying

Direction

- Soak vermicelli in warm water for half an hour; drain.
- Stir garlic, vermicelli, fish sauce, eggs, soy sauce, onion, pepper, mushrooms, bean sprouts, shrimp, crabmeat, pork, carrot, and vegetable oil together in a big bowl.
- Using a damp tea towel, dampen the rice wrappers one at a time; fill each wrapper with 2-3tbsp of vermicelli mixture then roll. Let the rolls stand for half an hour.

- Heat oil in a big pot until it reaches 190°C or 375°Fahrenheit.
- Fry 1-2 spring rolls at a time for 3mins until golden brown; place on paper towels to drain.

Nutrition Information

- Calories: 161 calories;
- Total Carbohydrate: 5.9 g
- Cholesterol: 63 mg
- Total Fat: 11.8 g
- Protein: 7.8 g
- Sodium: 268 mg

53. Swedish Chanterelle Mushroom Pate

"To make this dish more delicious, combine ground pork and golden chanterelle mushrooms and enjoy!"
Serving: 8 | Prep: 25m | Ready in: 1h40m

Ingredients

- 1 tbsp. butter
- 2 cloves garlic, minced
- 2 shallots, finely chopped
- 1 tbsp. butter
- 1 lb. fresh or frozen chanterelle mushrooms, torn
- 1/4 cup chopped fresh parsley
- 3/4 lb. ground pork
- 2 egg whites
- 1 1/2 tsps. salt
- 1/2 tsp. ground black pepper
- 1/2 cup whipping cream
- 10 thin slices smoked ham

Direction

- Prepare the oven by preheating to 300 degrees F (150 degrees C). Get an 8 1/2 x4 1/2 inch loaf pan and line with aluminum foil.
- Place a skillet on the stove and turn on to medium heat then melt 1 tbsp. butter. Mix in the shallots and garlic; stir and cook for about 5 minutes until shallots is soft and translucent. Then place it into a mixing bowl, and reserve to cool. Put the left tbsp. of butter using the same skillet over medium-high heat. Mix in the chanterelles, and let cook for 5 minutes until soft and edges are golden. Mix in the parsley and cook for 30 seconds more, and then transfer into the mixing bowl, and let it cool for 5 minutes.
- Add in the pepper, salt, egg whites and ground pork into the mushroom mixture using your hands to blend equally. Mix in the cream until absorbed well by pork mixture. Line with smoked ham the sides and bottom of the loaf pan. Put the meat mixture into the loaf pan and compress the top to flatten.
- Place inside the preheated oven for about 1 hour until no more pink color in the middle, and achieved the internal temperature of 160 degree F (72 degrees C). You can present it chilled or warm in slices.

Nutrition Information

- Calories: 229 calories;
- Total Carbohydrate: 6.8 g
- Cholesterol: 66 mg
- Total Fat: 16 g
- Protein: 13.4 g
- Sodium: 744 mg

54. Sweet And Spicy Barbecue Meatballs

"Sweet and spicy sauce for tasty barbecue meatballs."
Serving: 15

Ingredients

- Reynolds Wrap® Non Stick Aluminum Foil
- Meatballs:
- 2 1/2 lbs. ground chuck beef
- 2 lbs. ground pork
- 1/2 cup dry bread crumbs
- 2 tsps. steak seasoning
- 1/2 tsp. salt
- 1/4 tsp. pepper

- 1 tsp. garlic powder
- 2 eggs
- Sauce:
- 1 (32 oz.) container barbecue sauce
- 1 (32 oz.) jar grape jelly
- Hot sauce (optional)

Direction

- Set the oven at 375°F to preheat. Use Reynolds(R) Nonstick Aluminum Foil (set the dull side up) to line 4 baking sheets.
- Mix together the meat and all other meatball ingredients, then roll into 80 bite-size meatballs. On each pan, put 20 meatballs and bake until browned all the way through, about 35 minutes.
- While baking the meatballs, in a saucepan, pour the grape jelly and the barbecue sauce; over medium heat, heat until they are well blended. Add extra hot sauce to the mixture if you want to have a little extra flavor on the meatballs. When the meatballs are done, slide them off the pan into the serving dish. Pour the sauce on top and enjoy immediately. If you bring the final dish to a party, reheat it in the microwave.

Nutrition Information

- Calories: 536 calories;
- Total Carbohydrate: 64.2 g
- Cholesterol: 114 mg
- Total Fat: 18.8 g
- Protein: 26.7 g
- Sodium: 996 mg

55. Wicked Good Dip

"I make this tasty dip with Colby cheese, cream cheese, and ham. It has a zesty taste that comes from cayenne pepper, mustard, and olives."
Serving: 16

Ingredients

- 3 (8 oz.) packages cream cheese, softened
- 2 (4.5 oz.) cans deviled ham spread
- 1 lb. Colby cheese, shredded
- 1/4 cup chopped green olives
- 2 tbsps. prepared yellow mustard
- 1/2 tbsp. chopped black olives
- 1/2 tsp. mustard powder
- 1/2 tsp. celery salt
- 1/2 tsp. cayenne pepper
- 1/2 tsp. garlic salt

Direction

- Combine black olives, mustard, green olives, shredded cheese, deviled ham spread, and cream cheese together in a medium-sized bowl. Use garlic salt, cayenne pepper, celery salt, and mustard powder to season. Stir thoroughly, put a cover on and chill for a minimum of 15 minutes before using.

Nutrition Information

- Calories: 306 calories;
- Total Carbohydrate: 2.3 g
- Cholesterol: 81 mg
- Total Fat: 27.9 g
- Protein: 12.2 g
- Sodium: 585 mg

56. Witlof With Ham

"A great appetizer using Belgian endive or Witlof that's tasty and easy to make."
Serving: 4 | Prep: 15m | Ready in: 25m

Ingredients

- 4 medium heads Belgian endive
- 4 (1/2 oz.) slices prosciutto
- 1 cup grated Gruyere cheese

Direction

- Preheat grill for medium heat. When grill is ready, brush grate with oil lightly.
- In a shallow baking dish, put 1/4 cup water and endive. Use plastic wrap to cover.

Microwave until slightly tender for 2 minutes. Take out of dish. Pat dry.

- Wrap prosciutto around every whole endive. Secure by piercing with a toothpick. Directly put each piece on grill. Cook for 3 minutes, occasionally turning, until endive is tender and ham is browned.
- Put into disposable foil baking dish. Sprinkle cheese on. Put back onto the grill. Cover and continue cooking until cheese melts.

Nutrition Information

- Calories: 276 calories;
- Total Carbohydrate: 17.3 g
- Cholesterol: 49 mg
- Total Fat: 16.2 g
- Protein: 19 g
- Sodium: 498 mg

57. Wrapped Asparagus

"A sophisticated blend of lemon, delicate goat cheese, asparagus, garlic and delicious Margherita ® Prosciutto, create a delightful appetizer, an appealing buffet product or a delicious side dish."

Serving: 8 | Prep: 25m | Ready in: 40m

Ingredients

- 1 tbsp. lemon juice
- 1 tbsp. olive oil
- 1 clove garlic, minced
- 16 medium fresh asparagus spears, each trimmed to 5 inches
- 8 thin slices Margherita® Deli Prosciutto
- 1/3 cup soft goat cheese

Direction

- Preheat the oven to 425°F. Combine in a big bowl the olive oil, lemon juice, and garlic. Add asparagus, then toss to coat. In the baking pan, place asparagus.
- Bake for 8 minutes or until crisp-tender. Let cool to room temperature for about 15 minutes.
- Cut each prosciutto piece lengthways in half. Spread 1 tsp goat cheese on each piece. Wrap each slice around each spear of asparagus in a spiral. Serve right away, or cover and refrigerate until ready to serve.

Nutrition Information

- Calories: 85 calories;
- Total Carbohydrate: 1.8 g
- Cholesterol: 19 mg
- Total Fat: 6.1 g
- Protein: 6.3 g
- Sodium: 341 mg

Chapter 2: Buffalo Wings Recipes

***

58. Baked Spicy Chicken Wings

"Tasty chicken wings that are deliciously paired with a fresh salad and curried almond rice."

Serving: 6 main-dish or 12 appetizer servings. | Prep: 15m | Ready in: 55m

Ingredients

- 1 can (6 oz.) frozen orange juice concentrate, thawed
- 1 can (6 oz.) tomato paste
- 1/4 cup honey or packed brown sugar
- 2 to 3 garlic cloves, crushed
- 1 tsp. grated lime zest
- 1 tsp. grated lemon zest
- 1 tsp. grated orange zest
- 2 tbsps. lemon juice
- 2 tbsps. lime juice
- 1/2 tsp. seasoned pepper

- 1/2 tsp. salt
- 1/4 tsp. thyme
- Few drops hot pepper sauce
- 30 to 36 chicken wings or drumettes (about 3-1/2 lbs.)

Direction

- Blend all the ingredients but not chicken in a saucepan; heat them and stir until combined. Allow to cool to room temperature. In a shallow baking pan, arrange the chicken; pour sauce on top. Put a cover on and put in the fridge to marinate for 12-24 hours. Take the chicken out from the marinade to cook and arrange on a broiler pan. Retain the marinade. Bake at 375 degrees until tender or for approximately 40 minutes. Turn the chicken and brush from time to time using marinade.

59. Barbecued Hot Wings

"An ambrosial dish of spicy chicken wings that you cannot resist. You can serve them along with celery sticks and blue cheese dressing."

Serving: 6-8 servings. | Prep: 10m | Ready in: 30m

Ingredients

- 12 whole chicken wings (about 2-1/2 lbs.)
- 1 bottle (8 oz.) Italian salad dressing
- 1/2 to 3/4 cup hot pepper sauce
- 1/8 to 1/2 tsp. cayenne pepper
- 2 tbsps. butter, melted

Direction

- Divide the chicken wings into 3 sections; discard the wing tips.
- Blend the cayenne, pepper sauce, and salad dressing in a bowl. Take out 1/2 cup for basting; put a cover on and put in the fridge. In a large resealable plastic bag, arrange the remaining sauce; put in the chicken and coat by turning. Put a cover on and put in the fridge overnight.
- Discard the marinade. Put a cover on, grill the wings for 12-16 minutes on medium heat and turn from time to time. Put the butter into the retained sauce; brush on top of the wings.
- Remove the cover and grill until the juices run clear, or for 8-10 more minutes, turn and baste a few times.

60. Buffalo Chicken Wings

"A great recipe for tasty spicy chicken wings along with blue cheese dressing."

Serving: 4 | Prep: 20m | Ready in: 40m

Ingredients

- 1 cup vegetable oil
- 1 lb. chicken wings
- 1/2 tsp. salt
- 1/2 tsp. ground white pepper
- 1/2 cup butter
- 1/2 tsp. hot pepper sauce
- 1 cup mayonnaise
- 4 tbsps. minced onion
- 3 cloves garlic, minced
- 1/3 cup chopped fresh parsley
- 1/2 cup sour cream
- 1 tbsp. lemon juice
- 1 tbsp. distilled white vinegar
- 1/2 cup blue cheese, crumbled
- 1/8 tsp. salt
- 1/8 tsp. ground black pepper

Direction

- Set an oven to 175°C (350°F) and start preheating.
- Heat the oil to 190°C (375°F) in a large deep fryer or frying pan. Fry the wings for about 8 minutes. Place the wings onto a paper towel and drain them. Flavor with white pepper and salt. In a large mixing bowl, arrange the wings after the wings have been drained.
- Let the margarine or butter in a small saucepan. Add in the hot pepper sauce and stir. Top the chicken wings with the mixture,

toss the wings to coat. In a baking dish, arrange the wings.

- Bake for 15-20 minutes.
- Prepare the blue cheese dressing while the chicken wings are baking: Blend blue cheese, vinegar, lemon juice, sour cream, parsley, garlic, onion, and mayonnaise in a medium-size mixing bowl. Combine the mixture properly. On a serving platter, place the baked chicken wings. Serve together with blue cheese dressing.

Nutrition Information

- Calories: 870 calories;
- Total Carbohydrate: 6.6 g
- Cholesterol: 130 mg
- Total Fat: 89.4 g
- Protein: 13.1 g
- Sodium: 1131 mg

61. Buttery Hot Wings

"Hope you enjoy these."
Serving: about 3 dozen (2 cups sauce). | Prep: 20m | Ready in: 30m

Ingredients

- 20 whole chicken wings (4 lbs.)
- 2 cups whole wheat flour
- 1 cup all-purpose flour
- 1 tsp. salt
- 1 tsp. paprika
- 1/4 tsp. cayenne pepper
- Oil for deep-fat frying
- SAUCE:
- 1-1/2 cups butter, cubed
- 1/3 cup hot pepper sauce
- 3 tbsps. brown sugar
- 2 tbsps. chili sauce
- 2 tbsps. honey
- 1 tbsp. balsamic vinegar
- 3/4 tsp. salt
- 3/4 tsp. paprika
- 1/4 to 1/2 tsp. cayenne pepper

Direction

- Cut chicken wings into 3 parts; remove the wing tip parts. Combine cayenne, paprika, salt, and flours in a large resealable plastic bag. Put in the wings, a few at a time, then shake well to coat.
- Heat 1 in. of oil to 375° in a deep-fat fryer or an electric skillet. Fry 6-8 wings at a time until juices run clear, for 3-4 minutes on each side; add more oil if necessary. Drain on paper towels. Move them to a large bowl and keep warm.
- Combine the sauce ingredients in a large saucepan. Cook and stir over medium heat until butter is melted, for 10 minutes. Then pour over the chicken wings and toss to coat. Serve immediately.

62. Chicken Wings With Spicy Apricot Sauce

"Flavorful sweet-and-sour sauce for a delicious appetizer."
Serving: 6 dozen. | Prep: 15m | Ready in: 25m

Ingredients

- 3 dozen whole chicken wings
- 1-1/2 cups cornstarch
- 1 tbsp. baking powder
- 1-1/2 tsps. salt
- 1/2 tsp. pepper
- 1/2 tsp. sugar
- 3 eggs, beaten
- Oil for deep-fat frying
- SAUCE:
- 1 cup (3 oz.) dried apricots
- 1-1/4 cups water
- 2 tbsps. sugar
- 2 tbsps. cider vinegar
- 2 tbsps. honey
- 1/8 to 1/4 tsp. cayenne pepper

Direction

- Cut chicken wings into 3 parts; remove the wing tip part. In a large resealable plastic bag or shallow bowl, combine sugar, pepper, salt, baking powder, and cornstarch. First, dip the chicken pieces in eggs, then generously coat with the cornstarch mixture.
- Heat oil to 350° in a deep-fat fryer or an electric skillet. Fry the chicken wings, a few at a time, until juices run clear, for about 9 minutes. Drain on paper towels and keep warm.
- In the meantime, combine water and apricots in a large saucepan; bring to a boil. Lower the heat; simmer, covered, until the apricots are softened.
- Transfer to a food processor or blender. Add cayenne, honey, vinegar, and sugar; process until smooth on high. Cool slightly. Enjoy with the chicken wings.

63. Cola Hot Wings

"Simple yet tasty chicken wings to enjoy at any time throughout the year."

Serving: about 2-1/2 dozen. | Prep: 15m | Ready in: 55m

Ingredients

- 3 lbs. chicken wings
- 1 cup Louisiana-style hot sauce
- 1 can (12 oz.) cola
- 1 tbsp. soy sauce
- 1/4 tsp. cayenne pepper
- 1/4 tsp. pepper
- Blue cheese salad dressing

Direction

- Divide the chicken wings into 3 sections; discard the wing tip sections. Blend pepper, cayenne, soy sauce, cola, and hot sauce in a small bowl.
- Use a drip pan to prepare the grill for indirect heat. On an oiled rack, put a cover on and grill the chicken wings on indirect medium heat for 10 minutes. Grill, regularly basting with sauce and turn from time to time until the wings are glazed nicely, 30-40 more minutes. Then serve together with salad dressing.

Nutrition Information

- Calories: 57 calories
- Total Carbohydrate: 2 g
- Cholesterol: 15 mg
- Total Fat: 3 g
- Fiber: 0 g
- Protein: 5 g
- Sodium: 48 mg

64. Cranberry Hot Wings

"This recipe will warm up a winter night."

Serving: about 2-1/2 dozen. | Prep: 50m | Ready in: 02h50m

Ingredients

- 1 can (14 oz.) jellied cranberry sauce, cubed
- 2 tbsps. ground mustard
- 2 tbsps. hot pepper sauce
- 2 tbsps. reduced-sodium soy sauce
- 2 tbsps. honey
- 1 tbsp. cider vinegar
- 2 tsps. garlic powder
- 1 tsp. grated orange zest
- 3 lbs. chicken wings
- Blue cheese salad dressing and celery sticks

Direction

- Combine the first 8 ingredients in a 5-qt. slow cooker. Cover and cook on low until the cranberry sauce is melted, about 45 minutes.
- In the meantime, chop the wings into 3 parts; remove the wing tip parts. On a greased broiler pan, arrange the wings. Next, broil 4-6 in. from the heat until lightly browned, turning infrequently, about 15-20 minutes.
- Transfer the wings to the slow cooker; toss to coat well. Cook on high, covered, until

softened, about 2-3 hours. Enjoy with celery and dressing.

65. Deep-fried Spicy Chicken Wings

""Perfect appetizers and the best that I've ever tried.""
Serving: about 3 dozen. | Prep: 15m | Ready in: 30m

Ingredients

- 16 to 18 chicken wings (about 4 lbs.)
- Oil for deep-fat frying
- 1/2 cup butter, melted
- 1/2 cup hot pepper sauce
- 2 tbsps. cider vinegar
- Carrots and celery sticks
- Blue cheese dressing

Direction

- Slice wings into three sections; remove the wingtips. Fry the chicken in hot oil (5-7 minutes for small parts, 6-8 minutes for drumettes) until juices run clear and crisp.
- Mix vinegar, hot pepper sauce, and butter in a bowl; put in the chicken and toss to coat. Drain. Serve with dressing, celery, and carrots.

66. Favorite Hot Wings

""I enjoy making these wings ahead of time and put them in a slow cooker to keep them warm for parties with yummy mild sauce!""
Serving: 10 servings. | Prep: 10m | Ready in: 30m

Ingredients

- 20 whole chicken wings (about 4 lbs.)
- Vegetable oil for deep-fat frying
- 1/2 cup butter or margarine
- 1-1/2 tsps. brown sugar
- 1 tsp. lemon juice
- 1 garlic clove, minced
- 2 to 3 tbsps. Louisiana hot sauce
- 3 to 4 tsps. hot pepper sauce
- Celery and carrot sticks
- Ranch or blue cheese salad dressing

Direction

- Slice chicken wings into three parts; remove wingtips. Put oil in a deep-fat fryer or an electric skillet and heat to 375 degrees. Put in chicken wings a few at a time and fry until juices run clear. Transfer to paper towels to drain.
- Place butter in a large skillet to melt. Mix in the hot sauce, garlic, lemon juice, and brown sugar; bring to just a boil. Put in chicken wings; flip to coat. Cook and flip over for 5 to 10 minutes or until coated well. Serve with carrot sticks and celery and salad dressing for dipping.

67. Gingered Sweet & Spicy Hot Wings

"These wings are the champion of any day of the week thanks to the sweet and hot flavors bursting through in every bite."
Serving: about 3 dozen. | Prep: 15m | Ready in: 50m

Ingredients

- 1 cup orange marmalade
- 1/2 cup minced fresh cilantro
- 1/2 cup Sriracha Asian hot chili sauce
- 1/2 cup reduced-sodium soy sauce
- 1/4 cup lime juice
- 1/4 cup rice vinegar
- 1/4 cup ketchup
- 1/4 cup honey
- 4 garlic cloves, minced
- 1 tbsp. minced fresh gingerroot
- 1 tbsp. grated lime zest
- 1 tbsp. sesame oil
- 1 tsp. salt
- 1 tsp. pepper
- 4 lbs. chicken wingettes and drumettes

Direction

- Combine the first 14 ingredients in a large bowl. Put in the chicken; flip to coat. Cover and chill for 8 hours or overnight.
- Set the oven at 375° to preheat. Drain the chicken, removing the marinade. Next, transfer the chicken to 2 greased 15x10x1-in. baking pans. Bake until juices run clear, for 35-45 minutes.

68. Grilled Spicy Chicken Wings

"Delicious wings pairing with a salad, beans, and spicy rice to serve as a party appetizer or family dinner."
Serving: 2 dozen. | Prep: 30m | Ready in: 50m

Ingredients

- 12 whole chicken wings (about 2-1/2 lbs.)
- 2 cans (10 oz. each) green enchilada sauce
- 3 tbsps. lime juice
- 1/2 cup mild green taco sauce
- 2 tbsps. butter, melted

Direction

- Divide the chicken wings into 3 sections; discard the wing tip sections. Blend the lime juice and enchilada sauce in a large resealable plastic bag. Put in wings; seal the bag and coat by turning. Put in the fridge for 6 hours or overnight.
- Blend the butter and the taco sauce in a small bowl. Let the chicken wings drain and discard the marinade. Put a cover on and grill the wings for 10 minutes on indirect medium heat. Turn and grill until the juices run clear, or for 10-20 more minutes, turn and baste from time to time with the sauce.

Nutrition Information

- Calories: 68 calories
- Total Carbohydrate: 1 g
- Cholesterol: 18 mg
- Total Fat: 5 g
- Fiber: 0 g
- Protein: 5 g
- Sodium: 110 mg

69. Hot Wings

"These hot wings are addicting."
Serving: 15 | Prep: 5m | Ready in: 30m

Ingredients

- 4 lbs. chicken wings
- 1 tsp. garlic powder
- 1/2 tsp. ground black pepper
- 1 cup tomato-based hot pepper sauce
- 2 tbsps. vinegar-based hot pepper sauce
- 1 tsp. garlic powder
- 1/4 cup grated Parmesan cheese
- 3 tbsps. butter, melted

Direction

- Set an indoor or outdoor grill to high heat to preheat. Grease the grill lightly.
- Season the wings with ground black pepper and garlic powder. On the preheated grill, cook until they are very crispy. Flip the wings often as they're easily burned.
- While grilling the wings, combine melted butter, Parmesan cheese, both hot sauces with garlic powder in a large bowl.
- When the cooking the wings is done, in the large bowl of the hot sauce mixture, put them in and stir until they are covered.

Nutrition Information

- Calories: 317 calories;
- Total Carbohydrate: 4.9 g
- Cholesterol: 101 mg
- Total Fat: 22.2 g
- Protein: 23.4 g
- Sodium: 386 mg

70. Like 'em Hot Wings

"Well-seasoned spicy chicken wings are a simple and delightful snack."
Serving: about 2 dozen. | Prep: 10m | Ready in: 40m

Ingredients

- 2-1/2 lbs. chicken wings
- 1 bottle (2 oz.) hot pepper sauce (about 1/4 cup)
- 1 to 2 garlic cloves, minced
- 1-1/2 tsps. dried rosemary, crushed
- 1 tsp. dried thyme
- 1/4 tsp. salt
- 1/4 tsp. pepper
- Celery sticks, carrot sticks and blue cheese salad dressing, optional

Direction

- Divide the chicken wings into 3 sections; discard the wingtips. Blend the seasonings, garlic, and hot pepper sauce in a large resealable plastic bag. Put in wings; toss to cover evenly. Place into a well-greased 13x9-inch baking dish.
- Remove the cover, bake at 425 degrees until the chicken juices run clear, or for 30-40 minutes and turn every 10 minutes. If desired, serve together with blue cheese dressing, carrots, and celery.

Nutrition Information

- Calories: 43 calories
- Total Carbohydrate: 0 g
- Cholesterol: 12 mg
- Total Fat: 3 g
- Fiber: 0 g
- Protein: 4 g
- Sodium: 51 mg

71. Orange-pecan Hot Wings

"“I enjoy using orange juice and oranges in many different ways and these chicken wings are a yummy appetizer that our friends enjoy.”"
Serving: 8-10 servings. | Prep: 25m | Ready in: 01h20m

Ingredients

- 3 lbs. whole chicken wings
- 3 eggs
- 1 can (6 oz.) frozen orange juice concentrate, thawed
- 2 tbsps. water
- 1 cup all-purpose flour
- 1/2 cup finely chopped pecans
- 1/2 cup butter, melted
- RED HOT SAUCE:
- 2 cups ketchup
- 3/4 cup packed brown sugar
- 2 to 3 tbsps. hot pepper sauce

Direction

- Slice chicken wings into three sections; remove wingtips.
- Mix water, orange juice concentrate, and eggs in a bowl. Mix pecans and flour in another bowl or a resealable plastic bag. Dunk wings in egg mixture, then toss or roll in flour mixture.
- Pour the butter into a 15x10x1-inch baking pan. Put wings in the pan and arrange them in one single layer. Bake for 25 minutes at 375 degrees, without cover.
- In the meantime, mix the sauce ingredients. Scoop half over the wings; flip over. Put the remaining sauce on top. Bake for 30 more minutes or until meat juices run clear.

Nutrition Information

- Calories: 480 calories
- Total Carbohydrate: 46 g
- Cholesterol: 132 mg
- Total Fat: 25 g
- Fiber: 2 g
- Protein: 19 g

- Sodium: 749 mg

72. Pressure Cooker Cranberry Hot Wings

"Such a good recipe of cranberry wings."
Serving: about 4 dozen. | Prep: 45m | Ready in: 01h20m

Ingredients

- 1 can (14 oz.) jellied cranberry sauce
- 1/2 cup orange juice
- 1/4 cup hot pepper sauce
- 2 tbsps. soy sauce
- 2 tbsps. honey
- 1 tbsp. brown sugar
- 1 tbsp. Dijon mustard
- 2 tsps. garlic powder
- 1 tsp. dried minced onion
- 1 garlic clove, minced
- 5 lbs. chicken wings (about 24 wings)
- 1 tsp. salt
- 4 tsps. cornstarch
- 2 tbsps. cold water

Direction

- In a bowl, whisk the first 10 ingredients together. To prepare the chicken: cut through 2 wing joints using a sharp knife; remove the wingtips. In a 6-qt. electric pressure cooker, put the wing pieces and dust with salt. Pour over the top with the cranberry mixture. Lock the lid and make sure that the vent is closed. Choose the manual setting; set the pressure to high and the timer for 10 minutes. When the cooking is done, quickly release the pressure following the manufacturer's directions.
- Transfer the wings to a 15x10x1-in. pan and place in a single layer. Next, preheat the broiler. In the meantime, skim the fat from the cooking juices in a pressure cooker. Select the sauté setting and set for high heat. Boil the juices; cook for 20-25 minutes, occasionally stirring, until the mixture is reduced by half. Mix water and cornstarch in a small bowl until smooth; put into the juices and stir. Bring back to a boil, stirring continuously; cook and stir for 1-2 minutes, or until the glaze is thickened.
- Broil the wings 3-4 in. from heat for 2-3 minutes, until lightly browned. Before serving, sweep wings with glaze. Enjoy with the remaining glaze.

Nutrition Information

- Calories: 71 calories
- Total Carbohydrate: 5 g
- Cholesterol: 15 mg
- Total Fat: 4 g
- Fiber: 0 g
- Protein: 5 g
- Sodium: 122 mg

73. Spicy BBQ Chicken Wings

"These wings will warm you up from the inside."
Serving: 16 servings. | Prep: 25m | Ready in: 01h10m

Ingredients

- 4 lbs. chicken wings
- 2 cups white vinegar
- 2 cups water
- 1 cup all-purpose flour
- 1 tbsp. adobo seasoning
- 1 tsp. garlic salt
- 1 tsp. coarsely ground pepper
- 1 tsp. kosher salt
- 1 tsp. onion powder
- Canola oil for frying
- 1 cup honey barbecue sauce
- 1 cup hickory smoke-flavored barbecue sauce
- 1/4 cup honey
- 1 jalapeno pepper, seeded and minced

Direction

- Cut through the 2 wing joints using a sharp knife; remove the wingtips. In a large bowl, put the wings, then add water and vinegar. Cover and chill for 45 minutes. Drain and rinse, removing the vinegar mixture. Combine seasonings and flour; put in the chicken and toss to coat.

- Set the oven at 375° to preheat. Heat 1 in. oil to 375° in a deep skillet. Fry the wings, a few at a time, until golden brown, for 3-4 minutes each side. Drain on paper towels and cool for 10 minutes.
- In the meantime, cook and stir jalapeno, honey, and barbecue sauces in a small saucepan over medium heat. Bring to a boil; reduce the heat and simmer for 10-15 minutes, stirring sometimes, to allow the flavors to combine.
- Dip the wings in the sauce; arrange on greased foil-lined baking pans. Then bake for about 10 minutes, until glazed.

Nutrition Information

- Calories: 317 calories
- Total Carbohydrate: 23 g
- Cholesterol: 36 mg
- Total Fat: 19 g
- Fiber: 0 g
- Protein: 12 g
- Sodium: 816 mg

74. Spicy Breaded Chicken Wings

"“Baked chicken wings that everybody loves and are lovely even without the dipping sauce.”"

Serving: 20 pieces. | Prep: 25m | Ready in: 50m

Ingredients

- 1 large egg
- 1 tbsp. water
- 2/3 cup dry bread crumbs
- 1 tsp. onion powder
- 1 tsp. dried basil
- 1 tsp. cayenne pepper
- 1/2 tsp. garlic salt
- 1/2 tsp. paprika
- 10 whole chicken wings
- DIPPING SAUCE:
- 2 tbsps. ketchup
- 2 tbsps. honey
- 1 tbsp. Worcestershire sauce
- 1/2 tsp. hot pepper sauce

Direction

- Whisk water and egg in a shallow bowl. Mix the paprika, garlic salt, cayenne, basil, onion powder, and bread crumbs in another shallow bowl.
- Slice chicken wings into three parts; remove wingtip sections. Dunk chicken wings into the egg mixture, and press into crumb mixture to coat. Put in a 15x10x1-inch baking pan that is greased. Bake for 25-30 minutes at 425 degrees or until juices run clear, flipping over every 10 minutes.
- Mix the sauce ingredients in a small bowl. Serve it with chicken wings.

Nutrition Information

- Calories: 77 calories
- Total Carbohydrate: 5 g
- Cholesterol: 24 mg
- Total Fat: 4 g
- Fiber: 0 g
- Protein: 5 g
- Sodium: 121 mg

75. Spicy Butterscotch Wings

"“I balance the heat with a caramel sauce but you use melted brown sugar as well to glaze the wings.”"

Serving: 20 servings. | Prep: 25m | Ready in: 50m

Ingredients

- 2 lbs. chicken wings
- 2 tbsps. soy sauce
- 2 tbsps. ketchup
- 2 tbsps. Sriracha Asian hot chili sauce
- 1 tsp. pepper
- 1 tsp. crushed red pepper flakes
- 1 tsp. onion powder

- 1/2 tsp. salt
- BUTTERSCOTCH SAUCE:
- 1/2 cup sugar
- 1/2 cup 2% milk, warmed
- 2 tbsps. butter
- CRUMB TOPPING:
- 1 tbsp. butter
- 1/2 cup panko (Japanese) bread crumbs
- 2 green onions, sliced diagonally, divided
- 1 garlic clove, minced
- 1/2 tsp. salt
- 1/2 tsp. pepper
- 2 red bird's eye chili peppers, minced, optional

Direction

- Prepare the oven by preheating to 400 degrees. Cut through the two wing joints with a sharp knife; remove wingtips. Mix the next seven ingredients; put in wings and toss to coat.
- Use foil to line a 15x10-inch pan; grease with cooking spray. Place wings into prepared pan and bake for 10 minutes; lower the heat to 350 degrees and bake for 12-15 minutes until juices run clear. Remove from the oven; keep warm.
- In the meantime, spread sugar in a small skillet; cook over medium heat, without stirring, until it starts to melt. Drag melted sugar gently to the center of the pan to melt evenly. Cook until melted sugar becomes amber, without stirring. Carefully mix in butter and warm milk. Simmer for 5 to 7 minutes, stirring frequently, until thickened. Keep warm.
- Put butter in a large skillet and melt over medium heat; put in pepper, salt, garlic, one green onion, and bread crumbs. Stir and cook for about 2 minutes until bread crumbs are golden brown. Put aside.
- Toss wings in butterscotch sauce to serve. Dust with sliced peppers, leftover green onion, and crumb topping, if wished. Serve hot.

Nutrition Information

- Calories: 100 calories
- Total Carbohydrate: 8 g
- Cholesterol: 20 mg
- Total Fat: 5 g
- Fiber: 0 g
- Protein: 5 g
- Sodium: 312 mg

76. Spicy Chicken Wings

"A delicious dish of Spicy Chicken Wings."
Serving: Makes 20 servings, about 1 wing each. | Prep: 10m | Ready in: 25m

Ingredients

- 2 cups prepared GOOD SEASONS Italian Dressing Mix
- 1 cup honey
- 2 Tbsp. hot pepper sauce
- 2 Tbsp. soy sauce
- 2 lb. chicken wings (about 20 wings), cooked

Direction

- Set an oven to 350°F and start preheating. In a medium bowl, combine the soy sauce, hot pepper sauce, honey, and dressing.
- Divide the sauce in half. Plunge the cooked chicken wings into half of the sauce; on a foil-wrapped baking sheet, arrange in one layer.
- Bake until the wings are bubbling and hot, or for 15 minutes. Serve along with the remaining sauce.

Nutrition Information

- Calories: 250
- Total Carbohydrate: 15 g
- Cholesterol: 30 mg
- Total Fat: 18 g
- Fiber: 0 g
- Protein: 9 g
- Sodium: 410 mg
- Sugar: 15 g
- Saturated Fat: 3 g

77. Spicy Chicken Wings With Blue Cheese Dip

"Tender wings combined with blue cheese dressing together are the perfect blend of flavors for dipping."
Serving: 2 dozen (1-3/4 cups dip). | Prep: 25m | Ready in: 02h25m

Ingredients

- 1 cup reduced-sodium soy sauce
- 2/3 cup sugar
- 2 tsps. salt
- 2 tsps. grated orange zest
- 2 garlic cloves, minced
- 1/2 tsp. pepper
- 3 lbs. chicken wingettes and drumettes
- 3 tsps. chili powder
- 3/4 tsp. cayenne pepper
- 3/4 tsp. hot pepper sauce
- BLUE CHEESE DIP:
- 1 cup mayonnaise
- 1/2 cup blue cheese salad dressing
- 1/3 cup buttermilk
- 2 tsps. Italian salad dressing mix

Direction

- Blend the pepper, garlic, orange zest, salt, sugar, and soy sauce in a small bowl. Put 1/2 marinade into a large resealable plastic bag. Put in the chicken; seal the bag closed and turn to coat the chicken. Put in the fridge for an hour. Put a cover on and put the remaining marinade in the fridge.
- Drain off the marinade and discard. Place the chicken into a greased 13x9-inch baking dish. Put a cover on and bake at 325 degrees until the chicken juices run clear, or for 1 1/2 hours.
- Place the chicken into a greased 15x10x1-inch baking pan with tongs. Blend the retained marinade, pepper sauce, cayenne, and chili powder in a small bowl. Lightly sprinkle them over chicken.
- Remove the cover, bake for half an hour and turn once. Beat the dip ingredients in a small bowl. Serve together with wings.

Nutrition Information

- Calories: 237 calories
- Total Carbohydrate: 4 g
- Cholesterol: 47 mg
- Total Fat: 19 g
- Fiber: 0 g
- Protein: 11 g
- Sodium: 588 mg

78. Spicy Hot Wings

""Everyone will go wild with these finger-licking' good baked chicken wings paired with a creamy dipping sauce.""
Serving: 8 servings. | Prep: 25m | Ready in: 01h15m

Ingredients

- 10 chicken wings (about 2 lbs.)
- 1/2 cup butter, melted
- 2 to 5 tsps. hot pepper sauce
- 3/4 tsp. garlic salt
- 1/4 tsp. paprika
- DIPPING SAUCE:
- 3/4 cup sour cream
- 1 tbsp. dried minced onion
- 1 tbsp. milk
- 1/2 cup crumbled blue cheese
- 1/4 tsp. garlic salt
- 1/8 tsp. ground mustard
- Paprika, optional
- Celery sticks, optional

Direction

- Slice chicken wings into three parts and remove the wingtips. Transfer wings to a 15x10x1-inch baking pan that is greased. Mix the paprika, garlic salt, hot pepper sauce, and butter; pour over wings. Bake for 30 minutes at 375 degrees. Flip over; bake for 20-25 more minutes or until chicken juices run clear.
- In the meantime, to make the sauce, mix the mustard, garlic salt, cheese, milk, onion, and sour cream in a blender. Cover and process until smooth. Transfer into a bowl; dust with

paprika if wished. Keep in the refrigerator, covered, until serving. Strain wings. Serve with celery and sauce if wished.

Nutrition Information

- Calories: 122 calories
- Total Carbohydrate: 1 g
- Cholesterol: 35 mg
- Total Fat: 10 g
- Fiber: 0 g
- Protein: 6 g
- Sodium: 191 mg

79. Spicy Maple Chicken Wings

""Spicy and sweet chicken wings that my kids enjoy!""
Serving: about 2 dozen. | Prep: 20m | Ready in: 30m

Ingredients

- 3 lbs. chicken wings
- Oil for deep-fat frying
- 1/2 cup butter, cubed
- 1/2 cup maple syrup
- 1/2 cup Louisiana-style hot sauce
- 1/4 cup packed brown sugar
- 1/2 tsp. salt
- 1/4 tsp. pepper
- 2 tbsps. water
- 1-1/2 tsps. cornstarch

Direction

- Slice chicken wings into three parts; remove wingtip sections.
- Put oil in a deep-fat fryer or an electric skillet and heat to 375 degrees. Put in the chicken and fry a few pieces at a time for 8 minutes or until juices run clear and chicken is golden brown, flipping occasionally. Transfer to paper towels to drain.
- Put butter in a small saucepan to melt. Mix in the pepper, salt, brown sugar, hot sauce, and syrup. Mix cornstarch and water; mix into the sauce. Bring to a boil; stir and cook for 2 minutes or until thickened.
- Put wings in a large bowl; pour the sauce over and toss to coat.

Nutrition Information

- Calories: 161 calories
- Total Carbohydrate: 7 g
- Cholesterol: 26 mg
- Total Fat: 13 g
- Fiber: 0 g
- Protein: 5 g
- Sodium: 89 mg

80.Spicy Ranch Chicken Wings

"A finger-licking chicken wings for different occasions."
Serving: about 4 dozen. | Prep: 20m | Ready in: 60m

Ingredients

- 4 lbs. whole chicken wings
- 3/4 cup hot pepper sauce
- 1/4 cup butter, melted
- 3 tbsps. cider vinegar
- 1 envelope ranch salad dressing mix
- 1/2 tsp. paprika

Direction

- Divide the chicken wings into 3 sections; discard the wing tip sections. Blend the vinegar, butter, and hot pepper sauce in a gallon-size resealable plastic bag. Put in the chicken wings; seal the bag and toss to cover them evenly. Put in the fridge for 4-8 hours.
- In 2 greased 15x10x1-inch baking pans, arrange the chicken on racks. Dust with paprika and the dressing mix. Remove the cover and bake at 350 degrees until the juices run clear, or for 40-50 minutes.

Nutrition Information

- Calories: 175 calories
- Total Carbohydrate: 1 g

- Cholesterol: 49 mg
- Total Fat: 13 g
- Fiber: 0 g
- Protein: 14 g
- Sodium: 286 mg

81. Spicy-good Chicken Wings

"Delicious chicken wings for special occasions for a large group."
Serving: about 1-1/2 dozen. | Prep: 30m | Ready in: 50m

Ingredients

- 1 cup self-rising flour
- 1 tsp. celery salt
- 1 tsp. garlic powder
- 1 tsp. onion salt
- 1 tsp. barbecue seasoning
- 1/2 tsp. salt
- 2 lbs. chicken wingettes
- Oil for frying
- 1/2 cup butter, melted
- 1 bottle (2 oz.) hot pepper sauce
- Blue cheese salad dressing

Direction

- Combine the first 6 ingredients in a large resealable plastic bag. Add a few pieces of the chicken at a time; close and shake the bag to cover.
- Heat an inch of oil to 375 degrees in an electric skillet. Fry a few wingettes a time until they are browned, or for 4-5 minutes per side. Put on the paper towels to drain. Set an oven to 350 degrees and start preheating.
- Combine the pepper sauce and melted butter in a 13x9-inch baking dish. Put in the wings and turn them to cover. Remove the cover and bake for 10 minutes. Turn and bake until the chicken juices run clear, or for 10-15 more minutes. Serve together with the dressing.

Nutrition Information

- Calories: 225 calories
- Total Carbohydrate: 5 g
- Cholesterol: 51 mg
- Total Fat: 18 g
- Fiber: 0 g
- Protein: 10 g
- Sodium: 473 mg

82. Sweet & Spicy Chicken Wings

"Tasty wings pairing with sprinkled red pepper flakes that will satisfy any spice lovers."
Serving: about 2-1/2 dozen. | Prep: 25m | Ready in: 05h25m

Ingredients

- 3 lbs. chicken wings
- 1-1/2 cups ketchup
- 1 cup packed brown sugar
- 1 small onion, finely chopped
- 1/4 cup finely chopped sweet red pepper
- 2 tbsps. chili powder
- 2 tbsps. Worcestershire sauce
- 1-1/2 tsps. crushed red pepper flakes
- 1 tsp. ground mustard
- 1 tsp. dried basil
- 1 tsp. dried thyme
- 1 tsp. pepper
- Ranch Dressing and celery stalks, optional

Direction

- Slice the wings into 3 sections and discard the wing tip sections. In a 4-quart slow cooker, arrange the chicken. Blend the remaining ingredients in a small bowl. Place over the chicken and stir until covered. Cook, covered, on low until the chicken juices run clear or for 5-6 hours. If desired, serve along with celery stalks and ranch dressing.

Nutrition Information

- Calories: 95 calories
- Total Carbohydrate: 11 g
- Cholesterol: 14 mg

- Total Fat: 3 g
- Fiber: 0 g
- Protein: 5 g
- Sodium: 195 mg

83. Sweet 'n' Spicy Wings

"These are hot, spicy, and super delicious chicken wings."
Serving: about 4 dozen. | Prep: 20m | Ready in: 30m

Ingredients

- 5 lbs. chicken wings
- 1/2 cup butter, cubed
- 1/2 cup Louisiana-style hot sauce
- 1/4 cup balsamic vinegar
- 1/4 cup soy sauce
- 3 tbsps. brown sugar
- 3 tbsps. honey
- 2 tbsps. plus 1 tsp. celery seed, divided
- 2 tbsps. lemon juice
- 2/3 cup all-purpose flour
- 1 tsp. each salt, paprika and cayenne pepper
- 1/2 tsp. garlic powder
- Oil for deep-fat frying

Direction

- Cut wings into 3 parts; remove the wing tip parts. Boil lemon juice, 2 tbsps. celery seed, honey, brown sugar, soy sauce, vinegar, hot sauce, and butter in a large saucepan. Reduce the heat; uncover and simmer until reduced by half.
- In the meantime, combine the remaining celery seed, garlic powder, cayenne, paprika, salt, and flour in a large resealable plastic bag. Put in the wings a few at a time, and shake to coat well.
- Heat oil to 375° in a deep-fat fryer or an electric skillet. Fry the wings until no longer pink, a few at a time, about 3-4 minutes on each side. Drain on paper towels. Put in a large bowl, then add the sauce and toss to cover.

Nutrition Information

- Calories: 129 calories
- Total Carbohydrate: 4 g
- Cholesterol: 20 mg
- Total Fat: 10 g
- Fiber: 0 g
- Protein: 5 g
- Sodium: 156 mg

Chapter 3: Jerky Recipes

***

84. Amazing Turkey Jerky

"Inexpensive and very easy."
Serving: 10 | Prep: 25m | Ready in: 7h25m

Ingredients

- 1 1/2 lbs. ground turkey
- 1/2 cup soy sauce
- 1 tbsp. honey
- 1 tbsp. Worcestershire sauce
- 1 tbsp. apple cider vinegar
- 1 tbsp. liquid smoke
- 1 tbsp. garlic powder
- 1 tbsp. coarsely ground black pepper
- 1 1/2 tsps. ground ginger
- 1 tsp. olive oil
- 1/2 cube beef bouillon
- wooden paint stir sticks

Direction

- Mix together beef bouillon, olive oil, ginger, pepper, garlic powder, liquid smoke, apple cider vinegar, honey, Worcestershire sauce, honey, soy sauce and ground turkey in a big bowl; stir well and cover. Marinate for 2-12 hours in the fridge.

- Tape 2 paint stir sticks on a flat work surface, 2-in. apart; use a big plastic wrap piece to cover. Put a golf ball-sized turkey mixture piece between sticks; use another plastic wrap piece to cover. Use a rolling pin to roll turkey mixture into a thin strips; put strip on a dehydrator tray. Repeat the process using the leftover turkey mixture.
- Dehydrate for 5-8 hours till thoroughly dried at 70°C or 160°F.

Nutrition Information

- Calories: 137 calories;
- Total Carbohydrate: 4.3 g
- Cholesterol: 50 mg
- Total Fat: 7 g
- Protein: 14.6 g
- Sodium: 821 mg

85. Atwood's Peppered Micro-wave Jerky

"A cheap and simple but delicious recipe for peppered beef jerky."

Serving: 24 | Prep: 15m | Ready in: 3days4h15m

Ingredients

- 6 tbsps. Demerara sugar
- 3 tbsps. salt
- 1 tsp. curing salt (Prague powder #1)
- 2 tbsps. crushed dried chile pepper
- 2 tsps. cayenne pepper
- 2 tbsps. garlic pepper seasoning
- 1 tbsp. onion powder
- 1 tbsp. finely ground juniper berries
- 6 lbs. beef round steak, cut into 6x1/2 inch strips

Direction

- Combine juniper berries, cayenne pepper, chile pepper, curing salt, salt, and Demerara sugar together in a medium bowl. Divide the mixture evenly into thirds and arrange each into its own bowl.
- Combine 2 lbs. of meat strips into the mixture in each bowl until they are coated evenly with the spice mixture. Arrange lengthwise all the meat into a plastic bowl or a large glass, use plastic wrap to cover and put in the fridge for 3 days.
- Set the oven to 65°C (150°F) and start preheating. Place 6 or 8 meat strips at a time on a big plate and put in a microwave oven. Cook on High for 3 minutes. Transfer the meat strips onto a baking sheet and keep them in the warm oven until dry, or for 3-4 hours. The Jerky is supposed to be chewy, not crispy, so don't over dry.

Nutrition Information

- Calories: 244 calories;
- Total Carbohydrate: 3.5 g
- Cholesterol: 71 mg
- Total Fat: 14.6 g
- Protein: 23.2 g
- Sodium: 1146 mg

86. Beef Jerky

"You can keep these for months."

Serving: 5 | Prep: 10m | Ready in: 19h10m

Ingredients

- 1 lb. eye of round
- 1/4 cup soy sauce
- 1/2 tsp. ground black pepper
- 1 tsp. brown sugar
- 1 tsp. hot pepper sauce

Direction

- Combine brown sugar, ground black pepper, and soy sauce to taste in a medium bowl. Mix well and put in the steak slices. Next, put meat and the whole mixture into a sealed plastic container and chill for 12-24 hours.
- Put 1 rack on the lowest setting and 1 rack on the highest setting in the oven. To catch any drippings, put a baking sheet or a piece of aluminum foil on the lowest rack.
- Preheat the oven to 70° C (160° F).
- Insert a wooden toothpick through the end of each slice of meat, then hang each slice from the top rack in the oven using toothpicks.
- Bake in the preheated oven at 70° C (160° F) with the oven door propped open to let the moisture escape; depending on the thickness of slices, bake for about 6-8 hours. The jerky should be curled but not snap.

Nutrition Information

- Calories: 204 calories;
- Total Carbohydrate: 2 g
- Cholesterol: 55 mg
- Total Fat: 13 g
- Protein: 18.7 g
- Sodium: 791 mg

87. Beef Or Moose Jerky

"This beef jerky is made in only 12 hours with liquid smoke, brown sugar, and soy sauce."
Serving: 6 | Prep: 1h | Ready in: 13h

Ingredients

- 3 lbs. rump roast
- 3 cups soy sauce
- 3 cups packed brown sugar
- 4 fluid oz. hickory-flavored liquid smoke

Direction

- Slice the roast in roughly 1/4 inch-thick slabs, or you can ask your butcher or the grocery store to do this. Trim all the fat off the edges and cut them into pencil-like strips around 1/4 inches wide and 4 inches long.
- Combine hickory-flavored liquid smoke with brown sugar and soy sauce in a big bowl, blending well. Place in all the meat to marinate, cover, and keep refrigerated for a minimum of 30 minutes.
- Put the meat into a food dehydrator for around 12-20 hours, depending on how dry you want your jerky to be. Rotate each tray after 6 hours, like placing the bottom tray to the top and the top tray to the bottom, then the second tray from the bottom to the second tray from the top, and so on.

Nutrition Information

- Calories: 1129 calories;
- Total Carbohydrate: 117.6 g
- Cholesterol: 138 mg
- Total Fat: 50.5 g
- Protein: 52.9 g
- Sodium: 7357 mg

88. Dad's Jerky Marinade

""This marinade for beef jerky is homemade and passed down from generation to generation. Pick out roasts with less fat and as little marbling as possible.""
Serving: 8 | Prep: 10m | Ready in: 10m

Ingredients

- 1/2 cup soy sauce
- 1/4 cup Worcestershire sauce
- 1/2 tsp. liquid smoke flavoring
- 1 tsp. hot pepper sauce (e.g. Tabasco™), or to taste
- 1 tsp. garlic powder
- 1 tsp. onion powder
- 1/2 tsp. black pepper
- 1/2 cup brown sugar

Direction

- In a bowl, stir together hot pepper sauce, liquid smoke, Worcestershire sauce, and soy sauce. Mix and season with sugar, pepper, onion powder, and garlic powder, stirring until well combined.
- Marinate one lb. of thin slices of meat until the meat is well coated. Secure in a resealable plastic bag and squeeze to remove the air. Marinate in the refrigerator for 48 hours and mix it twice. Remove meat from the resealable plastic bag and discard the marinade. Prepare the jerky by following the directions of your dehydrator or smoker.

Nutrition Information

- Calories: 72 calories;
- Total Carbohydrate: 16.9 g
- Cholesterol: 0 mg
- Total Fat: 0.3 g
- Protein: 1.1 g
- Sodium: 993 mg

89. Doc's Best Beef Jerky

"You can use an oven/other dehydrators; check manual for the proper times."

Serving: 10 | Prep: 20m | Ready in: 12h20m

Ingredients

- 2 lbs. beef round steak, cut into thin strips
- 1/4 cup soy sauce
- 2 tbsps. Worcestershire sauce
- 2 tbsps. liquid smoke
- 2 tbsps. brown sugar
- 2 tsps. salt
- 1 tsp. ground black pepper
- 1 tsp. meat tenderizer
- 1 tsp. garlic powder
- 1 tsp. onion powder
- 1 tsp. paprika

Direction

- Put beef strips onto the bottom of a big bowl. Put paprika, onion powder, garlic powder, meat tenderizer, pepper, salt, brown sugar, liquid smoke, Worcestershire sauce and soy sauce on top of beef; mix to make sure evenly coat all the meat. Cover; marinade for 8 hours or overnight in the fridge.
- Take meat out of the bowl; transfer between 2 plastic wrap pieces then lb. to 1/8-in. thickness.
- Place meat strips on a dehydrator tray; dry for 4 hours minimum till done to your liking on dehydrator's highest setting; keep in a resealable bags or airtight container.

Nutrition Information

- Calories: 137 calories;
- Total Carbohydrate: 4.5 g
- Cholesterol: 31 mg
- Total Fat: 7.9 g
- Protein: 11.6 g
- Sodium: 934 mg

90. Dylan's Salmon Jerky

"A very simple recipe for salmon jerky for family gatherings or parties."

Serving: 16 | Prep: 10m | Ready in: 8h55m

Ingredients

- 1 cup soy sauce
- 6 tbsps. brown sugar
- 1 tbsp. rock salt
- 2 tsps. ground black pepper
- 4 lbs. salmon fillets

Direction

- Blend together the black pepper, rock salt, brown sugar, and soy sauce in a saucepan; boil and cook for 2-3 minutes until salt and sugar have dissolved. Take the saucepan away from the heat and allow the marinade to cool.

- Slice the salmon into strips without or with the skin. Put the marinade in a shallow bowl and place the salmon strips into the shallow bowl. Put in the fridge for 45 minutes.
- Set an oven to 85°C (185°F). Use aluminum foil to line a baking sheet and top with a wire rack. Place the salmon strips on the wire rack and discarding surplus marinade.
- In the oven, arrange the sheet of salmon for 8 hours until dehydrated.

Nutrition Information

- Calories: 236 calories;
- Total Carbohydrate: 6.4 g
- Cholesterol: 67 mg
- Total Fat: 12.3 g
- Protein: 23.6 g
- Sodium: 1406 mg

91. Ground Beef Jerky

""The spice mixture is combined in with the ground beef in place of a dry rub or marinade to make this jerky a bit different from its more costly brothers.""
Serving: 8 | Prep: 15m | Ready in: 5h45m

Ingredients

- 2 tsps. canning salt
- 1 tsp. chili powder
- 1 tsp. garlic powder
- 1 tsp. onion powder
- 1/4 tsp. ground ginger
- 1/4 tsp. ground black pepper
- 1 pinch cayenne pepper, or to taste (optional)
- 1 lb. extra lean ground beef

Direction

- Mix cayenne pepper, black pepper, ginger, onion powder, garlic powder, chili powder, and salt in a large bowl; put in the ground beef and stir well.
- Pass beef mixture through a meat grinder set with the finest blade.
- Prepare the oven by preheating to 250°F (120°C). Put wire-racks onto baking sheets.
- Put 1/2 ground beef mixture between two sheets of heavy plastic on a solid, level surface. Form the beef mixture firmly to 1/8-inch thickness. Take off the top layer of plastic wrap, invert beef mixture onto the prepared baking sheet, and take off the bottom layer of plastic wrap. Repeat the process with the leftover beef mixture.
- Place beef mixture in the preheated oven and bake for 2 1/2 hours with the oven door slightly ajar. Rotate the baking sheet. Bake for 3 more hours, until jerky is cooked through. Take the jerky from the oven and slice into strips while warm.

Nutrition Information

- Calories: 126 calories;
- Total Carbohydrate: 0.7 g
- Cholesterol: 39 mg
- Total Fat: 8 g
- Protein: 12.2 g
- Sodium: 619 mg

92. Jerky Lover's Jerky - Sweet, Hot And Spicy!

"A sweet and hot recipe."
Serving: 4 | Prep: 10m | Ready in: 5h10m

Ingredients

- 1 tbsp. onion powder
- 1 tbsp. garlic powder
- 2 tsps. cracked black pepper, or to taste
- 1 lb. lean beef sirloin tip, sliced into 1/8 inch strips
- 1/2 cup brown sugar
- 2/3 cup soy sauce
- 1/4 cup teriyaki sauce
- 1/4 cup Worcestershire sauce
- 1/3 cup balsamic vinegar
- 5 tbsps. liquid smoke flavoring
- 1/2 cup pineapple juice

- 1 tsp. red pepper flakes, or to taste (optional)

Direction

- Mix some cracked black pepper, garlic powder and onion powder in small bowl/cup; use part of mixture to lightly season meat. Keep leftover spices. Put in bowl/airtight plastic container; refrigerate.
- Mix and heat pineapple juice, liquid smoke flavoring, balsamic vinegar, Worcestershire sauce, teriyaki sauce, soy sauce and brown sugar in saucepan on medium heat till brown sugar fully dissolve. Refrigerate marinade till cool.
- Put cooled marinade on seasoned meat; by hand, mix to coat. Seal bowl; refrigerate for no less than 3 hours.
- Put beef strips on dehydrator rack; sprinkle little extra spice mixture then red pepper flakes (optional). Dry to desired dryness or for 5 hours.

Nutrition Information

- Calories: 527 calories;
- Total Carbohydrate: 47.4 g
- Cholesterol: 60 mg
- Total Fat: 27.5 g
- Protein: 23.3 g
- Sodium: 3319 mg

93. Matt's Jerky Recipe

"This jerky recipe can be done with beef, venison, or elk. You can even keep them refrigerated or frozen to keep it longer."

Serving: 10 | Prep: 15m | Ready in: 1day2h35m

Ingredients

- 3 lbs. beef top round
- 2/3 cup soy sauce
- 1/4 cup Worcestershire sauce
- 1 tbsp. brown sugar
- 2 tsps. liquid smoke flavoring
- 2 tsps. onion powder
- 2 tsps. chili powder
- 2 tsps. garlic powder
- 2 tsps. cayenne pepper
- 2 tsps. finely ground black pepper

Direction

- Freeze the beef for around 20 minutes to make them easier to slice, then slice them against the grain into 1/4-inch thick strips.
- Whisk together pepper, cayenne, garlic powder, chili powder, onion powder, liquid smoke, brown sugar, Worcestershire sauce, and soy sauce in a big bowl, then add in the beef strips. Cover and marinate them in the refrigerator for around 18-24 hours, mixing them at least 2 times.
- Place the beef strips onto dehydrator trays and dehydrate them at 70 degrees C or 160 degrees F for roughly 8 hours, or until they are dried.

Nutrition Information

- Calories: 180 calories;
- Total Carbohydrate: 5.5 g
- Cholesterol: 68 mg
- Total Fat: 5 g
- Protein: 26.9 g
- Sodium: 1084 mg

94. Mckagen's Beef Jerky

""Enjoy this recipe I made that has a perfect after-taste and not too strong.""

Serving: 8 | Prep: 20m | Ready in: 1day3h20m

Ingredients

- 1/4 cup teriyaki sauce
- 1/4 cup Worcestershire sauce
- 1/4 cup balsamic vinaigrette
- 1 tsp. garlic powder
- 1 tsp. onion powder
- 2 tsps. liquid smoke flavoring
- 1/2 tsp. salt

- 3 drops hot sauce (such as Dave's Insanity Sauce ®), or to taste
- 1 lb. top round steak, cut into 1/4 inch strips
- 1 tsp. ground black pepper

Direction

- Mix hot sauce, salt, liquid smoke, onion powder, garlic powder, balsamic vinaigrette, Worcestershire sauce, and teriyaki sauce in a resealable plastic bag. Put in the meat strips and coat evenly with the marinade. Keep in the refrigerator for 24 hours, sealed.
- Prepare the oven by preheating to 175°F (80°C). Use aluminum foil to line a baking sheet and put a wire rack on top.
- Take the beef strips from the marinade out and shake off the excess marinade. Get rid of the leftover marinade. Put the meat strips onto the wire rack and dust with black pepper. Place in the preheated oven and bake for at least 3 hours until dry and firm. Let the jerky to fully cool before keeping in a sealed container.

Nutrition Information

- Calories: 163 calories;
- Total Carbohydrate: 4.4 g
- Cholesterol: 51 mg
- Total Fat: 6.2 g
- Protein: 21.1 g
- Sodium: 696 mg

95. Mesquite Smoked Jerky

"You can use hickory smoked flavoring for this jerky recipe if you prefer."

Serving: 4 | Prep: 30m | Ready in: 8h30m

Ingredients

- 1 lb. beef eye of round sliced into 1/4 inch strips
- 1 cup soy sauce
- 1/2 cup packed brown sugar
- 2 tbsps. mesquite flavored liquid smoke concentrate
- 1 tbsp. ground paprika
- 3 cloves garlic, minced
- 1/4 tsp. salt

Direction

- Stir salt, garlic, paprika, liquid smoke, brown sugar, and soy sauce together in a shallow glass baking dish. Arrange strips of meat in the liquid in 1 layer. Cover and keep in the fridge for a minimum of 6 hours.
- Arrange beef strips in a dehydrator and allow to dry for about 6 hours, or to the dryness that you want.

96. Midg's Mouth Watering Beef Jerky

"Mouthwatering recipe."

Serving: 12 | Prep: 15m | Ready in: 17h45m

Ingredients

- 5 lbs. boneless beef sirloin
- 2 cups soy sauce
- 1 cup water
- 3 dashes Worcestershire sauce
- 3 tbsps. white sugar (optional)
- 3 tbsps. salt
- 1/2 tsp. onion powder
- 1/4 tsp. garlic powder
- 2 tsps. liquid smoke flavoring
- mesquite or hickory wood chips, as needed for smoker

Direction

- Cut beef to 1/4-in. thick slices. Mix liquid smoke, garlic powder, onion powder, salt, sugar, water, soy sauce and Worcestershire sauce. Put marinade in resealable heavy-duty bag; add beef. Stir well; seal bag then refrigerate for 12 hours.
- Take beef from marinade; use paper towels to pat dry. Stand for 30 minutes; throw used marinade. In the meantime, soak wood chips.
- Preheat a smoker for 10 minutes.

- Put beef on drying racks then smoke for 5-7 hours or depending on how you enjoy it; as needed, replenish wood chips.

Nutrition Information

- Calories: 279 calories;
- Total Carbohydrate: 6.5 g
- Cholesterol: 82 mg
- Total Fat: 11.6 g
- Protein: 35.5 g
- Sodium: 4219 mg

97. Mike's Peppered Beef Jerky

"Peppery and great."

Serving: 24 | Prep: 25m | Ready in: 1day10h25m

Ingredients

- 4 lbs. very lean beef, visible fat trimmed and cut against the grain into 1/4 inch-thick strips
- 3/4 cup Worcestershire sauce
- 3/4 cup soy sauce
- 1 1/2 tbsps. brown sugar
- 1 tbsp. onion powder
- 1 tbsp. garlic powder
- 1 tbsp. ground black pepper
- 1 tsp. liquid smoke, or more to taste
- 1/4 tsp. cayenne pepper
- 1/4 tsp. coriander seeds
- 3/4 cup water, or as needed
- 1/4 tsp. coriander seeds (optional)
- ground black pepper to taste (optional)

Direction

- On a solid, level surface, put beef strips; lb. beef firmly with tendering side of a meat mallet till meat fibers break slightly yet strips still hold shape.
- Mix coriander seeds, cayenne pepper, liquid smoke, black pepper, garlic powder, onion powder, brown sugar, soy sauce and Worcestershire sauce till brown sugar melts in a big bowl.
- Put beef strips into bowl; add enough water to let marinade cover meat. Mix to submerge beef in marinade and incorporate water; cover bowl. Refrigerate for 24 hours.
- Preheat an oven to 150°C/300°F.
- Take beef strips out of marinade and shake excess off; lay strips on ovenproof racks. Don't overlap strips.
- In preheated oven, bake beef strips till an inserted instant-read thermometer in thickest strip reads a minimum of 65°C/150°F.
- Take strips out of oven; put on racks of a food dehydrator so strips won't overlap.
- Sprinkle black pepper and extra coriander seeds on strips if desired.
- Turn dehydrator on; set machine temperature to 70°C/155°F. Dry jerky for 9 hours till leathery. Rotate racks every 1 1/2 hours from top to bottom to dry evenly; a jerky piece should crack yet not break in half when you fold it. Keep in fridge.

Nutrition Information

- Calories: 169 calories;
- Total Carbohydrate: 3.8 g
- Cholesterol: 68 mg
- Total Fat: 4 g
- Protein: 27.9 g
- Sodium: 569 mg

98. Minnesota Whitetail Jerky

"This delicious and hot venison jerky is an ideal snack when fishing, comping, hiking, etc."

Serving: 6 | Prep: 20m | Ready in: 21h20m

Ingredients

- 1 tbsp. sugar-based curing mixture (such as Morton® Tender Quick®)
- 1 tbsp. dark brown sugar
- 1/4 tsp. garlic powder
- 1/4 tsp. onion powder
- 1/4 tsp. whole mustard seed
- 1/8 tsp. freshly ground black pepper

- 1/8 tsp. crushed red pepper flakes
- 1/8 tsp. liquid smoke
- 1 lb. lean venison roast, trimmed of all fat and sinew

Direction

- in a large bowl, mix onion powder, curing mixture, liquid smoke, sugar, ground pepper, red pepper, garlic powder, and mustard seed. Combine until blended evenly and reserve.
- Cut the venison with the grain into strips 2-inches wide and 3/16-inch thick. Place in the curing mixture and gently combine together until each piece is covered with curing mix. Transfer into a plastic bag, and press out all air before sealing or put in a plastic or glass bowl and then cover. Chill for a minimum of 18 hours to cure.
- Set the oven to 65 degrees C (150 degrees F). Use cooking spray to spritz 2 wire racks and transfer onto cookie sheets.
- Press the excess liquid from venison and then spread the strips onto the wire racks. Ensure the pieces are not touching each other. Put jerky into oven and let to cook for 3 to 8 hours, depends on the temperature of the oven until dried.
- The meat is done if it no longer bends and easily to break off a piece. Meat should not be too dry as crisp and break. Better if less dry than being over dried since you can leave it to air dry to perfection. The color changes of the jerky should not bother you because it will become lighter and harder as it dries over time. You can freeze the jerky or store in sealed containers in your fridge.

Nutrition Information

- Calories: 86 calories;
- Total Carbohydrate: 2.5 g
- Cholesterol: 53 mg
- Total Fat: 1.7 g
- Protein: 14.3 g
- Sodium: 1189 mg

99.Paleo Jerky

"Yummy jerky without high-fructose corn syrup."
Serving: 5 | Prep: 10m | Ready in: 1day5h10m

Ingredients

- 2/3 cup soy sauce
- 1/3 cup hot water
- 1/4 cup Worcestershire sauce
- 1 tbsp. liquid smoke flavoring
- 1 tbsp. onion powder
- 1 tbsp. garlic powder
- 1 1/2 tsps. cayenne pepper
- 1 1/2 tsps. Creole-style seasoning (such as Emeril's Essence®)
- 1 1/2 tsps. Cajun seasoning blend (such as Tony Chachere's®)
- 2 1/2 lbs. London Broil sliced roast beef

Direction

- Whisk Cajun seasoning, creole seasoning, cayenne pepper, garlic powder, onion powder, liquid smoke, Worcestershire sauce, hot water and soy sauce in microwave-safe bowl then microwave for 1 minute; mix well. Add roast beef; toss to coat evenly. Use plastic wrap to cover bowl; marinate for 8 hours - overnight in the fridge. Take meat from marinade; use hot water to rinse.
- Preheat an oven to 70°C/160°F; put pan on bottom of oven to get drips.
- Put meat strips on rack, 1-in. apart; dehydrate in oven till desired consistency is reached for 5-6 hours.

Nutrition Information

- Calories: 68 calories;
- Total Carbohydrate: 8.5 g
- Cholesterol: 0 mg
- Total Fat: 2.9 g
- Protein: 2.7 g
- Sodium: 2344 mg

100. Spicy Salmon Jerky

"We usually catch a lot of red salmon during the summer every year. Some of it is usually used to make salmon jerky. This delicious marinade makes the best salmon jerky and I've never had a better recipe than this!"
Serving: 12 | Prep: 10m | Ready in: 10h10m

Ingredients

- 3 lbs. salmon fillet, skin removed
- 1 cup soy sauce
- 2 tbsps. molasses
- 2 tbsps. white sugar
- 2 tbsps. Worcestershire sauce
- 2 tbsps. lemon juice
- 1 1/2 tbsps. ground black pepper
- 2 tsps. liquid smoke flavoring
- 12 dashes hot sauce (such as Tabasco®), or more to taste

Direction

- Cut the salmon fillets, width-wise, into four equal portions. Rotate each portion 90 degrees and chop lengthwise, approximately 1/4-inch thick. Use needle-nose pliers to remove pin bones. Avoid cutting the bony parts near the center of fillet.
- In a glass or plastic bowl, combine Worcestershire sauce, soy sauce, liquid smoke, molasses, sugar, lemon juice, hot sauce, and black pepper together until the marinade is mixed well. Put the salmon into the marinade and make sure every strip is covered. Cover the bowl and chill for 4 hours.
- Take out the salmon from the bowl and then use a colander to drain of liquid. Pat dry the salmon with paper towels.
- Transfer each salmon strip to a dehydrator and then start the dehydrator following the instructions of the manufacturer for about 6 hours until the doneness desired is reached. Keep checking after every few hours for doneness.

Nutrition Information

- Calories: 232 calories;
- Total Carbohydrate: 7.5 g
- Cholesterol: 77 mg
- Total Fat: 10.5 g
- Protein: 25.6 g
- Sodium: 1317 mg

101. Sweet And Spicy Venison Jerky

"Sweet with a bit of a kick."
Serving: 8 | Prep: 15m | Ready in: 1day4h15m

Ingredients

- 1/2 cup brown sugar
- 1 tbsp. ground black pepper
- 1 tbsp. onion powder
- 1 tbsp. garlic salt
- 1 tbsp. lemon juice
- 3 tbsps. liquid smoke flavoring
- 1 tsp. paprika
- 1 tsp. hot pepper sauce
- 1/2 cup Worcestershire sauce
- 1/2 cup teriyaki sauce
- 1/3 cup soy sauce
- 1 lb. venison, cut into 1/4 thick strips

Direction

- In big glass/ceramic bowl, whisk soy sauce, teriyaki sauce, Worcestershire sauce, hot pepper sauce, paprika, liquid smoke, lemon juice, garlic salt, onion powder, black pepper and sugar. Add venison strips; evenly coat by tossing. Use plastic wrap to cover bowl. Marinate for 24 hours in the fridge. Mix venison several times while marinating to make sure the marinade gets absorbed.
- Take venison strips out of marinade; squeeze excess off. Discard leftover marinade. Put venison on food dehydrator's racks without overlapping.
- On high, dry venison for about 4 hours till dry yet still pliable. Jerky should bend but not break. In a resealable plastic bag/airtight container to store the jerky.

Nutrition Information

- Calories: 208 calories;
- Total Carbohydrate: 22.1 g
- Cholesterol: 48 mg
- Total Fat: 6.5 g
- Protein: 15 g
- Sodium: 2186 mg

102. Swen's Smokehouse Beef Jerky

"A new recipe to try."
Serving: 8 | Prep: 30m | Ready in: 14h30m

Ingredients

- 2 cups soy sauce
- 1 cup Worcestershire sauce
- 1 cup cranberry-grape juice
- 1 cup teriyaki sauce (such as Soy Vay®)
- 1 tbsp. hot pepper sauce (such as Tabasco®)
- 2 tbsps. steak sauce (such as A1®)
- 1 cup light brown sugar
- 1/2 tsp. ground black pepper, or to taste
- 2 lbs. flank steak, cut into 1/4 inch slices against the grain
- 4 cups wood chips, or as needed

Direction

- In a bowl, whisk black pepper, brown sugar, steak sauce, hot sauce, teriyaki sauce, cranberry-grape juice, Worcestershire sauce, and the soy sauce; then pour into a resealable plastic bag. Put in the flank steak and cover with the marinade, squeeze to remove the excess air and seal the bag. Then marinate for about 8-10 hours in the fridge.
- Next, remove the flank steak from the marinade and get rid of the excess. On the wire racks of the smoker, place the flank steak. It is fine if the meat is touching, but do not let them stack.
- Put the racks into the smoker, and smoke following the manufacturer's directions, using 4 pans of wood chips (1 pan/hour) for 6-8 hours, until the jerky has dried and will be broken when you bend.

Nutrition Information

- Calories: 317 calories;
- Total Carbohydrate: 49 g
- Cholesterol: 25 mg
- Total Fat: 4.7 g
- Protein: 20 g
- Sodium: 5423 mg

103. T Bird's Beef Jerky

"Let try this very good jerky recipe."
Serving: 64 | Prep: 30m | Ready in: 1day4h30m

Ingredients

- 4 lbs. round steak
- 4 tbsps. onion powder
- 1 1/3 tsps. black pepper
- 1 1/3 tsps. garlic powder
- 2 pinches salt
- 1 tsp. dry Italian-style salad dressing mix
- 1 cup Worcestershire sauce
- 1 cup soy sauce
- 1 tsp. hot pepper sauce

Direction

- Slice meat into strips no thicker than 1/4 inch. Mix Italian seasoning, salt, garlic powder, pepper, and onion powder in a large bowl. Stir in pepper sauce, soy sauce and Worcestershire sauce. Put the meat into a container and blend with marinade. Cover and chill for 24 hours.
- Put the oven rack on the highest level. To catch drips, on the bottom of the oven, place aluminum foil. Set the oven at 65°C (150°F) to preheat.
- Through the tops of the strips of meat, insert round toothpicks and hang them from the oven rack. In the preheated oven, bake until dry to the desired consistency, for 4 hours.

Nutrition Information

- Calories: 65 calories;
- Total Carbohydrate: 1.5 g
- Cholesterol: 18 mg
- Total Fat: 3.6 g
- Protein: 6.1 g
- Sodium: 285 mg

104. Teriyaki Beef Jerky

"Delicious beef strips marinated in the garlic-pineapple mixture, soy sauce, and teriyaki sauce"
Serving: 12 | Prep: 15m | Ready in: 12h15m

Ingredients

- 2 cups teriyaki sauce
- 1 cup soy sauce
- 1 cup brown sugar
- 1 dash Worcestershire sauce
- 1/4 lb. fresh pineapple, peeled
- 2 cloves garlic
- 2 lbs. beef round, cut into 1/2-inch thick strips

Direction

- In a large bowl, mix together Worcestershire sauce, brown sugar, soy sauce, and teriyaki sauce.
- In a blender or a food processor, arrange garlic and pineapple; blend until they become smooth. Place the teriyaki mixture and pineapple mixture into a resealable plastic bag. Put in beef and use the marinade to coat, then squeeze to remove the excess air and seal the bag. Put in the fridge for 6-8 hours to marinate.
- Set the smoker to 110-120°C (225-250°F) and start preheating. Drain the beef and discard the marinade.
- In the prepared smoker, smoke the beef for 6-8 hours until the jerky becomes dry and chewy without getting crispy. Place the jerky in the fridge to store.

Nutrition Information

- Calories: 207 calories;
- Total Carbohydrate: 28.5 g
- Cholesterol: 26 mg
- Total Fat: 4.3 g
- Protein: 13.4 g
- Sodium: 3068 mg

105. The Ultimate Beef Jerky

"An amazing and simple recipe."
Serving: 15 | Prep: 10m | Ready in: 1h40m

Ingredients

- 1/4 cup soy sauce
- 1/4 cup balsamic vinegar
- 1/4 cup Worcestershire sauce
- 2 tsps. liquid smoke flavoring
- 1 1/2 tbsps. steak seasoning rub
- 1 (1 1/2-lb.) London broil roast, thinly sliced along the grain

Direction

- Mix together steak seasoning, liquid smoke, Worcestershire sauce, balsamic vinegar and soy sauce then boil in a saucepan; lower the heat to low. Simmer for approximately 10 minutes; take off the heat. Put aside; cool.
- Transfer marinate into a plastic or glass bowl; add meat slices. Mix to coat; cover. Refrigerate for a maximum of 2 days; occasionally mix or turn to marinate meat evenly.
- Preheat an oven to 80°C/175°F. Place beef strips on a wire rack set above a baking sheet; if desired, at this point, sprinkle a little extra steak seasoning.
- In the preheated oven, bake till dry but pliable for 60-90 minutes; keep in an airtight container in fridge.

Nutrition Information

- Calories: 89 calories;
- Total Carbohydrate: 2.1 g

- Cholesterol: 18 mg
- Total Fat: 4.3 g
- Protein: 9.8 g
- Sodium: 585 mg

106. Tofu Jerky I

""A modification of a regular jerky recipe.""
Serving: 6 | Prep: 30m | Ready in: 2days8h30m

Ingredients

- 1 tsp. garlic powder
- 1 tbsp. salt
- 2 tsps. ground black pepper
- 1 lb. firm tofu, drained

Direction

- In a small bowl, mix pepper, salt, and garlic powder.
- Cut tofu in thin strips. Rub spices into tofu strips. Keep in the refrigerator for 2 days, covered.
- Prepare the oven by preheating to 115°F (45°C), or lowest oven setting. Line oven rack with foil, and put the rack in the lowest oven position.
- Put tofu strips straightly on the foil. Bake for 6-8 hours.

Nutrition Information

- Calories: 113 calories;
- Total Carbohydrate: 4 g
- Cholesterol: 0 mg
- Total Fat: 6.6 g
- Protein: 12.1 g
- Sodium: 1174 mg

107. Tofu Jerky II

"This tofu jerky is flavorful and tangy."
Serving: 8 | Prep: 2h | Ready in: 10h

Ingredients

- 1 (14 oz.) package firm tofu, drained
- 3 tbsps. soy sauce
- 2 tsps. maple syrup
- 1/4 tsp. liquid smoke flavoring
- 1 tsp. garlic powder
- 1/2 tsp. ground black pepper
- 3 tbsps. barbecue sauce
- 2 tsps. brown sugar

Direction

- Place the block of tofu onto a plate between paper towels, setting another plate on top. Place a weight on the top of the plate like a can to press the water out of the tofu block as you make the sauce.
- Stir together brown sugar, barbeque sauce, black pepper, garlic powder, liquid smoke, maple syrup, and soy sauce in a medium bowl until smooth.
- Slice the tofu into slices with 1/4 inch thick and dip into the sauce for them to coat. Place them into a tightly sealed container and place inside the refrigerator; marinate for roughly 1-2 hours.
- Heat up the oven to the lowest temperature, about 200 degrees Fahrenheit or 95 degrees Celsius. Use heavy duty aluminum foil to line the oven rack and place it in the lowest part of the oven; place the slices of tofu onto the foil.
- Bake around 8 hours, checking on the tofu and turning them over every couple of hours. The tofu jerky is done once it is evenly dark and hard.

Nutrition Information

- Calories: 58 calories;
- Total Carbohydrate: 6 g
- Cholesterol: 0 mg
- Total Fat: 2.2 g

- Protein: 4.5 g
- Sodium: 410 mg

108. Venison Jerky

"You can use either ground beef or venison for this jerky recipe."
Serving: 15 | Prep: 15m | Ready in: 5h25m

Ingredients

- 2 lbs. lean ground venison or beef
- 2 1/2 tsps. salt
- 2 tsps. monosodium glutamate (MSG)
- 1 tsp. hot pepper sauce
- 2 tsps. sugar-based curing mixture (such as Morton® Tender Quick®)
- 1 1/2 tsps. barbeque seasoning
- 2 tsps. water
- 2 tsps. hickory-flavored liquid smoke
- 2 tsps. garlic powder
- 1/2 tsp. pepper

Direction

- Combine pepper, garlic powder, liquid smoke, water, barbeque seasoning, curing mixture, hot sauce, MSG, salt, and ground venison in a big bowl; mix well. Keep covered in the refrigerator for 2 hours.
- Use plastic wrap to line the food dehydrator trays and pat the meat mixture onto the trays in a very thin layer. Place the trays in the dehydrator set following the manufacturer's instructions. Once the meat firms up, after roughly 2 hours, take the meat out of the plastic, cut them into strips, and place back onto the racks. Continue to dehydrate until the meat finishes drying, around 5-10 hours in total depending on the machine.
- Once done, blot any of the grease off using a paper towel. Store them in a jar with a tight-fitting lid inside the refrigerator.

Nutrition Information

- Calories: 81 calories;
- Total Carbohydrate: 0.4 g
- Cholesterol: 51 mg
- Total Fat: 2.1 g
- Protein: 14 g
- Sodium: 895 mg

109. Western Style Beef Jerky

"This beef jerky is a healthy snack to keep around."
Serving: 8 | Prep: 30m | Ready in: 6h30m

Ingredients

- 3/4 cup beer
- 3/4 cup teriyaki sauce
- 1/2 cup Worcestershire sauce
- 1/3 cup soy sauce
- 1/3 cup water
- 3 tbsps. liquid smoke
- 4 1/2 tsps. ketchup
- 1 tsp. red pepper flakes
- 1 1/2 tsps. salt
- 1/2 tsp. onion salt
- 1/4 tsp. cracked black pepper, or to taste
- 1/4 tsp. garlic powder
- 1 lb. beef round steak

Direction

- In a big bowl, stir together ketchup, liquid smoke, water, soy sauce, Worcestershire sauce, teriyaki sauce, and beer. Stir in garlic powder, pepper, onion salt, salt, and red pepper flakes until everything is mixed.
- Cut the round steaks into 1x1/4-inch long strips and toss the meat into the marinade to coat well. Cover the bowl tightly and marinate inside the refrigerator a minimum of 6 hours.
- Prepare the jerky using a food dehydrator following the manufacturer's instructions.

Nutrition Information

- Calories: 161 calories;
- Total Carbohydrate: 10.2 g
- Cholesterol: 20 mg

- Total Fat: 8.4 g
- Protein: 9.3 g
- Sodium: 2400 mg

Chapter 4: Turkey Recipes

***

110. Asian Roll Lettuce Wrap

"You'll need a minimum of 8 10-inch bamboo skewers to cook the meat."
Serving: 4 | Prep: 35m | Ready in: 1h

Ingredients

- 1 lb. ground turkey
- 1 tbsp. light soy sauce
- 1 tsp. minced garlic
- 2 tsps. minced fresh ginger root
- 1 cup brown rice
- 1 cup water
- 16 large lettuce leaves
- 1 cup shredded carrots
- 1 cup green onions, thinly sliced
- 1 cup sliced red bell pepper
- 1 cup sliced radishes
- 1/3 cup light soy sauce
- 1/3 cup water
- 3 tbsps. fresh lemon juice
- 2 tsps. minced garlic
- 1 tbsp. minced fresh ginger root
- 1 tsp. sugar

Direction

- Mix 2 tsp. ginger, 1 tsp. minced garlic, 1 tbsp. soy sauce and ground turkey in a medium bowl. Shape to 16 meatballs. Roll to ovals. Cover and refrigerate.
- Mix 2 cups water and rice in a medium saucepan on medium heat. Bring to a boil. Lower heat. Simmer until rice is tender for 20 minutes.
- Preheat broiler or grill. Put into every small bowl or serving platter red peppers, radishes, scallions, carrots, lettuce leaves and rice. Mix sugar, 1 tbsp. ginger, 2 tsp. garlic, lemon juice, 1/3 cup water and 1/3 cup soy sauce in a medium bowl. Divide to 4 small dipping bowls.
- On each 10-inch skewer, thread 2 meatballs. Broil or grill for 10-12 minutes, occasionally turning to brown all sides. Broiling: line aluminum foil on a broiler pan. After 6 minutes, drain fat.
- Eating: On the palm of your hand, put a lettuce leaf. Spoon a bit of rice, meat roll, and a few veggies. Roll up. Dip into dipping sauce or spoon sauce on.

Nutrition Information

- Calories: 369 calories;
- Total Carbohydrate: 42.8 g
- Cholesterol: 84 mg
- Total Fat: 9.9 g
- Protein: 28.6 g
- Sodium: 951 mg

111. Asian Turkey Lettuce Wraps

"An easy and quick wrap recipe."
Serving: 6 | Prep: 15m | Ready in: 30m

Ingredients

- 1 large DOLE® Onion, chopped
- 1 tbsp. peanut oil
- 1 (20 oz.) package ground turkey
- 1 cup bottled Thai peanut satay sauce, divided
- 2 tbsps. soy sauce, divided
- 1 tbsp. hoisin sauce
- 1 medium cucumber peeled and chopped

- 1/4 cup coarsely chopped fresh mint
- 6 (10 inch) flour tortillas
- 1 (6 oz.) package DOLE Butter Bliss
- small fresh mint leaves (optional)

Direction

- In peanut oil, sauté onion in big skillet for 3-5 minutes on medium high heat till onion begins to soften. Add turkey; sauté till cooked through for 7-8 minutes.
- Mix hoisin sauce, 1 tbsp. of soy sauce and 1/2 cup of satay sauce in. Add chopped mint and cucumber; heat till hot.
- In small bowl, whisk 1 tbsp. of soy sauce and leftover 1/2 cup of satay sauce.
- Assemble every wrap by putting 3/4 cup of turkey mixture on every tortilla; top with mint leaves (optional) and salad. Fold tortilla sides in; roll up. Slice in half. Serve with the satay soy sauce mixture.

Nutrition Information

- Calories: 530 calories;
- Total Carbohydrate: 46 g
- Cholesterol: 70 mg
- Total Fat: 25.5 g
- Protein: 30.7 g
- Sodium: 955 mg

112.Baked Hawaiian Sandwiches

""Simple, and fast to make sandwiches and a hit all the time. You can present them at any parties or occasions! I have prepared huge quantities and they turned out always. Prepare the sandwiches ahead and keep in the refrigerator until ready to bake. Taste them and have fun!""
Serving: 24 | Prep: 30m | Ready in: 45m

Ingredients

- 24 Hawaiian bread rolls (such as King's®), split
- 12 thin slices of honey-cured deli ham, halved
- 12 slices Swiss cheese, halved
- 12 thin slices deli smoked turkey, halved
- 12 thin slices provolone cheese, halved
- 1/2 cup butter
- 1/4 cup white sugar
- 1/4 cup dried onion flakes
- 2 tbsps. poppy seeds
- 1 tbsp. honey mustard

Direction

- Set a rack into the lower half of the oven then prepare the oven by preheating to 400°F (200°C).
- On a baking sheet, arrange bottom halves of Hawaiian rolls. Then put a half slice each of ham, provolone cheese, smoked turkey, and Swiss cheese onto every roll bottom. Put top halves on every bottom to form sandwiches.
- In a saucepan set on low heat, dissolve butter and mix in honey mustard, poppy seeds, dried onion flakes, and sugar for approximately 2 minutes, until mixture is smoothly blended, creamy, and the sugar is melted; then sweep on the tops of every sandwich.
- Place sandwiches on preheated oven at the lower rack and bake for approximately 15 minutes until tops become golden brown and fillings become hot.

Nutrition Information

- Calories: 426 calories;
- Total Carbohydrate: 46.6 g
- Cholesterol: 78 mg
- Total Fat: 11.4 g
- Protein: 23 g
- Sodium: 488 mg

113.Baked Sloppy Joe Egg Rolls

"Easy and quick for busy days!"
Serving: 7 | Prep: 15m | Ready in: 40m

Ingredients

- cooking spray
- 1 lb. ground turkey
- 1 small onion, diced (optional)

- 1 (15 oz.) can sloppy joe sauce
- 1 cup shredded Cheddar cheese (optional)
- 14 egg roll wrappers (such as Nasoya®), or as needed
- 1/3 cup olive oil

Direction

- Preheat an oven to 200°C/400°F. Prep baking sheet using cooking spray.
- Heat big skillet on medium high heat. Mix and cook onion and turkey in hot skillet for 5-7 minutes till turkey is browned completely.
- Mix sloppy joe sauce into onion and turkey mixture; simmer for 5 minutes till slightly thickened. Take skillet off heat. Mix cheddar cheese into turkey mixture till melted.
- On flat surface, lay egg roll wrapper. Put 2 tbsps. turkey mixture down middle of wrapper with a spoon, creating line reaching within 1-in. of 2 opposite corners. Over filling, fold near corners so points overlap filling. Fold a leftover corner on filling; roll to make a log. Repeat rolling and filling with leftover wrappers and filling till you use all the filling. Brush rolls to coat with olive oil; put on prepped baking sheet.
- In preheated oven, bake rolls for 12-15 minutes till crispy and lightly browned.

Nutrition Information

- Calories: 337 calories;
- Total Carbohydrate: 18.1 g
- Cholesterol: 66 mg
- Total Fat: 20.8 g
- Protein: 19.3 g
- Sodium: 560 mg

114. Baked Turkey Croquettes

"Delicious served with cranberry sauce."
Serving: 6 | Prep: 20m | Ready in: 35m

Ingredients

- 1/2 cup panko bread crumbs
- 1 tsp. melted butter
- 1 cup mashed potatoes
- 1 cup prepared stuffing
- 1 cup chopped cooked turkey
- 1 egg, beaten

Direction

- Set the oven at 230°C (450°F) to preheat. Use parchment paper to line a baking sheet.
- In a shallow bowl, stir melted butter and panko bread crumbs; put aside to moisten.
- In a bowl, stir turkey, stuffing, and mashed potatoes. Roll into a ball or log shapes with about 1 1/2 tbsps. of the turkey mixture; next, dip into the beaten egg, then roll in the panko bread crumb mixture, and arrange on the lined baking sheet. Repeat the process with the remaining turkey mixture.
- In the preheated oven, bake about 15 minutes, or until golden and crisp.

Nutrition Information

- Calories: 168 calories;
- Total Carbohydrate: 19.7 g
- Cholesterol: 51 mg
- Total Fat: 6 g
- Protein: 10.6 g
- Sodium: 364 mg

115.Barbecue Turkey Meatballs

"Use small scoop to make meatballs to easily shape. Use crunchy pretzel sticks instead of wooden sticks!"
Serving: 11 | Prep: 45m | Ready in: 1h5m

Ingredients

- 1 egg, lightly beaten
- 1 (5.3 oz.) container VOSKOS® Nonfat Honey Greek Yogurt
- 1 cup soft bread crumbs
- 2 tbsps. finely chopped onion
- 1 tsp. Italian seasoning blend
- 1/4 tsp. salt

- 1/4 tsp. black pepper
- 1 1/2 lbs. ground turkey
- Pretzel sticks
- Marmalade Barbecue Sauce:
- 1 cup bottled barbecue sauce
- 1/4 cup orange marmalade or apricot preserves

Direction

- Preheat an oven to 350°F. Mix pepper, salt, Italian seasoning, onion, bread crumbs, yogurt and eggs in big bowl. Put ground turkey in; stir well.
- Form turkey mixture to 1-inch meatballs. Put meatballs in 15x10x1-inch foil-lined baking pan. Bake till meatballs aren't pink for 20 minutes. Drain on paper towels. Put meatballs in warm Marmalade Barbecue Sauce in a big saucepan. Use pretzel sticks as picks; serve.
- Marmalade Barbecue Sauce: in a big saucepan, boil marmalade and barbecue sauce; lower heat. Simmer for 5 minutes then serve with meatballs.

Nutrition Information

- Calories: 533 calories;
- Total Carbohydrate: 92 g
- Cholesterol: 64 mg
- Total Fat: 6.8 g
- Protein: 23.5 g
- Sodium: 3086 mg

116. Big Game Sunday Chili Dip

"Eliminate meat for vegetarians and you can also add whatever you want like corn or pinto beans!"
Serving: 8 | Ready in: 1h5m

Ingredients

- 1 (14 oz.) can black beans, drained
- 1 (8 oz.) jar salsa
- 1 lb. ground turkey
- salt and ground black pepper to taste
- 1 (8 oz.) package shredded Mexican cheese blend

Direction

- In slow cooker set on low, mix salsa and black beans.
- In skillet, break ground turkey on medium heat; season with pepper and salt. Mix and cook turkey for 5-7 minutes till browned completely. Mix turkey into black bean mixture. Sprinkle the cheese on bean and turkey mixture.
- Cook mixture for 1 hour on high. Lower to low setting while serving to keep dip hot.

Nutrition Information

- Calories: 246 calories;
- Total Carbohydrate: 10.9 g
- Cholesterol: 69 mg
- Total Fat: 13.6 g
- Protein: 21 g
- Sodium: 630 mg

117. Caroline And Brian's Stuffed Mushrooms

"Even mushroom haters love this!"
Serving: 5 | Prep: 30m | Ready in: 1h10m

Ingredients

- 5 portobello mushrooms
- 1 turkey sausage link, without casing
- 3 cloves garlic, peeled and chopped
- 1 tbsp. crushed garlic
- 1/2 tsp. ground cayenne pepper
- 1 tsp. ground black pepper
- 1/2 cup seasoned bread crumbs
- 1/2 cup cream cheese, softened
- 2 tbsps. grated Parmesan cheese

Direction

- Remove portobello mushroom's stems. Put mushroom caps on medium baking sheet, bottoms up. Chop stems; put aside.
- On small baking sheet, put turkey sausage link. In preheated oven, cook for 15 minutes, uncovered, till interior isn't pink. Take off heat; chop.
- Mix seasoned breadcrumbs, black pepper, cayenne pepper, crushed garlic, chopped garlic, chopped sausage and chopped mushroom stems in a medium saucepan on medium heat. Mix and cook slowly for 5-7 minutes till breadcrumbs start to brown; take off heat. Cool for 10 minutes; put in medium bowl.
- Preheat an oven to 175°C/350°F.
- Mix Parmesan cheese and cream cheese in mushroom stem mixture. Use mixture to stuff mushroom caps.
- In preheated oven, bake stuffed mushrooms till stuffing is lightly browned for 20 minutes.

Nutrition Information

- Calories: 171 calories;
- Total Carbohydrate: 16.1 g
- Cholesterol: 27 mg
- Total Fat: 9.6 g
- Protein: 7.3 g
- Sodium: 318 mg

118.Chinese Firecrackers

"Delicious appetizers."
Serving: 14 | Prep: 35m | Ready in: 55m

Ingredients

- 1 tsp. vegetable oil
- 1/2 lb. ground turkey
- 1 cup shredded cabbage
- 1/2 cup shredded carrots
- 2 green onions, finely chopped
- 1 tbsp. chile paste
- 1 tsp. cornstarch
- 1 tbsp. white wine
- 14 sheets phyllo pastry dough, halved into triangles
- 4 tsps. vegetable oil
- 3/4 cup sweet and sour sauce for dipping

Direction

- Preheat oven to 190°C/375°F. Grease the baking sheet.
- In skillet, heat 1 tsp. of vegetable oil on medium heat. Cook turkey in skillet till not pink; add green onions, carrots and cabbage. Cook for 5-7 minutes till veggies are slightly tender; mix chile paste through vegetable mixture.
- In small bowl, whisk cornstarch into white wine; add to mixture in skillet. Mix and cook till liquid in skillet is slightly thick; take off heat. Put aside; cool.
- On a flat surface, put 1 1/2 of phyllo dough sheet; brush a small amount vegetable oil on. Top with 2nd phyllo sheet. Put 2 tbsps. of turkey mixture on phyllo's short end. Form mixture to 4-inch log. Roll turkey mixture and phyllo. Twist log, 1-inch from every end to get firecracker shape; put on greased cookie sheet then repeat with leftover mixture and phyllo till all get used. Brush vegetable oil lightly on firecrackers
- In preheated oven, bake for 18-22 minutes till phyllo dough is golden brown and crisp; serve with sweet and sour sauce.

Nutrition Information

- Calories: 120 calories;
- Total Carbohydrate: 15.2 g
- Cholesterol: 12 mg
- Total Fat: 4.5 g
- Protein: 4.8 g
- Sodium: 164 mg

119. Cocktail Turkey Meatballs

"Moist and savory turkey meatballs."
Serving: 8 | Prep: 20m | Ready in: 1h

Ingredients

- Meatballs:
- 1 cup panko bread crumbs
- 1 egg, beaten
- 1/4 cup minced onion
- 1/4 cup minced water chestnuts
- 1/4 cup applesauce (such as Mott's® Natural Applesauce)
- 1/4 cup finely grated Parmesan cheese
- 1 tbsp. finely chopped fresh parsley
- 1/2 tsp. salt
- 1/2 tsp. dry mustard powder (such as Coleman's®)
- 1/2 tsp. poultry seasoning
- 1 lb. ground turkey
- Sauce:
- 1 cup apple jelly
- 1 cup applesauce (such as Mott's® Natural Applesauce)
- 1/2 cup cider vinegar
- 1/2 cup minced onion
- 1/4 cup ketchup
- 1/4 cup chili sauce (such as Heinz®)
- 2 tbsps. tomato paste
- 1 tbsp. brown sugar
- 1 tbsp. Dijon mustard
- 1 tsp. dry mustard powder (such as Coleman's®)
- 1/2 tsp. salt
- 1 tbsp. chopped fresh parsley, or more to taste

Direction

- Set the oven at 175° C (350° F) to preheat. Use aluminum foil to line a baking sheet.
- In a large bowl, mix together poultry seasoning, 1/2 tsp. mustard powder, 1/2 tsp. salt, 1 tbsp. parsley, Parmesan cheese, 1/4 cup applesauce, water chestnuts, 1/4 cup minced onion, egg, and bread crumbs. Put in the ground turkey and mix together gently until just combined.
- Next, roll the turkey mixture into 1 1/2-inch meatballs and arrange on the prepared baking sheet.
- Bake for around 20 minutes in the preheated oven until cooked through. Insert an instant-read thermometer into the center and it should state at least 74° C (165° F).
- In a saucepan, whisk together 1/2 tsp. salt, 1 tsp. dry mustard, Dijon mustard, brown sugar, tomato paste, chili sauce, ketchup, 1/2 cup minced onion, cider vinegar, 1 cup applesauce, and apple jelly; bring to a simmer and cook for about 10 minutes, stirring irregularly, until the flavors combine.
- Next, transfer the cooked meatballs to the simmering sauce, use a lid to cover the saucepan and continue to simmer for 10 minutes more, or until the flavors blend. Decorate with the remaining parsley.

Nutrition Information

- Calories: 303 calories;
- Total Carbohydrate: 50.6 g
- Cholesterol: 67 mg
- Total Fat: 6.4 g
- Protein: 15.4 g
- Sodium: 716 mg

120. Colossal American Falafel

"A yummy dish my husband and I love!"
Serving: 6 | Prep: 20m | Ready in: 40m

Ingredients

- 2 (16 oz.) cans garbanzo beans (chickpeas), drained and rinsed
- 6 tbsps. olive oil
- 1/4 cup lemon juice
- 2 tbsps. minced garlic
- 2 tbsps. water
- 2 tbsps. tahini (optional)
- 2 eggs

- 1/2 cup fine bread crumbs
- 2 large carrots, finely shredded
- 1/2 onion, chopped
- 1 tsp. garlic salt
- 1 tsp. lemon pepper
- 1 tsp. onion powder
- 1 tsp. ground cumin
- 6 slices turkey bacon, sliced into small strips (optional)
- 2 tbsps. olive oil

Direction

- In a blender, puree tahini, water, garlic, lemon juice, 6 tbsps. olive oil and garbanzo beans till smooth and thick. Put mixture in big mixing bowl.
- Mix eggs into hummus mixture till mixed completely.
- Mix turkey bacon, cumin, onion powder, lemon pepper, garlic salt, onion, carrots and bread crumbs gently into hummus mixture till combined well,
- Heat 2 tbsps. olive oil in big skillet on medium heat.
- In hot oil, drop big spoonful of falafel mixture. Flatten to thick disc gently. Cook patties, 3 minutes per side, till golden brown. Put on wire racks that have paper towels underneath.

Nutrition Information

- Calories: 526 calories;
- Total Carbohydrate: 48.8 g
- Cholesterol: 87 mg
- Total Fat: 30.4 g
- Protein: 16.6 g
- Sodium: 1285 mg

121.Curried Fowl Balls

"Tasty appetizer/entrée."
Serving: 16 | Prep: 20m | Ready in: 40m

Ingredients

- 1 cup cooked rice
- 1/2 cup finely diced onion
- 1/2 cup mild curry powder
- 1/2 cup water
- 10 tortilla chips with a 'hint of lime', crushed, or as needed
- 1/4 cup vegetable oil
- 2 cloves garlic, minced
- 2 tsps. salt
- 1 tsp. dried tarragon
- 2 lbs. ground turkey
- 2 tsps. butter, or as needed

Direction

- In bowl, mix tarragon, salt, garlic, vegetable oil, tortilla chips, water, curry powder, onion and rice. Add turkey. Mix till combined thoroughly. Shape mixture to 1-in. balls.
- Preheat an oven to 60°C/140°F.
- Heat big nonstick skillet on medium heat; add butter. Place 12 balls in melted butter; press every ball using back of spatula to 1/2-in. thick patty. Cook, 2-3 minutes per side, till not pink in the middle anymore. Put cooked patties in oven-safe plate; keep warm in oven. Repeat with leftover balls, adding extra butter if needed.

Nutrition Information

- Calories: 159 calories;
- Total Carbohydrate: 7.2 g
- Cholesterol: 43 mg
- Total Fat: 9.3 g
- Protein: 12.2 g
- Sodium: 345 mg

122. Curried Turkey Meatballs

"Lean and yummy meatballs."
Serving: 4 | Prep: 15m | Ready in: 35m

Ingredients

- 1 lb. ground turkey
- 1 yellow onion, finely chopped
- 1/3 cup dry bread crumbs
- 1 egg, beaten
- 1 1/2 tsps. Madras curry powder
- 1 tsp. kosher salt
- 1/4 tsp. ground cumin
- 1/4 tsp. ground ginger
- 1 pinch ground cinnamon
- 2 tbsps. olive oil

Direction

- Preheat an oven to 175°C/350°F.
- Use your hands to mix cinnamon, ginger, cumin, salt, curry powder, egg, bread crumbs, onion and turkey in a bowl; shape to 20 balls.
- In a skillet, heat olive oil on medium high heat. In batches, cook meatballs in hot oil for 5 minutes till browned on all sides. Put browned meatballs in baking dish.
- In preheated oven, bake for 15 minutes till cooked through. An inserted instant-read thermometer in middle should register 70°C/160°F minimum.

Nutrition Information

- Calories: 294 calories;
- Total Carbohydrate: 9.9 g
- Cholesterol: 130 mg
- Total Fat: 17.2 g
- Protein: 25.7 g
- Sodium: 629 mg

123. David's Favorite Football Dip

"My husband's favorite dip!"
Serving: 8 | Prep: 10m | Ready in: 30m

Ingredients

- 1 lb. ground turkey
- 1 onion, chopped
- 1 green bell pepper, chopped
- 1 (28 oz.) can vegetarian baked beans
- 1 (16 oz.) can vegetarian refried beans
- 1 tbsp. coconut oil
- 1 cup salsa
- 1/2 cup taco seasoning mix
- 2 tbsps. ranch dressing
- 2 tsps. soy sauce
- 2 tsps. liquid smoke flavoring
- 1/2 cup shredded Cheddar cheese
- 1/2 cup shredded mozzarella cheese
- salt and ground black pepper to taste

Direction

- Heat big skillet on medium high heat; mix and cook ground turkey in hot skillet for 5-7 minutes till crumbly and browned. Add bell pepper and onion; cover skillet. Simmer for 5 more minutes till onion is softened. Put turkey mixture in bowl.
- In same skillet for turkey mixture, mix coconut oil, refried beans and baked beans; mix and cook on medium heat for 5-7 minutes till beans are heated through. Mix liquid smoke, soy sauce, ranch dressing, taco seasoning and salsa into bean mixture. Sprinkle mozzarella cheese and cheddar cheese. Cover skillet. Cook for 3-5 minutes till cheese melts.
- Stir bean mixture into ground turkey mixture well. Season with pepper and salt.

Nutrition Information

- Calories: 367 calories;
- Total Carbohydrate: 40.8 g
- Cholesterol: 55 mg
- Total Fat: 13.5 g
- Protein: 23.3 g

- Sodium: 1684 mg

124. Deluxe Egg Rolls

"A great egg roll recipe."
Serving: 20 | Prep: 45m | Ready in: 1h5m

Ingredients

- 2 quarts oil for deep frying
- 1/2 lb. ground turkey
- 2 tbsps. chopped fresh ginger root
- 3 cloves garlic, peeled and minced
- 2 tsps. sesame oil
- 1 medium head bok choy, shredded
- 3/4 cup shredded carrots
- 2 green onions, finely chopped
- 1 tsp. soy sauce
- 2 (12 oz.) packages wonton wrappers

Direction

- Heat oil in big heavy saucepan/deep-fryer to 190°C/375°F.
- In big deep skillet, put approximately 1/2 garlic, 1/2 ginger and ground turkey. Cook till evenly brown on medium high heat.
- In wok, heat sesame oil on medium high heat. Mix garlic and leftover ginger in. Mix soy sauce, green onions, carrots and bok choy in. Mix and cook till veggies are tender yet crisp; take off heat.
- Mix bok choy mixture and ground turkey in medium bowl.
- Use approximately 1 tbsp. bok choy and turkey mixture to fill double thickness of wonton wrappers. Fold wrappers on filling. To seal, moisten seam. Repeat with leftover filling and wrappers.
- Deep fry filled wontons in small batches for 3-5 minutes till golden brown and crisp.

Nutrition Information

- Calories: 206 calories;
- Total Carbohydrate: 21.1 g
- Cholesterol: 12 mg
- Total Fat: 10.8 g
- Protein: 6 g
- Sodium: 248 mg

125. Drunk Turkey Bites

"This is great for a quick appetizer or dinner."
Serving: 8 | Prep: 5m | Ready in: 25m

Ingredients

- 1 tbsp. olive oil
- 2 (16 oz.) packages turkey kielbasa, cut into bite-size pieces
- 1/2 cup diced onion
- 1 cup lager-style beer
- 2 tbsps. brown sugar
- 1 tbsp. Dijon mustard, or to taste
- salt and ground black pepper to taste

Direction

- In a skillet, heat oil over medium heat. Cook and stir onion and kielbasa in hot oil for about 5 minutes, or until the onion starts to soften.
- In a bowl, whisk mustard, brown sugar, and beer gently; pour into the skillet.
- Next, bring the mixture to a boil and cook for about 15 minutes, or until the liquid reduces by half in volume. Season with pepper and salt.

Nutrition Information

- Calories: 227 calories;
- Total Carbohydrate: 9.8 g
- Cholesterol: 70 mg
- Total Fat: 11.7 g
- Protein: 16.3 g
- Sodium: 1050 mg

126. Easy Snack Wraps

""These delicious bite-sized wraps are perfect to serve as appetizers at your parties!""
Serving: 60 | Prep: 15m | Ready in: 15m

Ingredients

- 12 (10 inch) flour tortillas
- 1 (8 oz.) package cream cheese
- 1 head lettuce
- 1 (6 oz.) package sliced deli-style turkey
- 2 cups shredded carrots
- 2 cups minced tomato

Direction

- Put cream cheese on tortillas evenly. Put lettuce leaves on top of the cream cheese. Put turkey slices in even layers on top of the lettuce leaves. Top with tomato and carrots. Roll tortillas into wraps then cut diagonally into small pieces. Use toothpicks to secure wraps.

Nutrition Information

- Calories: 65 calories;
- Total Carbohydrate: 8.5 g
- Cholesterol: 5 mg
- Total Fat: 2.5 g
- Protein: 2.1 g
- Sodium: 140 mg

127. Fried Pot Stickers

"Yummy fried pot stickers!"
Serving: 3 | Prep: 25m | Ready in: 28m

Ingredients

- 1/4 lb. ground turkey
- 1 egg, beaten, divided
- 1 tsp. minced water chestnuts
- 1 tsp. minced green onion
- 1/2 tsp. light soy sauce
- 1/2 tsp. minced fresh ginger
- 1/2 tsp. freshly ground black pepper
- 1/4 tsp. salt
- 1/4 tsp. garlic powder
- 1/4 tsp. red pepper flakes
- 12 wonton wrappers
- vegetable oil for frying

Direction

- In bowl, mix red pepper flakes, garlic powder, salt, black pepper, ginger, soy sauce, green onion, water chestnuts, 1 tbsp. beaten egg and turkey.
- Cut wonton wrappers to circles with a 3-in. biscuit cutter. In middle of every wonton wrapper, put 1 1/2 tsp. turkey filling. Brush beaten egg on one side of every wrapper. Fold wrapper on filling, pleating edges while sealing.
- In deep-fryer/big saucepan, heat oil to 190°C/375°F. 6 at a time, fry pot stickers for 3-6 minutes till browned. On paper towels, drain.

Nutrition Information

- Calories: 241 calories;
- Total Carbohydrate: 19.5 g
- Cholesterol: 93 mg
- Total Fat: 12.4 g
- Protein: 12.9 g
- Sodium: 472 mg

128. Gluten-free Turkey Meatballs

"Gluten-free meatball recipe."
Serving: 40 | Prep: 15m | Ready in: 45m

Ingredients

- 3/4 lb. ground turkey
- 1/2 lb. chicken sausage, casings removed
- 2/3 cup gluten-free bread crumbs
- 3 tbsps. chopped fresh basil
- 3 tbsps. milk
- 2 tsps. minced garlic

- 1/4 cup grated Parmesan cheese
- 1 tsp. kosher salt
- 1/2 tsp. ground black pepper
- 1 egg, lightly beaten

Direction

- Preheat an oven to 175°C/350°F. Line parchment paper on baking sheet.
- Mix black pepper, kosher salt, parmesan cheese, garlic, milk, basil, bread crumbs, chicken sausage and ground turkey in bowl; gently mix with fork. Drop mixture on prepped baking sheet with a spoon, 1 1/4-in. diameter per meatball.
- In preheated oven, bake for 30 minutes till lightly browned and cooked through. An inserted instant-read thermometer in middle should register 74°C/165°F minimum.

Nutrition Information

- Calories: 32 calories;
- Total Carbohydrate: 1.3 g
- Cholesterol: 15 mg
- Total Fat: 1.6 g
- Protein: 2.9 g
- Sodium: 114 mg

129. Hot Italian Turkey Sausage Spread

"An easy recipe that guests love!"
Serving: 5 | Prep: 10m | Ready in: 21m

Ingredients

- cooking spray
- 5 (10 inch) flour tortillas, cut into quarters
- 1 (14 oz.) package hot Italian turkey sausage, casings removed
- 1/2 red onion, chopped
- 5 slices American cheese

Direction

- Spray cooking spray on skillet; heat on medium heat. Fry tortilla quarters, 1 minute per side, till light brown and crisp. Take chips out of skillet.
- Put sausage in skillet on medium high heat. Mix and cook for 3 minutes then add onion. Mix and cook for 5 more minutes till turkey is crumbly and browned. Add American cheese; mix for 1 minute till completely melted. Put spread in serving dish then surround with chips using a spoon.

Nutrition Information

- Calories: 459 calories;
- Total Carbohydrate: 37.4 g
- Cholesterol: 87 mg
- Total Fat: 22.3 g
- Protein: 27 g
- Sodium: 1525 mg

130. King Of The Hill Frito® Pie

"I made this recipe based on a dish I saw on the TV. It's very tasty."
Serving: 4 | Prep: 10m | Ready in: 20m

Ingredients

- 1 lb. lean ground turkey
- 2 (8 oz.) cans tomato sauce
- 1 (10 oz.) can petite diced tomatoes with green chiles
- 1 (6 fluid oz.) can tomato juice, or more to taste
- 1 (1.25 oz.) package mild chili seasoning mix
- 1 (16 oz.) package corn chips (such as Fritos®)
- 1/2 cup shredded Cheddar cheese, or to taste

Direction

- Heat a big frying pan on medium-high heat. Stir and cook the turkey in the hot frying pan for 5-7 minutes until turning brown and crumbly. Strain and dispose the grease.

- Mix chili seasoning mix, tomato juice, diced tomatoes, and tomato sauce into the turkey; simmer for another 5 minutes until the chili is hot.
- In a big bowl, put corn chips and put turkey chili on top. Sprinkle over the chili with Cheddar cheese.

Nutrition Information

- Calories: 871 calories;
- Total Carbohydrate: 85.6 g
- Cholesterol: 98 mg
- Total Fat: 46 g
- Protein: 36.5 g
- Sodium: 2663 mg

131.Leftover Turkey Nachos

"After a holiday meal, there's usually some leftover turkey. Here's a good way to use some of it. If you prefer, cooked and cubed chicken breast can also be used. Prepare double size as a main dish or as an appetizer."

Serving: 8 | Prep: 10m | Ready in: 15m

Ingredients

- 10 oz. processed cheese food (such as Velveeta®), cubed
- 1 cup cubed cooked turkey
- 3/4 cup salsa
- 1/4 cup sour cream (optional)
- 1/4 cup sliced black olives (optional)
- 1 (13.5 oz.) package tortilla chips

Direction

- In a large microwavable bowl mix turkey, cheese food, and salsa.
- Heat the mixture for 3 minutes in the microwave on high. Stir after the first minute and after every 30 seconds after, until the cheese melts. Serve with tortilla chips topped with olives and sour cream.

Nutrition Information

- Calories: 403 calories;
- Total Carbohydrate: 35.8 g
- Cholesterol: 44 mg
- Total Fat: 22.7 g
- Protein: 15.9 g
- Sodium: 842 mg

132. Leftover Turkey Spring Rolls With Cranberry Sweet And Sour Dipping Sauce

"You may deep fry this for more flavor. If you use egg roll wrappers, deep-fry them."

Serving: 25 | Prep: 45m | Ready in: 1h15m

Ingredients

- 2 tbsps. olive oil
- 1 tsp. Asian (toasted) sesame oil (optional)
- 2 cups finely chopped cooked turkey
- 1/2 carrot, minced
- 2 cloves garlic, minced
- 1/8 tsp. ground black pepper
- 1/8 tsp. ground ginger
- 1/8 tsp. garlic and herb seasoning blend (such as Mrs. Dash®)
- 5 tbsps. soy sauce
- 6 cups finely shredded cabbage
- 1/2 tsp. oyster sauce (optional)
- 50 (7 inch square) egg roll wrappers
- 1/4 cup jellied cranberry sauce
- 1/4 cup white sugar
- 1/4 cup white vinegar
- 1 dash soy sauce

Direction

- Heat sesame oil and olive oil in big skillet/wok on medium high heat till it shimmers. Mix and cook herb seasoning, garlic, ginger, black pepper, garlic, carrot and turkey for 2 minutes till garlic is fragrant. Mix 2 tbsps. soy sauce in; cook for 5 minutes till carrots start to soften. Mix leftover 3 tbsps. soy sauce, oyster sauce and cabbage in. Keep mixing for 10 minutes till cabbage is cooked through and soft. Take mixture off heat; put aside. Drain any extra liquid off.

- Preheat an oven to 175°C/350°F. Line parchment paper on several baking sheets.
- Filling wrappers: Separate and put spring roll wrappers on work surface, square points pointing down and up like a diamond shape. Put 2 tbsps. turkey filling in a line across middle of wrapper. Fold bottom point up so filling is covered. Fold 2 side points in on the top of folded wrapper to enclose filling fully. 2 side points should be 1-in. apart. Gently but firmly, roll spring roll to tight cylinder. Roll wrapper over to press down leftover point firmly. Put filled wrappers on parchment-lined baking sheets, seam-side down to avoid touching. Rolls should be as thick as a finger.
- In preheated oven, bake filled rolls for 15 minutes till they start to brown. In a saucepan, mash cranberry sauce till sauce is smooth on medium sauce. Whisk dash of soy sauce, vinegar and sugar in. Boil mixture; simmer, whisking sauce, for 10 minutes till sauce slightly thickens and reduces and sugar melts. Put sauce in bowl. Serve rolls hot with sauce.

Nutrition Information

- Calories: 236 calories;
- Total Carbohydrate: 41.6 g
- Cholesterol: 14 mg
- Total Fat: 2.8 g
- Protein: 10 g
- Sodium: 562 mg

133. Lighter Cretons

"This recipe has lots of pork and lard in it. Lovely surprise awaits with this light version. Put on your desired crackers or bread."

Serving: 10 | Prep: 15m | Ready in: 2h

Ingredients

- 1 lb. ground turkey
- 1 1/2 cups water, divided
- 1 cup chopped onion
- 1/8 tsp. ground cloves
- 1/8 tsp. sage
- 1/8 tsp. ground cinnamon
- 1 (.25 oz.) package unflavored gelatin (such as Knox ®)

Direction

- Put together in a saucepan the cinnamon, sage, cloves, onion, 1 cup water and ground turkey. Make it boil, lower the heat and gently boil for 45 minutes, crushing the mixture regularly using a spatula while it's boiling; then get away from heat.
- Mix gelatin into left 1/2 cup water; add in the gelatin mixture into turkey mixture then mix. Then place it into a small container; let chill inside the refrigerator for 1 hour then serve.

Nutrition Information

- Calories: 76 calories;
- Total Carbohydrate: 1.5 g
- Cholesterol: 33 mg
- Total Fat: 3.4 g
- Protein: 9.8 g
- Sodium: 29 mg

134. Loaded Stuffed Jalapeno Poppers

"Great stuffed jalapeno poppers!"
Serving: 12 | Prep: 10m | Ready in: 1h

Ingredients

- 12 jalapeno peppers, seeded
- 8 turkey sausage
- 2 cups finely shredded sharp Cheddar cheese
- 1 (8 oz.) package cream cheese, softened
- 1 cup shredded Parmesan cheese
- 1 (1 oz.) package dry ranch-flavored seasoning mix
- 1 tsp. minced garlic, or more to taste
- 1 1/2 cups panko bread crumbs
- 2 tbsps. butter, melted

Direction

- Fill a big bowl with cold water and ice; put aside. Slice a thin piece from bottom of every pepper to keep peppers from rolling on sides while baking.
- Boil a big pot of water on medium high heat. Carefully drop every pepper in water; boil for 2 minutes. Take peppers from water; put in bowl with ice water.
- In skillet, cook turkey sausage on medium heat for 3 minutes till browned. Drain extra fat. Mix garlic, ranch-flavored seasoning, Parmesan cheese, cream cheese and Cheddar cheese in.
- Take peppers from water; drain. Use sausage mixture to fill each pepper, making a mound. Put filled peppers on a baking sheet. Put in freezer for 20 minutes till frozen.
- Preheat an oven to 175°C/350°F.
- Mix butter and breadcrumbs. Press into top of sausage filling.
- In the preheated oven, bake for 25-30 minutes till cheese begins to bubble and breadcrumbs are golden brown.

Nutrition Information

- Calories: 341 calories;
- Total Carbohydrate: 12.5 g
- Cholesterol: 98 mg
- Total Fat: 24.1 g
- Protein: 21.9 g
- Sodium: 1012 mg

135. Mexican Ground Turkey Dip

"A great ground turkey dip."
Serving: 18 | Prep: 20m | Ready in: 1h

Ingredients

- 1 lb. ground turkey
- 2 red bell peppers, chopped
- 1 large Spanish onion, chopped
- 1 jalapeno pepper, diced, or more to taste
- 2 cups salsa
- 1 cup sour cream
- 1 (1 oz.) packet taco seasoning
- 1 (1 lb.) package processed cheese (such as Velveeta®), cubed
- 1 cup grated Cheddar cheese

Direction

- Preheat an oven to 175°C/350°F.
- Heat big skillet on medium high heat. Mix and cook turkey in hot skillet for 5-7 minutes till crumbly and browned. Add jalapeno pepper, onion and red bell peppers; sauté for 5 minutes till onion is just translucent.
- In big oven-safe casserole dish, mix taco seasoning, sour cream and salsa. Add processed cheese and turkey mixture; stir well. Put cheddar cheese on top.
- In preheated oven, bake for 30 minutes till top is bubbling.

Nutrition Information

- Calories: 194 calories;
- Total Carbohydrate: 7.1 g
- Cholesterol: 51 mg
- Total Fat: 13.1 g
- Protein: 12.3 g

- Sodium: 667 mg

136. Mexican Turkey Dip

"A simple and wonderful ground turkey dip to enjoy together with tortilla chips."
Serving: 16 | Prep: 5m | Ready in: 25m

Ingredients

- 1 tbsp. olive oil
- 1 (16 oz.) package ground turkey
- 1/2 cup spicy salsa
- 1 (1.25 oz.) package dry taco seasoning mix
- 1 (16 oz.) can refried beans
- 1 (8 oz.) package tortilla chips
- 1/2 cup enchilada sauce
- 6 slices American cheese
- 1 (8 oz.) can sliced black olives (optional)

Direction

- Set an oven to 175°C (350°F) and start preheating.
- In a skillet, heat the olive oil on medium heat. Put in the ground turkey and cook it for 5 minutes until it is no longer pink. Combine in taco seasoning and salsa.
- In a 9x13-inch pan, place the American cheese, enchilada sauce, tortilla chips, refried beans, and turkey mixture in a layer in reverse order. Place with olives on top.
- In the prepared oven, bake for 15-20 minutes until heated thoroughly.

Nutrition Information

- Calories: 215 calories;
- Total Carbohydrate: 17.3 g
- Cholesterol: 33 mg
- Total Fat: 11.7 g
- Protein: 11 g
- Sodium: 675 mg

137. Originals Oven Roasted Turkey Cucumber Roll-ups

"Low-carb and full of protein!"
Serving: 2 | Prep: 12m | Ready in: 12m

Ingredients

- 1 cucumber
- 5 slices Dietz & Watson Originals Oven Roasted Turkey Breast
- 3 slices Dietz & Watson Originals Cheddar Cheese
- 4 oz. ranch veggie dip

Direction

- Peel cucumber to thin sliced strips with mandolin/vegetable peeler.
- Cut Dietz & Watson Originals turkey breast to thin sliced strips.
- Cut Dietz & Watson Originals Cheddar cheese to 1/2-in. sliced strips.
- On cucumber slices, layer 2 D&W cheese pieces and 1 D&W turkey slice, folded in half.
- Roll cucumber; put toothpick in center to hold roll together.
- Dipping: Serve with the ranch veggie dip.

Nutrition Information

- Calories: 447 calories;
- Total Carbohydrate: 6.2 g
- Cholesterol: 71 mg
- Total Fat: 39.6 g
- Protein: 16.6 g
- Sodium: 1021 mg

138. Santa Fe Turkey Crostini

"“This recipe of crostini is as flavorful as it is inspired by the flavors of the Southwest. It's well roasted with peppers and sun-dried tomatoes”"
Serving: 8 | Prep: 2m | Ready in: 8m

Ingredients

- 1 French baguette
- Olive oil cooking spray
- 8 tsps. Dietz & Watson Chipotle Mayo
- 8 slices Dietz & Watson Provolone Cheese, cut into 1-inch strips
- 8 slices Dietz & Watson Santa Fe Turkey Breast, cut into 1-inch strips
- 2 ripe avocados - peeled, pitted, and cubed
- 8 cherry or pear tomatoes, halved or quartered
- Salt and cracked pepper to taste

Direction

- Set the oven to 350°F for preheating.
- Using a serrated knife, divide the baguette into 16 slices. Spray olive oil cooking spray on both of their sides lightly. Arrange on baking sheets.
- Let it bake for 8 minutes until light golden brown. Set aside to cool.
- Coat each of the crostini with Dietz & Watson™ Chipotle Mayo.
- Top crostini with 2 strips of turkey and provolone. Place also a few pieces of tomato and avocado on top.
- Season it with pepper and salt.

Nutrition Information

- Calories: 290 calories;
- Total Carbohydrate: 25.3 g
- Cholesterol: 37 mg
- Total Fat: 11.8 g
- Protein: 18.1 g
- Sodium: 767 mg

139. Savory Turkey Meatballs With Tangy Mustard Dip

"Don't get extra-lean turkey breast because it easily dries out."
Serving: 10 | Prep: 20m | Ready in: 1h40m

Ingredients

- Meatballs:
- 1 slice day-old whole-grain bread, torn into 2-inch pieces
- 1/4 cup 1% low-fat milk
- 1 onion, quartered
- 1 red bell pepper, seeded and quartered
- 2 cloves garlic
- 1 lb. 93% lean ground turkey
- 1 egg, lightly beaten
- 2 tbsps. chopped fresh Italian parsley
- 1 tbsp. grainy Dijon mustard
- 3/4 tsp. salt
- 1/2 tsp. ground black pepper
- cooking spray
- Dip:
- 1/3 cup non-fat Greek yogurt
- 1/4 cup light mayonnaise
- 4 tsps. grainy Dijon mustard

Direction

- In food processor, pulse torn bread till you make fine crumbs. Put bread crumbs in big bowl; add milk. Put aside till bread is soaked completely.
- In food processor, pulse garlic, red bell pepper and onion till chopped finely. Mix into bread mixture. Add pepper, salt, 1 tbsp. mustard, parsley, egg and turkey into bread crumb mixture; stir well. Use plastic wrap to cover bowl and refrigerate for an hour.
- Preheat an oven to 230°C/450°F. Spray cooking spray on rimmed baking sheet.
- Form turkey mixture to 1-in. balls; put on prepped baking sheet.
- In preheated oven, bake for 15 minutes till cooked through and firm. An inserted instant-read thermometer in middle should read

74°C/165°F minimum. For 5 minutes, let meatballs stand.

- In a bowl, mix 4 tsps. mustard, mayonnaise and yogurt; serve with meatballs.

Nutrition Information

- Calories: 120 calories;
- Total Carbohydrate: 5.1 g
- Cholesterol: 55 mg
- Total Fat: 6.2 g
- Protein: 11.2 g
- Sodium: 353 mg

140. Savory Turkey Sausage Quinoa Bites

"Tasty small bites!"

Serving: 10 | Prep: 20m | Ready in: 40m

Ingredients

- cooking spray
- 1/2 lb. ground turkey sausage
- 4 cloves garlic, minced
- 1 tsp. ground dried sage
- 2 cups cooked quinoa
- 1 cup shredded sharp Cheddar cheese
- 1/2 cup grated Parmesan cheese
- 3 green onions, diced
- 2 eggs, whisked
- 2 tbsps. all-purpose flour
- 1/2 tsp. coarsely ground black pepper

Direction

- Preheat an oven to 175°C/350°F. Spray cooking spray on a mini-muffin pan lightly.
- Mix sage, garlic and turkey sausage in skillet on medium high heat. Mix and cook for 6 minutes till browned; drain.
- Mix black pepper, flour, eggs, green onions, parmesan cheese, cheddar cheese, quinoa and browned sausage mixture till blended well in medium bowl. Put mixture in prepped muffin cups using spoon.
- In preheated oven, bake for 20 minutes till golden brown.

Nutrition Information

- Calories: 166 calories;
- Total Carbohydrate: 10.2 g
- Cholesterol: 65 mg
- Total Fat: 8.8 g
- Protein: 11.6 g
- Sodium: 335 mg

141. Southwestern Mini Turkey Meatballs

"Great for parties!"

Serving: 24 | Prep: 15m | Ready in: 45m

Ingredients

- 2 lbs. ground turkey
- 1 cup finely crushed tortilla chips
- 1 egg
- 2 cups Dannon Oikos Plain Greek Nonfat Yogurt
- 1/2 cup chopped cilantro
- 1 cup prepared (jar) picante sauce or salsa, divided
- 1 cup frozen corn kernels, thawed
- 1 cup black beans
- 1 tsp. cumin
- 1 tsp. ground chipotle chili powder, divided

Direction

- Mix chipotle chili powder, cumin, salsa and yogurt in a bowl. In the fridge, put aside 1 1/2 cups.
- Mix black beans, corn, cilantro, leftover seasoned yogurt, egg, crushed chips and turkey in another bowl. Make tbsp. sized balls with small scoop spoon; put on lightly greased shallow baking sheet. In preheated 400°F oven, bake till lightly browned for 20-25 minutes.
- On shredded lettuce, serve meatballs with leftover sauce for a dip.

Nutrition Information

- Calories: 111 calories;
- Total Carbohydrate: 8.7 g
- Cholesterol: 37 mg
- Total Fat: 3.5 g
- Protein: 11.8 g
- Sodium: 103 mg

142. Tangy Turkey Taco Cups

"A great snack or even a main dish."
Serving: 12 | Prep: 14m | Ready in: 14m

Ingredients

- 1 (16.3 oz.) can refrigerated flaky biscuit dough
- 2 tsps. vegetable oil
- 1 lb. ground turkey
- 1 (1.25 oz.) package taco seasoning mix
- 1 (15 oz.) can sloppy joe sauce
- 3 slices Borden® American Singles, cut into 4 small squares

Direction

- Preheat an oven to 175°C/350°F.
- Separate 6 biscuits to 2 rounds each. Stretch every round to 5-in. circle gently. Press into nonstick muffin tin's cups.
- Oil skillet lightly; put on medium high heat. In skillet, cook turkey, separating to small pieces while browning. When turkey isn't pink anymore, lower heat to medium low. Put in taco seasoning, mixing to combine. Mix sloppy joe sauce in; cook for 5 minutes till heated through.
- Use turkey mixture to fill biscuit-lined muffin cups.
- In preheated oven, bake for 13 minutes till hot and browned.
- Divide each cheese slice to quarters; on top of every filled cup, put one quarter slice.
- Bake till cheese melts or for 3 more minutes.
- Cool for 5 minutes in pan. Put on rack till cool enough to serve.

Nutrition Information

- Calories: 227 calories;
- Total Carbohydrate: 23.4 g
- Cholesterol: 31 mg
- Total Fat: 9.5 g
- Protein: 11.5 g
- Sodium: 890 mg

143. Thanksgiving Leftover Wontons With Cranberry Salsa

"You can put a bit of cilantro in cranberry salsa if you want."
Serving: 10 | Prep: 30m | Ready in: 50m

Ingredients

- 3/4 cup lemon juice
- 1 cup dried cranberries
- 1 1/2 cups shredded cooked turkey
- 1 cup prepared stuffing
- 4 oz. cream cheese, softened
- 1/4 cup thick turkey gravy
- 1 (14 oz.) package wonton wrappers
- salt to taste
- 3 cups canola oil for frying
- 2 tbsps. minced onion
- 1 tbsp. lime juice
- 1 tsp. seeded and minced jalapeno pepper - or to taste
- 1 tsp. minced garlic
- 1 tsp. water

Direction

- Put lemon juice on dried cranberries in bowl; put aside. Mix turkey gravy, cream cheese, stuffing and turkey in another bowl till combined well.
- On work surface, put wonton wrapper; put 1 tbsp. filling in middle of wrapper using a spoon. Use a finger dipped into water to moisten 2 opposite wrapper's edges. Fold wrapper in half the long way. Use a fork to

press edges together. Sprinkle salt on wrapper. Repeat with leftover wrappers and filling.
- Heat canola oil in big deep skillet on medium heat. In batches, pan-fry filled wontons, 2 minutes per side, till golden brown and crisp. On paper towels, drain fried wontons. Cool for 5 minutes to let filling set.
- Drain lemon juice from dried cranberries. In a food processor, pulse cranberries a few times till cranberries are chopped finely. Put in bowl; mix water, garlic, jalapeno pepper, lime juice and onion in. Serve with hot fried wontons.

Nutrition Information

- Calories: 330 calories;
- Total Carbohydrate: 39.6 g
- Cholesterol: 32 mg
- Total Fat: 14.1 g
- Protein: 11.7 g
- Sodium: 427 mg

144. Thanksgiving Won Tons

"Yummy wontons."

Serving: 20 | Prep: 30m | Ready in: 45m

Ingredients

- 1 1/2 cups cooked turkey breast meat, shredded
- 2/3 cup dried cranberries
- 1/3 cup slivered almonds
- 1/2 cup cranberry sauce
- 1 (14 oz.) package wonton wrappers
- 1 quart vegetable oil for frying

Direction

- In a bowl, mix cranberry sauce, almonds, cranberries and turkey. In middle of every wonton wrapper, put 1 tsp. of mixture. Fold the wrapped over the filling and moisten edges. Use a fork to press edges to seal.
- In big skillet/deep fryer, heat oil.
- In hot oil, fry wontons till golden brown then drain on paper towels.

Nutrition Information

- Calories: 146 calories;
- Total Carbohydrate: 17.8 g
- Cholesterol: 10 mg
- Total Fat: 6 g
- Protein: 5.6 g
- Sodium: 120 mg

145. Totchos

"A twist on nachos!"

Serving: 8 | Prep: 20m | Ready in: 1h

Ingredients

- 1 (32 oz.) package frozen tater tots
- 8 oz. lean ground turkey
- 1/2 cup salsa
- 2 tsps. Mexican seasoning blend
- 1 1/2 cups shredded reduced-fat Mexican cheese blend
- 1/2 cup diced tomatoes
- 1/3 cup diced bell pepper
- 1/3 cup sliced ripe olives
- 1/2 cup sliced green onions
- Optional Toppings:
- Light sour cream
- Guacamole
- Salsa
- Chopped fresh cilantro

Direction

- Preheat an oven to 425°F. In 1 layer, put tater tots in a single layer on a big baking sheet. Cook till very crisp and browned, mixing once halfway through cooking, for 30 minutes.
- As tater tots cook, cook ground turkey in big skillet on medium heat till cooked through. Mix seasoning and salsa in; cook for several more minutes.
- Slightly mound tater tots on baking sheet; sprinkle 1/2 of the cheese on. Top using turkey mixture. Sprinkle leftover cheese then top with olives, bell pepper and tomatoes.

- Cook till cheese melts for 10 more minutes. Sprinkle green onions. Serve with any toppings you want.

Nutrition Information

- Calories: 302 calories;
- Total Carbohydrate: 30.7 g
- Cholesterol: 33 mg
- Total Fat: 16.2 g
- Protein: 16.3 g
- Sodium: 823 mg

146. Turkey Bacon-wrapped Jalapeno Poppers

"Ingredient amount depends on how many you are making."

Serving: 20 | Prep: 20m | Ready in: 30m

Ingredients

- 2 (8 oz.) packages cream cheese, softened
- 2 cups shredded Cheddar cheese
- 10 jalapeno peppers, halved and seeded
- 1 (12 oz.) package turkey bacon

Direction

- Preheat an oven to 175°C/350°F.
- Mix cheddar cheese and cream cheese well in a bowl. Put mixture in middle of jalapeno halves using a spoon; spread.
- Crosswise, cut bacon slices in half. Around middle of every jalapeno half, wrap 1 bacon strip. Put jalapeno poppers on nonstick baking sheet.
- In preheated oven, bake for 10-15 minutes till jalapenos are a bit tender and bacon is cooked.

Nutrition Information

- Calories: 140 calories;
- Total Carbohydrate: 1.2 g
- Cholesterol: 42 mg
- Total Fat: 12.7 g
- Protein: 5.4 g
- Sodium: 204 mg

147. Turkey Cocktail Meatballs With Orange Cranberry Glaze

"You can make it ahead of time then freeze without glaze. Defrost and reheat in sauce to serve."

Serving: 8 | Prep: 15m | Ready in: 35m

Ingredients

- 1 1/4 lbs. ground turkey
- 1/4 tsp. poultry seasoning
- 1/2 tsp. garlic salt
- 1 tsp. onion powder
- 1 tsp. salt
- 1/2 tsp. ground black pepper
- 1/4 tsp. Worcestershire sauce
- 1 pinch cayenne pepper
- 1 large egg, beaten
- 1/4 cup milk
- 1/2 cup plain bread crumbs
- 1 tbsp. olive oil
- 1 cup canned jellied cranberry sauce
- 1/2 cup orange marmalade
- 1/2 cup chicken broth
- 1 tbsp. minced jalapeno pepper (optional)
- 1 tbsp. minced Fresno pepper (optional)
- salt and ground black pepper to taste

Direction

- In a bowl, mix cayenne pepper, Worcestershire sauce, pepper, salt, onion powder, garlic salt, poultry seasoning and turkey. Mix bread crumbs, milk and egg in. Use plastic to cover; refrigerate for an hour.
- In skillet, heat olive oil on medium heat. Roll turkey mixture to balls, 1 tbsp. each. In 1 layer, put meatballs in skillet. Brown all sides of meatballs, occasionally flipping. On clean baking sheet, put browned meatballs; put aside.
- In skillet used to cook meatballs, mix chicken broth, marmalade and cranberry sauce on medium heat. Mix Fresno peppers and

jalapeno in; put meatballs in skillet. Lower heat to medium low. Cook till glaze reduces and meatballs aren't pink in the middle anymore. Season with pepper and salt.

Nutrition Information

- Calories: 264 calories;
- Total Carbohydrate: 32.5 g
- Cholesterol: 80 mg
- Total Fat: 8.7 g
- Protein: 14.5 g
- Sodium: 555 mg

148. Turkey Croquettes

"A great recipe for leftover chicken/turkey."
Serving: 3 | Prep: 15m | Ready in: 3h50m

Ingredients

- 2 slices bread, or more as needed
- 2 tbsps. butter
- 3 tbsps. all-purpose flour
- 1/2 cup milk
- 1/2 cup chicken broth
- 2 cups diced cooked turkey
- 1 tbsp. chopped fresh parsley
- 1/4 tsp. dried rosemary
- salt and ground black pepper to taste
- 1 egg, beaten

Direction

- In a blender, blend bread till you make soft crumbs. Put breadcrumbs in shallow bowl.
- In a saucepan, heat butter till melted on medium heat. Mix flour in melted butter till dissolved. Mix broth and milk into flour-butter mixture; mix and cook for 5 minutes till thick. Take saucepan off heat. Cool mixture.
- Mix pepper, salt, rosemary, parsley and turkey in cooled mixture. Shape turkey mixture to balls. Cool on a plate in the fridge until chilled for at least 3 hours.
- Preheat an oven to 175°C/350°F.
- In beaten egg, dip balls; let excess drip back in bowl. Press balls in bread crumbs till coated. Put balls on baking sheet.
- In preheated oven, bake for 25-30 minutes till browned and cooked through.

Nutrition Information

- Calories: 346 calories;
- Total Carbohydrate: 16.7 g
- Cholesterol: 157 mg
- Total Fat: 15.5 g
- Protein: 33.2 g
- Sodium: 486 mg

149. Turkey Lettuce Wraps With Shiitake Mushrooms

"You can serve the filling with hoisin sauce on flour tortillas or on top of brown rice and veggies."
Serving: 4 | Prep: 40m | Ready in: 1h

Ingredients

- 2 cups water
- 2 oz. mai fun (angel hair) rice noodles
- 1 tsp. vegetable oil
- 4 shiitake mushrooms, sliced
- 2 tsps. vegetable oil
- 1 (16 oz.) package ground turkey
- 6 green onions, chopped
- 1/4 cup chopped water chestnuts
- 4 tsps. finely minced fresh ginger root
- 2 tsps. minced garlic
- 3 tbsps. soy sauce
- 2 tbsps. brown sugar
- 1 tbsp. rice vinegar
- 1 tsp. sesame oil
- 1 tsp. finely grated orange zest
- 12 leaves green leaf lettuce
- Toppings
- 1/2 cup bean sprouts
- 1 carrot, grated
- 1/2 cup salted peanuts
- 1/2 cup chopped fresh cilantro

- 1/2 cup sweet chili sauce

Direction

- Boil 2 cups of water in a small saucepan. Turn heat off. Mix in rice noodles. Cover and let noodles soak for 5-7 minutes until soft. Rinse using cold water. Thoroughly drain.
- In a big skillet, heat 1 tsp. oil on medium-high heat. Cook mushrooms in hot oil for about 2 minutes until soft and brown. Take mushrooms out of pan. Put aside.
- Heat leftover 2 tsps. oil in the pan. Sauté turkey in oil for 5-7 minutes until it's not pink. Mix in green onions, garlic, ginger, and water chestnuts. Keep cooking for a minute. Mix in brown sugar, soy sauce, and reserved mushrooms. Briefly simmer to merge flavors. Take pan off heat. Mix in orange zest, sesame oil, and rice vinegar.
- Put a little turkey filling on every lettuce leaf to make lettuce wraps. Place cooked noodles on top of each one. Add a sprinkle of cilantro, peanuts, carrots, and bean sprouts. Use sweet chili sauce as a dip.

Nutrition Information

- Calories: 481 calories;
- Total Carbohydrate: 43.5 g
- Cholesterol: 84 mg
- Total Fat: 22.4 g
- Protein: 29.9 g
- Sodium: 1284 mg

150. Turkey Meatballs

"A great main dish!"
Serving: 4 | Prep: 15m | Ready in: 3h15m

Ingredients

- 2 (1 oz.) envelopes dry onion soup mix
- water as needed
- 2 lbs. ground turkey
- 1 (6.8 oz.) package beef flavored instant rice mix (e.g. Rice A Roni)
- 2 eggs, beaten

Direction

- Mix enough water to halfway fill slow cooker and onion soup mix in slow cooker. Put slow cooker to 175°C/350°F till soup boils.
- Meanwhile, make meatballs: Mix flavoring mix, rice and turkey in a big bowl. Add beaten egg; stir well. Shape mixture to 2-inch balls. Brown on medium high heat in a big skillet.
- When soup boils, put browned meatballs in slow cooker. Cook on medium setting for 3 hours or on low setting for 6 hours.

Nutrition Information

- Calories: 567 calories;
- Total Carbohydrate: 43.6 g
- Cholesterol: 272 mg
- Total Fat: 22.2 g
- Protein: 48.4 g
- Sodium: 2213 mg

151.Turkey Nacho Bake

"Easy and fast nachos!"
Serving: 6 | Prep: 20m | Ready in: 45m

Ingredients

- 1 lb. ground turkey
- 2 cloves garlic, chopped
- freshly ground black pepper to taste
- 2 tsps. crushed red pepper flakes
- 2 tbsps. chopped fresh chives
- 2 tbsps. hot sauce (optional)
- 1 (1 oz.) package dry taco seasoning mix
- 1 (14 oz.) can refried beans
- 1 (14.5 oz.) package tortilla chips
- 2 cups shredded Cheddar cheese
- 1 (4 oz.) can sliced black olives
- 1 ripe tomato, diced
- 1 bunch green onions, sliced

Direction

- Preheat an oven to 175°C/350°F.
- Start browning ground turkey in big skillet on medium heat. Mix 1 tbsp. of chives, 1 tsp. of red pepper flakes, pepper and garlic in; mix 1 tbsp. of hot sauce in. Mix taco seasoning mix in following package instructions when turkey browns.
- Put beans in microwave safe bowl; heat till soft in microwave. Mix 1 tbsp. of hot sauce ant 1 tbsp. of chives in.
- Across the bottom of baking sheet, spread tortilla chips. Put beans mixture on chips; spread turkey mixture across top. Sprinkle the cheese then leftover 1 tsp. of crushed red pepper flakes, green onions, tomatoes and olives on top.
- In preheated oven, bake for 15 minutes till cheese melts.

Nutrition Information

- Calories: 717 calories;
- Total Carbohydrate: 64.2 g
- Cholesterol: 105 mg
- Total Fat: 37.7 g
- Protein: 32.8 g
- Sodium: 1424 mg

152. Turkey Roll Sushi

"An easy wrap recipe."
Serving: 4 | Prep: 15m | Ready in: 15m

Ingredients

- 3/4 cup fresh spinach, chopped
- 1/4 cup cream cheese, softened
- 1/4 cup shredded Cheddar cheese, or more to taste
- 4 pickled peppers, chopped
- 1/2 spring onion (green part only), chopped, or more to taste
- 2 tsps. garlic powder
- 3/4 tsp. ground black pepper
- 2 pinches red pepper flakes
- 2 flour tortillas
- 1/2 lb. sliced deli turkey meat

Direction

- In bowl, mix red pepper flakes, black pepper, garlic powder, spring onion, pickled peppers, cheddar cheese, cream cheese and spinach. Spread, 1-in. wide, cream cheese mixture on top portion of every tortilla. Keep 1 tbsp. cream cheese mixture to seal later.
- Below cream cheese mixture section, put turkey on each tortilla. Spread thin line of leftover cream cheese mixture under turkey section of every tortilla to seal. Roll every tortilla around filling, starting at end with the most cream cheese mixture, sealing together with opposing end with a bit of cream cheese mixture. Cut roll to 1/2-in. wide slices to make turkey "sushi "rolls.

Nutrition Information

- Calories: 225 calories;
- Total Carbohydrate: 18.9 g
- Cholesterol: 46 mg
- Total Fat: 10.3 g
- Protein: 14.9 g
- Sodium: 943 mg

153. Turkey Spinach Crispy Baked Egg Rolls

"These are fantastic and crunchy turkey spinach egg rolls."
Serving: 12 | Prep: 20m | Ready in: 38m

Ingredients

- 1 lb. lean ground turkey
- 1 onion, diced
- 1 tsp. ground cumin
- 1 tsp. garlic powder
- 1/2 tsp. onion powder
- 1/4 tsp. salt
- 1/4 tsp. ground black pepper

- 2 1/2 cups fresh spinach
- 1 cup black beans, rinsed and drained
- 1/2 cup finely chopped red cabbage
- 1 tbsp. low-sodium soy sauce
- 1 tbsp. red chile paste
- 2 tsps. garlic paste
- 12 egg roll wrappers
- 3/4 cup bean sprouts
- coconut oil cooking spray

Direction

- Preheat the oven to 210 degrees C (415 degrees F). Use parchment paper to line a baking sheet.
- In a nonstick skillet, combine turkey, onion powder, garlic powder, cumin, onion, pepper, and salt. Over medium heat, cook and stir for 3 minutes. Then add garlic paste, red chile paste, soy sauce, cabbage, black beans, and spinach. Cook for 3-5 minutes, until the turkey is no longer pink. Let drain the excess grease.
- Put egg roll wrappers on a flat surface, sweep the edges with water. In the center, place a few bean sprouts diagonally; use 3 tbsps. of the turkey mixture to cover. Fold the bottom corner over the filling and roll up halfway. Tightly fold in both sides. Wet the edges of the last flap, then roll up and seal the top corner. Arrange the flap-side down on the baking sheet. Next, repeat the process with the remaining filling and wrappers.
- Use coconut oil spray to spray the tops of egg rolls lightly.
- Bake for 12-15 minutes in the preheated oven, or until golden brown.

Nutrition Information

- Calories: 112 calories;
- Total Carbohydrate: 10.7 g
- Cholesterol: 29 mg
- Total Fat: 3.3 g
- Protein: 10.1 g
- Sodium: 283 mg

154. Turkey Wrap By Avocados From Mexico

"Delicious small pieces!"
Serving: 4

Ingredients

- 4 (8 to 10 inch) flour tortillas, any flavor
- 1/2 cup cream cheese
- 3 cups tightly packed leaf lettuce
- 1/2 lb. thinly sliced cooked turkey (from deli)
- 1 bell pepper, cut into strips
- 1 scallion, chopped
- 1 Avocado from Mexico, cubed

Direction

- Evenly spread cream cheese on each tortilla. Evenly put lettuce on cream cheese within 1-in. of top edge. Put 1 layer of bell pepper strips on top. Layer turkey slices evenly on bell pepper; sprinkle avocado and scallions.
- Tightly roll up every tortilla, starting at bottom edges.
- Serving: Trim uneven ends of rolls; slice rolls to 1-in. slices. Put on serving platter.
- Use thinly sliced radishes to garnish.

Nutrition Information

- Calories: 451 calories;
- Total Carbohydrate: 35.1 g
- Cholesterol: 75 mg
- Total Fat: 23.9 g
- Protein: 25 g
- Sodium: 377 mg

155. Yam Sausage Spread

"A great recipe!"
Serving: 16 | Prep: 1h | Ready in: 1h20m

Ingredients

- 1/2 cup whole wheat flour
- 1 cup heavy cream

- 3 eggs, beaten
- 4 medium beets, peeled and julienned
- 1/4 cup fresh chives, chopped
- 1 turkey sausage link, without casing, chopped
- 4 tbsps. ground allspice
- 2 tbsps. baking soda
- 1 tbsp. yam extract

Direction

- Mix heavy cream and flour in medium bowl. Let mixture stand for 1 hour till thick.
- Mix turkey sausage, chives, beets and eggs into heavy cream and flour. Mix yam extract, baking soda and allspice in.
- Put mixture in a medium saucepan; boil. Frequently mixing, cook for 20 minutes till liquid evaporates.

Nutrition Information

- Calories: 90 calories;
- Total Carbohydrate: 6.3 g
- Cholesterol: 55 mg
- Total Fat: 6.7 g
- Protein: 2.4 g
- Sodium: 477 mg

Chapter 5: Beef Recipes

***

156. Addictingly Spicy Cheeseburger Dip

""A must-have for every party and addicting. Make it thick enough to dip without the mess with Colby cheese.""
Serving: 24 | Prep: 5m | Ready in: 25m

Ingredients

- 1 lb. lean ground beef
- 1 (16 oz.) jar mild picante sauce (such as Pace®)
- 1 (16 oz.) jar hot picante sauce (such as Pace®), or less to taste
- 1/3 lb. shredded Colby cheese, or more to taste
- 1 (1 lb.) package processed cheese food (such as Velveeta®), cut into cubes

Direction

- Place a large skillet over medium-high heat. Stir and cook beef in the hot skillet for 5-7 minutes until crumbly and browned; drain and remove grease.
- Add hot and mild picante sauce over the ground beef; mix. Put in Colby cheese and processed cheese food, lower the heat to low, and cook for about 15 minutes, until the cheese is fully melted.

Nutrition Information

- Calories: 134 calories;
- Total Carbohydrate: 3.6 g
- Cholesterol: 34 mg
- Total Fat: 9.2 g
- Protein: 9.1 g
- Sodium: 531 mg

157. Antipasto Platter

" "A layered antipasto that you can cut in square slices cleanly and have all the items. Pretty dish that is a hit all the time! Vegetarians will be so jealous of this one. Add veggies based on your desire. Present with fresh Italian bread. Have fun!" "

Serving: 20 | Prep: 45m | Ready in: 45m

Ingredients

- 2 heads iceberg lettuce
- 1 tbsp. garlic powder
- 1 tbsp. dried oregano
- 1 (8 oz.) bottle Italian-style salad dressing
- 1 lb. thinly sliced cooked ham
- 2 1/2 lbs. sliced provolone cheese
- 1/2 lb. Genoa salami, thinly sliced
- 1/4 lb. Capacola sausage, sliced
- 1/4 lb. pepperoni sausage, sliced
- 1/4 lb. prosciutto, thinly sliced
- 1/4 lb. thinly sliced roast beef
- 1 cup fresh mushrooms
- 1 (6 oz.) can marinated artichoke hearts
- 1 (7 oz.) jar roasted red peppers
- 1 (6 oz.) can sliced black olives
- 3/4 cup sliced pepperoncini peppers
- 1 (5 oz.) jar sliced pimento-stuffed green olives
- 1/2 cup crumbled Gorgonzola cheese
- 1/2 lb. mozzarella cheese, sliced
- 1/4 cup grated Parmesan cheese

Direction

- From the heads of lettuce, take off large outer leaves. On a large serving platter, pile 1/3 in a layer. Drizzle with desired amount of Italian-style salad dressing, 1/3 crushed oregano, and 1/3 garlic powder. Layer with Provolone cheese and cooked ham.
- On the Provolone cheese layer another 1/3 of lettuce leaves, Capacola sausage, Genoa salami, desired amount of Italian-style salad dressing, 1/3 crushed oregano, and 1/3 garlic powder.
- Redo the layering with the left lettuce, roast beef, prosciutto, pepperoni sausage, Italian-style salad dressing, crushed oregano, and garlic powder.
- Layer with pimento-stuffed olives, pepperoncini, black olives, roasted red peppers, marinated artichoke hearts and mushrooms. Drizzle more Italian-style salad dressing on if desired.
- Place Parmesan cheese, mozzarella cheese and Gorgonzola cheese on top. Place inside the refrigerator to chill, covered until serving time.

Nutrition Information

- Calories: 503 calories;
- Total Carbohydrate: 7.4 g
- Cholesterol: 94 mg
- Total Fat: 39 g
- Protein: 31.3 g
- Sodium: 2209 mg

158. Asian Lettuce Wraps

"Asian lettuce wraps."

Serving: 4 | Prep: 20m | Ready in: 35m

Ingredients

- 16 Boston Bibb or butter lettuce leaves
- 1 lb. lean ground beef
- 1 tbsp. cooking oil
- 1 large onion, chopped
- 1/4 cup hoisin sauce
- 2 cloves fresh garlic, minced
- 1 tbsp. soy sauce
- 1 tbsp. rice wine vinegar
- 2 tsps. minced pickled ginger
- 1 dash Asian chile pepper sauce, or to taste (optional)
- 1 (8 oz.) can water chestnuts, drained and finely chopped
- 1 bunch green onions, chopped
- 2 tsps. Asian (dark) sesame oil

Direction

- Wash the entire lettuce leaves and pat dry, be cautious not damage them. Reserve.
- Over moderately-high heat, heat a big skillet. In hot skillet, cook and mix cooking oil and beef for 5 to 7 minutes till crumbly and browned. Let drain and throw the grease; turn beef onto a bowl. In the same skillet used for beef, cook and mix the onion for 5 to 10 minutes till slightly soft. Into the onions, mix chili pepper sauce, ginger, vinegar, soy sauce, garlic and hoisin sauce. Put cooked beef, sesame oil, green onions and water chestnuts; cook and mix for 2 minutes till onions barely start to wilt.
- Place the leaves of lettuce around outer edge of a big serving platter and stack the meat mixture in the middle.

Nutrition Information

- Calories: 388 calories;
- Total Carbohydrate: 24.3 g
- Cholesterol: 69 mg
- Total Fat: 22.3 g
- Protein: 23.4 g
- Sodium: 580 mg

159. Bachelors Flamin' Hot Mexican Bean Dip

"An easy, quick and hot dip for parties."
Serving: 12 | Prep: 5m | Ready in: 20m

Ingredients

- 1 tbsp. olive oil
- 1 clove garlic, minced
- 1 onion, chopped
- 1 (11 oz.) can chopped jalapeno peppers
- 1 (15 oz.) can black beans with green chilies, drained
- 1 (10 oz.) can diced tomatoes with green chilies, drained
- 1 (15 oz.) jar nacho cheese dip

Direction

- In a large saucepan, heat olive oil over medium heat. Place in garlic and onion, cook for 5 minutes, stirring, till onion turns translucent. Add cheese dip and green chilies with diced tomatoes, black beans and jalapenos. Heat through and stir till blended as necessary. Serve the dip hot.

Nutrition Information

- Calories: 165 calories;
- Total Carbohydrate: 10.1 g
- Cholesterol: 25 mg
- Total Fat: 10.3 g
- Protein: 8.6 g
- Sodium: 1093 mg

160. Bacon-wrapped Steak Bites (perfect For Campfires And Grilling!)

"A perfect grill to go with a beer."
Serving: 6 | Prep: 20m | Ready in: 25m

Ingredients

- 2 tbsps. barbeque seasoning (such as KC Masterpiece®), or to taste
- 2 lbs. beef tips, trimmed
- 1 lb. bacon, strips cut in half
- toothpicks

Direction

- Rub the barbeque seasoning into the beef tips for 3-5 minutes until the meat has an orange hue. Slice the beef into 1-inch cubes.
- In a bacon slice, wrap each beef cube and use a toothpick to secure bacon slice.
- Heat a skillet on medium. Cook the wrapped beef tips in batches in the heated skillet until beef is browned all over and bacon is crispy, 5 to 10 minutes.

Nutrition Information

- Calories: 423 calories;
- Total Carbohydrate: 1.4 g
- Cholesterol: 168 mg
- Total Fat: 22.9 g
- Protein: 49.8 g
- Sodium: 1544 mg

161. Baked BBQ Meatballs

"These meatballs have a wicked delicious taste with a sweet, tangy sauce."

Serving: 10 | Prep: 15m | Ready in: 1h

Ingredients

- 1 lb. ground beef
- 1 cup cracker crumbs
- 1/4 cup chopped onion
- 1/4 cup milk
- 2 eggs
- 3/4 tsp. salt
- 2/3 cup ketchup
- 1/3 cup water
- 6 tbsps. brown sugar
- 1/2 tsp. ground nutmeg

Direction

- Set the oven at 175°C (350°F) to preheat.
- In a large bowl, mix ground beef, salt, eggs, milk, chopped onion, and cracker crumbs. Roll out 20 meatballs and put them on a rimmed baking sheet. In a bowl, whisk nutmeg, brown sugar, water, and ketchup. Pour the mixture over the meatballs.
- In the preheated oven, bake for about 45 minutes, or until the center of the meatballs are not pink anymore.

Nutrition Information

- Calories: 264 calories;
- Total Carbohydrate: 26 g
- Cholesterol: 66 mg
- Total Fat: 13 g
- Protein: 10.8 g
- Sodium: 603 mg

162. Baked Curry Triangles

"Baked curry triangles."

Serving: 12 | Prep: 20m | Ready in: 40m

Ingredients

- 1/2 lb. ground beef
- 1/4 onion, chopped
- 5 tbsps. curry powder, or more to taste
- 1 sheet puff pastry, cut into 6 squares
- 1 egg, beaten

Direction

- Preheat an oven to 190 °C or 375 °F.
- In a nonstick skillet, cook and mix onion and beef for 5 minutes till beef is browned. Mix in curry powder for 1 to 2 minutes till heated through and aromatic.
- Diagonally slice puff pastry squares to form 12 triangles. Fold every triangle in 1/2, patting edges of 1 side together, and retaining a gap for filling. With curried beef, stuff every triangle and press edges to close.
- With a pastry brush, glaze every triangle with beaten egg. On a baking sheet, put the triangles.
- In the prepped oven, bake for 15 to 20 minutes till golden brown and they puffed up.

Nutrition Information

- Calories: 161 calories;
- Total Carbohydrate: 11.1 g
- Cholesterol: 27 mg
- Total Fat: 10.7 g
- Protein: 5.5 g
- Sodium: 68 mg

163. Bavarian Style Meatballs

"These are very yummy and easy to make."
Serving: 7 | Prep: 5m | Ready in: 4h5m

Ingredients

- 12 fluid oz. tomato-based chili sauce
- 1 (16 oz.) can whole cranberry sauce
- 27 oz. Bavarian-style sauerkraut, undrained
- 1 cup water
- 1 cup packed brown sugar
- 1 (16 oz.) package frozen meatballs

Direction

- Combine brown sugar, water, sauerkraut, cranberry sauce, and chili sauce in a medium-size mixing bowl. Mix well. Next, in a slow cooker, put the meatballs and the sauce, stir well.
- Cover and cook for 4 hours at a medium temperature. Stir infrequently to coat the meatballs.

Nutrition Information

- Calories: 494 calories;
- Total Carbohydrate: 76.7 g
- Cholesterol: 50 mg
- Total Fat: 17.1 g
- Protein: 11.5 g
- Sodium: 1954 mg

164. BBQ Nachos

"These simple nachos are delicious. It's great to enjoy while watching the TV."
Serving: 2 | Prep: 5m | Ready in: 6m

Ingredients

- 20 tortilla chips
- 1/4 lb. smoked beef sausage
- 1/2 cup Cheddar cheese
- 1/4 cup barbeque sauce

Direction

- On a microwave-safe dish, put tortilla chips. Use a cheese grater to shred sausage, evenly scatter over the chips, and put Cheddar cheese on top. Drizzle over the nachos with barbeque sauce.
- Put in the microwave and heat for 15-30 seconds until the cheese melts.

Nutrition Information

- Calories: 411 calories;
- Total Carbohydrate: 22.9 g
- Cholesterol: 68 mg
- Total Fat: 28.2 g
- Protein: 16.2 g
- Sodium: 1230 mg

165. Beef And Sausage Fried Wontons

"Wonton wrappers rolled over a lovely spiced sausage-and-beef filling! Best paired with a yummy Oriental-style sweet chile sauce as dip! Enjoy!"
Serving: 12 | Prep: 40m | Ready in: 55m

Ingredients

- 1 egg white
- 1 tbsp. water
- 1 lb. lean ground beef
- 1 lb. bulk hot Italian sausage
- 1 tbsp. Asian sweet chili sauce, or to taste
- 1 tbsp. Chinese five-spice powder
- 1 tsp. garlic powder
- 1 green onion, finely chopped
- salt and pepper to taste
- 1 (16 oz.) package wonton wrappers
- 3 cups vegetable oil for frying
- 1/2 cup Asian sweet chili sauce, for dipping

Direction

- In a small bowl, whisk the water and egg white together and put it aside. Combine the salt, five-spice powder, pepper, ground beef, green onion, 1 tbsp. of sweet chile sauce, garlic powder and sausage together and mix it gently. Fill a wonton wrapper, with one corner pointed towards you, with about 1 teaspoonful of the prepared meat mixture. Fold the opposite right and left corners of the wonton wrapper, partially overlap the filling and roll it up tightly starting from the corner pointed at you until it resembles a pocket. Keep rolling the wonton wrapper until you get to the last remaining corner; brush the tip of the last corner with the egg white mixture and seal the stuffed wonton rolls by.

- In a big saucepan or a deep-fryer, let the oil heat up to 350°F (175°C).
- Put the egg rolls into the deep-fryer or a saucepan and let it cook by batch in the hot oil for 3-5 minutes until it turns golden brown in color. Place the fried egg rolls onto a plate that is lined with paper towel to drain off any excess oil. Serve the egg rolls alongside 1/2 cup of sweet chili sauce.

Nutrition Information

- Calories: 338 calories;
- Total Carbohydrate: 27.6 g
- Cholesterol: 50 mg
- Total Fat: 17.5 g
- Protein: 16.6 g
- Sodium: 609 mg

166. Beef Bacon Rolls

""A dish that you can serve as a meal or an appetizer. If you want it for a meal, make it bigger, and if you want it for an appetizer, make it smaller.""
Serving: 10 | Prep: 10m | Ready in: 2h20m

Ingredients

- 1 1/2 lbs. lean top sirloin
- 1 lb. bacon
- 1 cup chopped onion
- 1 1/3 cups butter

Direction

- Slice the beef into strips about 1 inch in width, about 1/8 inch in thickness and the same (or close) length as that of the bacon strip.
- Put the bacon strip on top of the beef strip and roll both meats so that the beef is on the outside. Secure each roll by inserting a toothpick from the bottom left of the roll and out on the top right.
- Cook and stir the onions in a big skillet with butter for about 5 minutes or until soft. Put the beef bacon rolls in one layer on the skillet. Let it cook for about 5 minutes on medium heat or until browned, flip the beef bacon rolls 1 or 2 times. Cover the skillet with a lid and let it simmer for about 2 hours.

Nutrition Information

- Calories: 404 calories;
- Total Carbohydrate: 1.7 g
- Cholesterol: 118 mg
- Total Fat: 36.5 g
- Protein: 17.3 g
- Sodium: 545 mg

167. Beefy Cheese Dip

""A lovely dip that I place in a slow cooker and keep it warm paired with tortilla chips and serve.""
Serving: 72 | Prep: 5m | Ready in: 30m

Ingredients

- 1 lb. ground beef
- 1 lb. sausage
- 1 bunch green onions, chopped
- 1 (16 oz.) jar salsa
- 2 lbs. processed cheese, shredded

Direction

- Brown sausage and beef in a large skillet. Strain excess fat.

- Stir processed cheese, salsa, and green onions in another large skillet over low heat. Keep on mixing until cheese melts.
- Put the meat to the cheese mixture and simmer without cover until ready to use.

Nutrition Information

- Calories: 90 calories;
- Total Carbohydrate: 1.7 g
- Cholesterol: 20 mg
- Total Fat: 7.4 g
- Protein: 4.3 g
- Sodium: 244 mg

168. Best Cheese Dip

"A great dip made from the best ingredients."
Serving: 10 | Ready in: 1h40m

Ingredients

- 1/2 lb. bulk spicy pork sausage
- 1/2 lb. ground beef
- 1 onion, diced
- 1 (2 lb.) loaf processed cheese food (such as Velveeta®), cubed
- 1 (28 oz.) can diced tomatoes with green chile peppers (such as RO*TEL®)
- 1 (10.75 oz.) can condensed cream of mushroom soup

Direction

- Heat a large skillet on medium-high heat. Crumble ground beef and sausage into the skillet; put the onion. Stir and cook the beef mixture for 10 minutes until the meat is not pink anymore, becomes crumbly and evenly browned. Let drain and discard all the excess grease. Add into a slow cooker.
- Top the meat mixture with a layer of cheese food cubes.
- In a blender, combine the green chile peppers with diced tomatoes until the mixture becomes smooth; place over the cheese cubes together with the cream of the mushroom soup. Mix the mixture.
- Cook and stir from time to time on High for 90 minutes until the cheese melts completely.

Nutrition Information

- Calories: 445 calories;
- Total Carbohydrate: 14.3 g
- Cholesterol: 100 mg
- Total Fat: 32.3 g
- Protein: 24.9 g
- Sodium: 1876 mg

169. Best Football Dip Ever

"This dipping recipe is enough for 3 to 6 people."
Serving: 8 | Prep: 10m | Ready in: 35m

Ingredients

- 1 lb. ground beef
- 1 (8 oz.) package cream cheese, room temperature
- 1 (8 oz.) jar prepared salsa
- 1 (1 lb.) loaf processed cheese food, sliced

Direction

- Set the oven at 200°C (400°F) to preheat.
- Over medium-high heat, put the ground beef in a large skillet. Cook until no more pink, stirring to crumble. Drain off the grease.
- In the bottom of a 9-inch square baking dish, spread the cream cheese in an even layer. Continue to spread over the cream cheese with a layer of salsa, and finish with a layer of the ground beef. Put the processed cheese slices on top and wrap the plate with aluminum foil.
- Bake until heated through in the preheated oven, about 15 minutes. Serve hot.

Nutrition Information

- Calories: 391 calories;
- Total Carbohydrate: 6.9 g
- Cholesterol: 110 mg

- Total Fat: 30.6 g
- Protein: 22.3 g
- Sodium: 992 mg

170. Cape Cod Cocktail Meatballs

"Try out these cocktail meatballs which are great for any party that you wish to impress. They will finish fast and everyone will request for the recipe. This recipe comes from Cape Cod where cranberries are abundant.""

Serving: 20 | Prep: 30m | Ready in: 1h20m

Ingredients

- 2 lbs. ground beef
- 1 cup bread crumbs
- 1/4 cup chopped fresh parsley
- 2 eggs
- 2 tbsps. grated onion
- 2 tbsps. soy sauce
- 1/4 tsp. garlic powder
- 1 (16 oz.) can jellied cranberry sauce (such as Ocean Spray®)
- 1 1/2 cups ketchup
- 2 1/2 tbsps. packed brown sugar
- 1 tbsp. lemon juice

Direction

- Preheat the oven to 190 degrees C (375 degrees F).
- In a bowl, combine ground beef, grated onion, bread crumbs, garlic powder, eggs, parsley, and soy sauce until the resulting mix is well combined. Take approximately two tsps. of the meat mixture for each meatball and then fold into tiny meatballs. Spread the meatballs on a large and deep baking dish.
- Bake for about 25 minutes in the preheated oven until the meatballs turn brown. Drain off the excess grease.
- In a saucepan, mix together lemon juice, jellied cranberry sauce, brown sugar, and ketchup then put pan over medium heat. Mix sauce until the brown sugar has dissolved and cranberry sauce has melted.
- Spread sauce on top of meatballs and then bake for about 25 to 30 minutes until no pink color remains inside the meatballs and the sauce forms a glaze.

Nutrition Information

- Calories: 168 calories;
- Total Carbohydrate: 19.2 g
- Cholesterol: 46 mg
- Total Fat: 6.2 g
- Protein: 9.4 g
- Sodium: 371 mg

171. Celery Chesapeake

"As you see, it's a very simple dip with very simple ingredients. Just mix celery, cream cheese, and dried beef mixture. Your guests will surely love this."

Serving: 8 | Prep: 5m | Ready in: 1h10m

Ingredients

- 8 oz. dried beef, chopped
- 1 (8 oz.) package cream cheese, softened
- 3 tbsps. prepared horseradish
- 1/4 tsp. ground black pepper
- 1 tsp. lemon juice
- 1 bunch celery

Direction

- Mix cream cheese and beef in a small mixing bowl. Stir in black pepper, lemon juice, and horseradish until they're well-blended. Cover the bowl and store it inside the fridge for 60 minutes.
- Remove the ends and leaves from the celery and cut out its remaining stalks in half. Pour the cream cheese mixture into the celery stalks.

Nutrition Information

- Calories: 155 calories;
- Total Carbohydrate: 4.3 g
- Cholesterol: 53 mg
- Total Fat: 10.5 g

- Protein: 11.5 g
- Sodium: 946 mg

172. Certified Angus Beef® Jalapeno Beef Poppers

"A quick to prepare recipe made with Certified Angus Beef® that's tender, juicy and flavorful."
Serving: 42 | Prep: 15m | Ready in: 55m

Ingredients

- 2 lbs. Certified Angus Beef® ground chuck
- 12 oz. Food Club® Shredded Sharp Cheddar cheese
- 6 jalapenos, seeded and minced
- 1 tbsp. Food Club® Salt
- 1 tbsp. Food Club® Pure Ground Black Pepper
- 1 tsp. whole mustard seeds
- 12 Food Club® eggs
- 1 cup Food Club® Plain Bread Crumbs
- 1 cup Food Club® Plain Panko Bread Crumbs
- oil for frying

Direction

- In a big mixing bowl, mix together the mustard seeds, pepper, salt, jalapenos, cheese and ground beef. Portion into 42 popper-shaped balls using your hand, about 1 oz. each.
- Break and whisk the eggs, then put in a shallow dish. Mix breadcrumbs and place in the 2nd shallow dish.
- Prepare a pot with frying oil and heat it to 325°F. Roll the poppers in the egg mix, 6-8 at a time, then roll in the breadcrumbs; redo the process. Deep fry for 4 minutes in batches, then allow to dry on the paper towels.

Nutrition Information

- Calories: 134 calories;
- Total Carbohydrate: 4.1 g
- Cholesterol: 77 mg
- Total Fat: 9.7 g
- Protein: 8.2 g
- Sodium: 282 mg

173. Cheese Wizards

"Cocktail rye topped with cheese sauce and ground beef."
Serving: 15 | Prep: 5m | Ready in: 15m

Ingredients

- 1 lb. lean ground beef
- 1 (16 oz.) jar processed cheese sauce
- salt and pepper to taste
- 16 oz. cocktail rye bread

Direction

- Preheat broiler.
- Place a large, deep skillet over medium-high heat and cook the ground beef until evenly browned. Drain and crumble the beef.
- Mix pepper, salt, processed cheese sauce, and the crumbled beef together in a medium bowl. On slices of cocktail rye, evenly spread the mixture.
- Transfer the slices on a large baking sheet. Broil in the preheated broiler until the cheese sauce melts, for 5 minutes.

Nutrition Information

- Calories: 240 calories;
- Total Carbohydrate: 17.4 g
- Cholesterol: 45 mg
- Total Fat: 13.5 g
- Protein: 11.5 g
- Sodium: 710 mg

174. Cheesesteak Egg Rolls

"Such an easy and delicious appetizer."
Serving: 4 | Prep: 10m | Ready in: 15m

Ingredients

- 1 tbsp. vegetable oil
- 1 onion, chopped
- 1 (12.5 oz.) package frozen sandwich steak meat
- 1 (14 oz.) package egg roll wrappers
- 4 slices American cheese, halved
- 2 cups oil for frying, or as needed
- 1/4 cup ketchup

Direction

- Over medium heat, heat skillet with tbsp. oil. Put the onion; cook and mix for 5 minutes till onion is translucent. Into skillet, separate frozen steak portions; cook and mix for 10 minutes till steak is not pink anymore. Take off heat and reserve.
- On a flat area, place egg roll wrappers; put a 1/2 cheese slice on every one. To every cheese slice with an even amount of steak mixture. Roll up the egg rolls following packaging instructions, and enclose the edges, moisten with water if needed.
- In a big skillet, or preheat a deep-fryer to 190 °C or 375 °F, heat an-inch of oil.
- In hot oil, fry rolls for 5 minutes till golden brown on every side. Take off; let drain on paper towels. Serve while warm along with ketchup for dipping.

Nutrition Information

- Calories: 779 calories;
- Total Carbohydrate: 66.3 g
- Cholesterol: 106 mg
- Total Fat: 39.2 g
- Protein: 38.6 g
- Sodium: 1213 mg

175. Chef John's Hot Sloppy Joe Dip

"An easy, cheap and incredibly versatile dip. Great to serve at room temperature, warm or hot."
Serving: 12 | Prep: 15m | Ready in: 1h20m

Ingredients

- 2 lbs. extra lean ground beef
- 2 green bell peppers, diced
- 1 onion, diced
- 4 cloves garlic, minced
- 3 tbsps. all-purpose flour
- 2 tbsps. brown sugar
- 2 tsps. kosher salt, or to taste
- 1 tsp. ground black pepper
- cayenne pepper, to taste
- 2 cups chicken broth
- 1 cup ketchup
- 1 tbsp. Dijon mustard
- 1 tsp. Worcestershire sauce
- 1 cup shredded Cheddar cheese, divided

Direction

- In a heavy pot, place cayenne pepper, pepper, salt, brown sugar, flour, garlic, onion, bell pepper and ground beef.
- Set the pot over medium-high heat. Break up the mixture and stir while heating. Cook for 15 minutes, stirring, till the mixture starts to brown and crumbly and moisture is mostly evaporated. Stir in Worcestershire sauce, mustard, ketchup and chicken broth. Mix well and simmer the mixture. Lower to medium heat. Cook and stir occasionally for 45 minutes till thickened.
- 6 inches away from the heat source, place the oven rack and preheat the broiler of the oven.
- In an oven-proof saucepan, place the mixture and add 1/2 of the shredded cheese on top. Use a fork to poke and lightly stir the cheese down into the dip. Place the leftover cheese on top.

- Set pan under the broiler and broil for 5 minutes till the mixture is bubbly and hot and the cheese is browned.

Nutrition Information

- Calories: 230 calories;
- Total Carbohydrate: 11.6 g
- Cholesterol: 67 mg
- Total Fat: 11.7 g
- Protein: 19.2 g
- Sodium: 832 mg

176. Cocktail Meatballs I

"Simple but delicious meatballs unusually coated with grape jelly or chili sauce."
Serving: 8 | Prep: 25m | Ready in: 1h10m

Ingredients

- 1 lb. ground beef
- 1/2 cup dried bread crumbs
- 1/3 cup chopped onion
- 1/4 cup milk
- 1 egg
- 1 tsp. salt
- 1/2 tsp. Worcestershire sauce
- 1/8 tsp. ground black pepper
- 1/4 cup shortening
- 12 fluid oz. tomato-based chili sauce
- 1 1/4 cups grape jelly

Direction

- Blend ground black pepper, Worcestershire sauce, salt, egg, milk, onion, breadcrumbs, and ground beef in a large bowl. Combine them together and form into meatballs.
- Heat shortening in a large skillet on medium heat. Put meatballs and cook for 5-7 minutes until they are browned. Take out from the skillet and transfer to paper towels to drain.
- Place jelly and chili sauce into the skillet; heat and stir until the jelly melts. Bring the meatballs back to the skillet and stir until they are coated. Turn down the heat to low. Remove the cover and bring to a simmer for half an hour.

Nutrition Information

- Calories: 458 calories;
- Total Carbohydrate: 52.5 g
- Cholesterol: 72 mg
- Total Fat: 22.8 g
- Protein: 12.7 g
- Sodium: 1038 mg

177. Cocktail Wieners I

""Yummy little smoked cocktail wieners get simmered in a chile sauce and tangy cranberry sauce.""
Serving: 15 | Prep: 10m | Ready in: 20m

Ingredients

- 1 (16 oz.) can cranberry sauce
- 12 fluid oz. chili sauce
- 3 lbs. beef cocktail wieners

Direction

- Stir chili sauce and cranberry sauce in a 4-qt saucepan over medium heat. Use a wooden spoon to crumble the cranberry sauce into smaller pieces to quicken the melting process. Heat and stir until the cranberry sauce has melted. Put in the cocktail wieners then cook until the wieners are heated. Use toothpicks to serve.

Nutrition Information

- Calories: 341 calories;
- Total Carbohydrate: 19.8 g
- Cholesterol: 56 mg
- Total Fat: 24.3 g
- Protein: 11.8 g
- Sodium: 1230 mg

178. Connecticut Cheeseburger Dip

" "Get everything you enjoy about a juicy, big burger - and make it into a dip! This creamy, tantalizing appetizer is packed with pickles, tomatoes, Cheddar, onions, mustard, ketchup, and ground beef and seasoned with McCormick® Brown Gravy Mix. (We weren't joking when we told you EVERYTHING!) And bake until dissolved and present with breadsticks or steak fries. Enjoy!" "

Serving: 36 | Prep: 10m | Ready in: 35m

Ingredients

- 1 lb. lean ground beef
- 1/2 cup chopped onion
- 1/2 cup ketchup
- 2 tbsps. yellow mustard
- 1 (.87 oz.) package McCormick® Brown Gravy Mix
- 1 (8 oz.) package whipped cream cheese
- 1 cup shredded Cheddar cheese, divided
- 1/3 cup chopped tomatoes
- 3 tbsps. chopped pickles

Direction

- Prepare the oven by preheating to 350°F. In a big skillet, combine Gravy mix, mustard, ketchup, onion, and ground beef until well mixed. Stir and cook on medium-high heat until beef is not pink. Mix in 1/2 cup of shredded cheese and cream cheese.
- Scoop in a 2-qt baking dish. Dust with the rest of the 1/2 cup of shredded cheese.
- Place in the preheated oven and bake for 10-15 minutes or until cheese is dissolved. Top with pickles and tomatoes.

Nutrition Information

- Calories: 62 calories;
- Total Carbohydrate: 1.9 g
- Cholesterol: 18 mg
- Total Fat: 4.5 g
- Protein: 3.7 g
- Sodium: 149 mg

179. Dale's Swedish Meatballs

"Small tasty meatballs in a sour and creamy sauce that will deliciously go with rice or egg noodles. They can also be a nice appetizer."

Serving: 6 | Prep: 15m | Ready in: 45m

Ingredients

- 1 lb. ground beef
- 2 eggs
- 1/2 cup bread crumbs
- 1/2 onion, chopped
- 4 cloves garlic, minced
- 2 tbsps. Worcestershire sauce
- 1/2 green bell pepper, chopped
- 3/4 cup shredded Cheddar cheese
- 1 tbsp. butter
- 3 tbsps. all-purpose flour
- 1 tsp. instant coffee granules
- 2 tsps. beef bouillon
- 2 cups water
- 3 tbsps. sour cream, or more to taste

Direction

- Combine the Cheddar cheese, green pepper, Worcestershire sauce, garlic, onion, breadcrumbs, eggs, and ground beef together in a medium bowl until combined thoroughly. Shape into walnut-sized balls.
- In a large skillet, let the butter melt on medium-high heat. Drop in meatballs and evenly brown. Take away from the skillet, then put aside. Stir the instant coffee and flour into the pan drippings. Place water and beef bouillon into the pan and combine properly. Boil and thicken. Add in sour cream and stir.
- Put the meatballs back into the skillet and bring them to a simmer in the sauce for 20-40 minutes. Serve over egg noodles or the rice as the main course, or as an appetizer.

Nutrition Information

- Calories: 325 calories;
- Total Carbohydrate: 13.5 g
- Cholesterol: 134 mg

- Total Fat: 20.3 g
- Protein: 21.4 g
- Sodium: 463 mg

180. Dilly Rye Boat Dip

"This dip is very classic. You can serve this dish at any gatherings or parties. You can use chipped beef instead of corned beef, as well as add more celery salt."
Serving: 10 | Prep: 20m | Ready in: 1h20m

Ingredients

- 1 (1 lb.) loaf round rye bread
- 1 cup sour cream
- 1 cup mayonnaise
- 1 (4 oz.) jar dried chipped beef, chopped
- 1 tsp. Beau Monde ™ seasoning
- 2 tsps. celery salt
- 3 tbsps. dried dill weed

Direction

- Cut off the 'crown' of the bread with a bread knife. Scoop out the inside of the loaf, and slice into bite-sized cubes for dipping.
- Combine dill weed, celery salt, Beau Monde seasoning, chipped beef, mayonnaise, and sour cream in a medium-sized bowl. Blend well, put a cover on and refrigerate for a minimum of 1 hour.
- Ladle the chilled dip into the emptied bread loaf, and enjoy with cubed bread for dipping.

Nutrition Information

- Calories: 227 calories;
- Total Carbohydrate: 2.6 g
- Cholesterol: 27 mg
- Total Fat: 22.6 g
- Protein: 4.6 g
- Sodium: 749 mg

181.Dog Food Dip

"A recipe handed by a friend 15 or more years ago. Created it for a buffet at work, then it was all gone all the time from nurse's station than the rest of the food! An easy combination of cheese and beef, make sure to make it a day prior to let the flavor enhance. Pair with desired corn chips when served."
Serving: 48 | Prep: 15m | Ready in: 8h35m

Ingredients

- 2 lbs. lean ground beef
- 1 onion, chopped
- 1 (10.75 oz.) can condensed cream of mushroom soup
- 1 lb. processed cheese food, cubed
- pickled jalapeno pepper slices, to taste (optional)

Direction

- Place a large, deep skillet pan on the stove and turn on to medium high heat, then put the ground beef and onion together. Stir and cook until onion becomes soft beef is equally brown. Turn the stove to medium low heat then let the liquid dry out.
- Add in the condensed cream of mushroom soup. Then stir in your wish amount of jalapeno pepper and processed cheese food. Mix and let it cook for about 10 minutes until all are well combined.
- Place the mixture in medium size bowl. Use a plastic wrapper to cover the bowl and let it chill in the refrigerator for 8 hour or overnight.
- Using a slow cooker to reheat the mixture, you can 1 tbsp. of water to make it thin if needed, then serve.

Nutrition Information

- Calories: 88 calories;
- Total Carbohydrate: 1.5 g
- Cholesterol: 20 mg
- Total Fat: 6.6 g
- Protein: 5.3 g
- Sodium: 166 mg

182. Dried Beef Ball

"This old-school recipe is made with dried beef and cream cheese."
Serving: 10 | Prep: 10m | Ready in: 10m

Ingredients

- 5 oz. dried beef, chopped
- 2 (8 oz.) packages cream cheese, softened
- 6 green onions, chopped
- 1 tbsp. Worcestershire sauce
- 1/2 tsp. seasoned salt

Direction

- Store about 1/2 cup of chopped dried beef.
- Combine seasoned salt, Worcestershire sauce, green onions, cream cheese, and the remaining beef in a separate medium bowl. Mix well and form into a ball.
- Next, roll ball in the reserved beef, covering the whole outside of the ball.

Nutrition Information

- Calories: 182 calories;
- Total Carbohydrate: 2.6 g
- Cholesterol: 60 mg
- Total Fat: 15.9 g
- Protein: 8 g
- Sodium: 592 mg

183. Dt's Beef Dip

"This dip goes well with beer."
Serving: 32 | Prep: 10m | Ready in: 8h10m

Ingredients

- 3 (8 oz.) packages cream cheese
- 15 green onions, chopped
- 2 (2 oz.) packages dried beef, chopped
- 3/4 cup milk
- 2 tbsps. Beau Monde ™ seasoning

Direction

- Beat cream cheese in a medium bowl until smooth. Stir in beef and onion. Add milk, a little at a time, beating until the dip gets the thick pea soup's consistency. Stir in the seasoning. Before serving, chill for 8 hours or overnight.

Nutrition Information

- Calories: 84 calories;
- Total Carbohydrate: 1.5 g
- Cholesterol: 27 mg
- Total Fat: 7.5 g
- Protein: 3.1 g
- Sodium: 175 mg

184. Easy Beer And Ketchup Meatballs

"A simple but tasty appetizer for parties or potlucks."
Serving: 8 | Prep: 40m | Ready in: 3h40m

Ingredients

- 1 (28 oz.) bottle ketchup
- 24 fluid oz. beer
- 1 1/2 lbs. ground beef
- 2 tsps. garlic powder
- 1 onion, chopped

Direction

- Set an oven to 200°C (400°F) and start preheating.
- In a slow cooker on a high setting, arrange the ketchup and beer and bring to a simmer.
- At the same time, blend the onion, garlic powder, and ground beef in a large bowl and mix thoroughly. Shape the mixture into meatballs with a diameter of about 3/4 inch. In a 9x13-inch baking dish, arrange meatballs.
- Bake for 20 minutes at 200°C (400°F).
- Place the meatballs into the slow cooker with the ketchup and beer and bring to a simmer for 3 hours; the sauce will become thickened.

Nutrition Information

- Calories: 405 calories;
- Total Carbohydrate: 29.6 g
- Cholesterol: 72 mg
- Total Fat: 22.9 g
- Protein: 16.5 g
- Sodium: 1154 mg

185. Easy German Bierocks (runza)

"An easy and quick version of German Bierocks."
Serving: 36 | Prep: 35m | Ready in: 1h35m

Ingredients

- 1 tbsp. vegetable oil
- 2 lbs. ground beef
- 1 small onion, chopped
- 1 head cabbage, finely chopped
- 1/2 tsp. salt
- 1/2 tsp. ground black pepper
- 36 frozen dinner rolls, thawed
- 2 quarts vegetable oil for deep frying

Direction

- In a big pot over medium-high heat, heat a tbsp. of vegetable oil. Mix in the ground beef, and allow to cook for 5 minutes till not pink anymore and crumbly. Mix in chopped onion, and let cook for 5 minutes longer till onion has turned translucent and softened. Put chopped cabbage; cook for 10 minutes and mix till the cabbage has become tender. Put pepper and salt to season, then onto a baking sheet, scatter the mixture to cool till enough to handle.
- Flatten a dinner roll when mixture has cooled, and in the middle, put a few tbsps. of cabbage mixture. Fold edges of dough on top of filling and pinch to secure. Redo with leftover filling and dough.
- In an electric skillet or deep-fryer, heat oil to 175 °C or 350 °F.
- In the prepped oil, fry bierocks for 5 to 7 minutes several at a time on each side till golden brown; allow to drain on paper towels.

Nutrition Information

- Calories: 224 calories;
- Total Carbohydrate: 22.9 g
- Cholesterol: 17 mg
- Total Fat: 10.8 g
- Protein: 9 g
- Sodium: 267 mg

186. Easy Spring Rolls (air Fried)

"An easy spring roll recipe."
Serving: 20 | Prep: 35m | Ready in: 54m

Ingredients

- 2 oz. dried rice noodles
- 1 tbsp. sesame oil
- 7 oz. ground beef
- 1 cup frozen mixed vegetables
- 1 small onion, diced
- 3 cloves garlic, crushed
- 1 tsp. soy sauce
- 1 (16 oz.) package egg roll wrappers
- 1 tbsp. vegetable oil, or to taste

Direction

- In a bowl of hot water, submerge the noodles for 5 minutes till tender. Slice noodles making shorter strips.
- In a wok, heat the sesame oil over medium-high heat. Put the garlic, onion, mixed vegetables and ground beef. Let cook for 6 minutes till beef is nearly browned completely. Take off heat. Mix in noodles; allow to sit till juices have been soaked in. To filling, put soy sauce.
- Preheat an air fryer to 175 °C or 350 °F.
- Onto a flat work area, spread out an egg roll wrapper; put strip of filling diagonally along the wrapper. Fold upper corner on top of

filling; fold in 2 side corners; with cold water, brush the middle and roll over to secure. Redo with the rest of the filling and wrappers.

- With vegetable oil, brush the surfaces of spring rolls. Into the air fryer basket, set a batch of spring rolls; let cook for 8 minutes till browned lightly and crisped. Redo till everything are cooked.

Nutrition Information

- Calories: 112 calories;
- Total Carbohydrate: 16.4 g
- Cholesterol: 8 mg
- Total Fat: 3.2 g
- Protein: 4.1 g
- Sodium: 155 mg

187. Egg Roll Reuben Wraps

""Yum-fusion: egg rolls meet the Reuben. These are truly great. I had them in Connecticut's restaurant, and I have to duplicate theirs. With a dipping sauce of thousand islands to serve.""

Serving: 10 | Prep: 30m | Ready in: 45m

Ingredients

- 1 (16 oz.) package egg roll wrappers
- water in a small bowl
- 1/2 cup drained sauerkraut
- 1/2 lb. thinly sliced corned beef (from deli), chopped
- 1 cup shredded Gruyere cheese
- 1 quart oil for frying, or as needed

Direction

- In a workspace big enough to have everything in one area without it getting crowded, place Gruyere cheese, corned beef, sauerkraut, water, and egg roll wrappers in a line.
- Get one wrapper and put in front of you with a corner pointing towards you.
- Sink fingers in water and dampen the wrapper side that is facing up.
- On the third of the wrapper nearest you, put small, equal amounts of sauerkraut, the corned beef, and the Gruyere cheese, in order. Then turn the corner that is opposite you over the fillings and slightly roll to cover the filling with the wrapper. Fully seal the fillings by folding the sides, rolling it to fully enclose. Place finished rolls on a tray. Continue until all the ingredients are finished. Keep the rolls in the refrigerator until oil is hot.
- In a big saucepan or a deep-fryer, heat oil to 350°F (175°C).
- Add egg rolls and fry in hot oil (in batches), for approximately 5 minutes for each batch, until it is golden brown.

Nutrition Information

- Calories: 286 calories;
- Total Carbohydrate: 26.5 g
- Cholesterol: 31 mg
- Total Fat: 14.5 g
- Protein: 12.1 g
- Sodium: 645 mg

188. Famous Meatballs

"This meatballs recipe will be a favorite for any occasion."

Serving: 6 | Prep: 10m | Ready in: 2h20m

Ingredients

- 1 (13.25 oz.) can pineapple chunks in juice
- 1 green bell pepper, sliced
- 1/2 cup brown sugar
- 2 tbsps. cornstarch
- 2 tbsps. soy sauce
- 2 tbsps. lemon juice
- 1 (3 lb.) bag frozen cooked meatballs, thawed

Direction

- Pour pineapple chunks with juice into a saucepan. Stir lemon juice, soy sauce, cornstarch, brown sugar, and green bell pepper through the pineapple chunks until the cornstarch and sugar dissolve.

- Next, bring the mixture to a boil; then cook and stir for about 10 minutes, until thickened.
- Put the meatballs into slow cooker crock; pour over the meatballs with the pineapple mixture.
- Cook for 2 hours on medium, stirring every half an hour.

Nutrition Information

- Calories: 611 calories;
- Total Carbohydrate: 46.4 g
- Cholesterol: 189 mg
- Total Fat: 29.2 g
- Protein: 38.9 g
- Sodium: 587 mg

189. Favorite Hamburger Bites

"A wonderful recipe for hamburgers that everyone will ask for."

Serving: 12 | Prep: 20m | Ready in: 40m

Ingredients

- 1 lb. ground beef
- 1 (1 oz.) package dry onion soup mix
- 1/2 cup dried minced onion
- 3/4 cup mayonnaise
- 1 cup shredded Cheddar cheese
- 2 (8 oz.) packages dinner rolls
- 1 (16 oz.) jar dill pickle slices, drained

Direction

- Set an oven to 175°C (350°F) and start preheating. Use aluminum foil to line a medium baking sheet.
- Stir the dry minced onion, dry onion soup mix, and ground beef together in a medium skillet on medium-high heat. Cook them until the beef turns brown evenly. Take away from the heat, let drain and stir in Cheddar cheese and mayonnaise.
- Remove the tops from the dinner rolls. On the baking sheet, place the rolls. Top each roll with some of the ground beef mixture. Decorate with pickle slices. Arrange the tops back on rolls.
- Use aluminum foil to wrap the baking sheet tightly. In the prepared oven, bake for 20 minutes.

Nutrition Information

- Calories: 276 calories;
- Total Carbohydrate: 5.6 g
- Cholesterol: 47 mg
- Total Fat: 24.2 g
- Protein: 9.4 g
- Sodium: 848 mg

190. Hanky Panky

"This recipe is made of Worcestershire sauce, hamburger, mild sausage and topped the processed melted cheese. It makes a quick meal or tasty snack. You can serve it on top of toasted slices of the bread you love."

Serving: 10 | Prep: 5m | Ready in: 15m

Ingredients

- 1 1/2 lbs. lean ground beef
- 1 (12 oz.) package sausage
- 1 tsp. Worcestershire sauce
- 1 (8 oz.) package processed cheese

Direction

- Put sausage and ground beef in a large, deep skillet and then cook over medium high heat until browned evenly.
- Drain meat, add in the Worcestershire sauce and stir. Pour the processed cheese on top of the meat and let it to melt. You can serve warm over slices of bread.

Nutrition Information

- Calories: 255 calories;
- Total Carbohydrate: 1.9 g
- Cholesterol: 69 mg
- Total Fat: 19.8 g
- Protein: 16.2 g

- Sodium: 337 mg

191. Hearty Egg Rolls

"Potatoes and beef make these deep-fried a hearty filling flavor."
Serving: 8 | Prep: 30m | Ready in: 1h15m

Ingredients

- 3 potatoes, cubed
- 2 lbs. ground beef
- 2 eggs
- 2 cups chopped cabbage
- soy sauce to taste
- salt and pepper to taste
- 1 quart oil for frying
- 1 (14 oz.) package egg roll wrappers

Direction

- In a medium saucepan, place potatoes with enough water to cover. Bring to a boil, cook for about 15 minutes, until tender. Remove from the heat and let drain.
- In a large saucepan, put ground beef over medium-high heat. Then cook until equally brown; allow to drain.
- In the saucepan, place potatoes, pepper, salt, soy sauce, cabbage, and eggs with the ground beef. Cook and stir over medium heat until the eggs are cooked and the cabbage is softened, for about 10 minutes. Shift to a medium bowl.
- In a large, heavy saucepan, heat oil to 190 degrees C (375 degrees F).
- In the center of each egg roll wrapper, put approximately 1 tbsp. of the potato mixture and the ground beef. Then roll the wrappers around the mixture and fold all edges inward to seal tight.
- In the hot oil, fry these egg rolls until golden brown. Let drain on paper tissues.

Nutrition Information

- Calories: 526 calories;
- Total Carbohydrate: 43.7 g
- Cholesterol: 120 mg
- Total Fat: 26.4 g
- Protein: 27.3 g
- Sodium: 372 mg

192. Holiday Cheese Ball

"This cheese ball is ideal for an appetizer at a party that has extra zing when coated with a little hot pepper sauce."
Serving: 8 | Prep: 10m | Ready in: 10m

Ingredients

- 1 (8 oz.) package cream cheese
- 1 (2.5 oz.) package smoked sliced beef, chopped
- 3 green onions, finely chopped
- 1 dash hot pepper sauce

Direction

- Use an electric mixer or hands to mix pepper sauce, onions, beef and cream cheese together. Form into a ball and refrigerate for a minimum of an hour before serving together with crackers.

Nutrition Information

- Calories: 112 calories;
- Total Carbohydrate: 1.2 g
- Cholesterol: 37 mg
- Total Fat: 10.3 g
- Protein: 3.9 g
- Sodium: 210 mg

193. Korean Mandu (egg Roll)

"A unique egg roll or mandu!"
Serving: 24 | Prep: 30m | Ready in: 40m

Ingredients

- 1 cup shredded cabbage
- 1/2 lb. ground beef

- 1/2 lb. ground pork
- 1 (14 oz.) can bean sprouts - drained, rinsed, and finely chopped
- 1/3 cup minced celery
- 1 green onion, chopped (white part only)
- 1 tbsp. soy sauce
- 1 1/2 tsps. cornstarch
- 1 tsp. sesame oil
- 1 tsp. salt
- 1/2 tsp. ground black pepper
- 2 (12 oz.) packages wonton wrappers
- 1 egg, beaten
- vegetable oil for frying

Direction

- In a saucepan, put a steamer insert. Fill water to reach just below the bottom of the steamer. Boil. Add cabbage, steam, covered, for 2-4 minutes until tender.
- Heat a big skillet on medium-high heat. Sauté pork and beef in hot skillet for 5-7 minutes until crumbly and brown. Drain and throw out grease. Place meat mixture in a big bowl, break any big chunks using a wooden spoon.
- In a big saucepan or deep-fryer, heat oil to 182 degrees C/360 degrees F.
- Mix pepper, salt, sesame oil, cornstarch, soy sauce, green onion, celery, bean sprouts, and cabbage in meat mixture. Place mixture in the middle of every wonton wrapper. Spread beaten egg on 2 wrapper edges. Fold wrapper around the filling. Seal the edges together.
- Fry wontons for 3-5 minutes in hot oil until brown. Place on a plate lined with paper towels with a slotted spoon.

Nutrition Information

- Calories: 139 calories;
- Total Carbohydrate: 17.2 g
- Cholesterol: 22 mg
- Total Fat: 4.6 g
- Protein: 6.6 g
- Sodium: 314 mg

194. Korean Sushi

"Korean-style sushi that uses canned tuna and minced beef instead of raw fish."

Serving: 6 | Prep: 30m | Ready in: 1h

Ingredients

- 2 cups uncooked short-grain white rice
- 2 cups water
- 2 tbsps. cider vinegar
- 2 leaves chard
- 2 eggs, well beaten
- 2 tbsps. soy sauce, divided
- 3 tbsps. water
- 1 onion, diced
- 1 tbsp. vegetable oil
- 3/4 lb. beef tenderloin, minced
- 1 (5 oz.) can tuna, drained
- 1 carrot, julienned
- 1 cucumber, julienned
- 6 sheets nori (dry seaweed)

Direction

- Boil cider vinegar and 2 cups water in a medium saucepan. Add rice then stir. Reduce heat, simmer for 20 minutes, covered, until rice grains are soft and sticky.
- Cover chard with enough water in a medium saucepan then boil. Cook until tender. Slice to thin strips.
- Whisk eggs with 3 tbsps. water and soy sauce. Place in medium skillet on medium heat. Cook until thick. Take off heat. Slice to strips.
- In a medium saucepan heat vegetable oil on medium-high heat. Slowly sauté onion until tender. Mix beef in with 1 tbsp. soy sauce. Cook until browned evenly. Drain then put aside.
- Preheat oven to 175 degrees C/350 degrees F. Put nori sheets onto a medium baking sheet. Heat in the preheated oven for 1-2 minutes until a little crisp.
- One by one, put nori sheets on the bamboo rolling mat. Evenly line nori sheets with approximately 3/4 inch/2 cm depth of rice. Be sure rice doesn't cover nori edges. Start with

one nori sheet end, top rice with a line of beef, a cucumber slice, a line of tuna, and a stick of carrot, repeat process until you food reaches approximately the middle of the nori sheet. Carefully roll sheets tightly. Seal with one or two grains of sticky rice. Slice every roll to approximately 4 pieces then serve.

Nutrition Information

- Calories: 492 calories;
- Total Carbohydrate: 58 g
- Cholesterol: 109 mg
- Total Fat: 17.6 g
- Protein: 23.1 g
- Sodium: 409 mg

195. Lahmajoon

"“Little meat pizzas that are normally made with lamb but works well too with beef.”"
Serving: 24 | Prep: 30m | Ready in: 3h50m

Ingredients

- 1 package active dry yeast
- 3 tbsps. white sugar
- 2 cups warm water
- 6 cups all-purpose flour
- 1 1/2 tsps. salt
- 5 tbsps. shortening
- 2 lbs. ground beef
- 1 (16 oz.) can whole peeled tomatoes, drained and chopped
- 2 onions, finely chopped
- 1/2 cup chopped fresh parsley
- 1/2 cup finely chopped green bell pepper
- 2 tsps. salt
- 1 pinch cayenne pepper
- 1 pinch ground black pepper

Direction

- Combine 1/2 cup warm water, 1 tbsp. sugar, and active dry yeast in a small bowl. Let it stand for about 5 minutes.
- Combine the yeast preparation, remaining water, remaining sugar, 3 tbsp. shortening, salt, and flour in a large bowl. Knead until smooth. Remove any dough sticking to the sides of the bowl using the remaining shortening, and to discard the dough from fingers. Use a towel to cover it and put it in a warm place for about 2-3 hours until double in size.
- Stir black and cayenne pepper, salt, green bell pepper, parsley, onions, tomatoes, and ground beef in a medium bowl. Keep in the refrigerator to chill until ready to use.
- Prepare the oven by preheating to 450°F (230°C). Lightly coat a large baking sheet with flour.
- Roll the dough into 12 balls on a lightly floured surface. Separate each ball in half. Form halves into balls. Transfer balls to the prepared baking sheet. Let them stand for about 10 minutes.
- Form balls into 7-in. diameter circles. Spread about 1 1/2 tbsps. of meat mixture on each circle. Place in the preheated oven and bake for 15-20 minutes, or until the dough turned light brown and beef is not pink.

Nutrition Information

- Calories: 270 calories;
- Total Carbohydrate: 27.4 g
- Cholesterol: 32 mg
- Total Fat: 13.1 g
- Protein: 9.9 g
- Sodium: 394 mg

196. Lana's Sweet And Sour Meatballs

"An amazing sweet sauce and savory meatball recipe."
Serving: 8 | Prep: 20m | Ready in: 1h

Ingredients

- 2 lbs. lean ground beef
- 2 eggs

- 1 cup dry bread crumbs
- 1/2 cup finely chopped onion
- 1/2 tsp. ground ginger
- 1 tsp. seasoning salt
- 1/2 tsp. ground black pepper
- 2 tsps. Worcestershire sauce
- 2 tsps. granulated sugar
- 1 (20 oz.) can pineapple chunks, drained with juice reserved
- 1/3 cup water
- 3 tbsps. distilled white vinegar
- 1 tbsp. soy sauce
- 1/2 cup packed brown sugar
- 3 tbsps. cornstarch
- 1/2 tsp. ground ginger
- 1/2 tsp. seasoning salt
- 1 large carrot, diced
- 1 large green bell pepper, cut into 1/2 inch pieces

Direction

- Set the oven at 200°C (400°F) to preheat. Grease a large, shallow baking sheet lightly.
- Mix thoroughly onion, bread crumbs, eggs, and ground beef in a large bowl. Dust with sugar, Worcestershire sauce, pepper, seasoning salt, and ginger. Form into 1-inch balls.
- On the prepared baking sheet, place them in a single layer. In the preheated oven, bake for 10 to 15 minutes; put aside.
- To prepare the sauce: Mix the reserved pineapple juice with enough water to make 1 cup. Combine brown sugar, soy sauce, vinegar, 1/3 cup water, and the juice mixture in a large pot over medium heat. Stir in seasoning salt, ginger, and cornstarch until smooth. Cook, covered, until thickened.
- Stir the meatballs, green pepper, carrot, and pineapple chunks into the sauce. Stir gently with the sauce to coat the meatballs. Uncover and simmer until the meatballs are completely cooked, for about 20 minutes.

Nutrition Information

- Calories: 427 calories;
- Total Carbohydrate: 42.1 g
- Cholesterol: 124 mg
- Total Fat: 16.5 g
- Protein: 27.4 g
- Sodium: 479 mg

197. Magic Pickle Dip

"This simple snack is a family favorite. You can prepare them as a wrap but this is easier! You can serve alongside whole wheat crackers."

Serving: 16 | Prep: 10m | Ready in: 10m

Ingredients

- 1 (8 oz.) package softened cream cheese
- 6 dill pickle spears, diced
- 1 (2 oz.) package thinly sliced dried beef, chopped

Direction

- Combine together the chopped beef, softened cream cheese, and diced pickle until mixed thoroughly. Refrigerate until when ready to serve.

Nutrition Information

- Calories: 57 calories;
- Total Carbohydrate: 0.9 g
- Cholesterol: 19 mg
- Total Fat: 5 g
- Protein: 2.4 g
- Sodium: 296 mg

198. Meat Candy

""Excellent for any casual get-together and these meaty treats will disappear first once serve on the buffet!""

Serving: 20 | Prep: 20m | Ready in: 1h10m

Ingredients

- 1 pinch cayenne pepper

- 2 cups brown sugar, or as needed
- 2 (14 oz.) packages little smoked sausages
- 1 (16 oz.) package bacon slices, cut into thirds (or as needed)
- 1 box toothpicks

Direction

- Prepare the oven by preheating to 400°F (200°C). Use aluminum foil to line a baking sheet.
- Mix brown sugar and cayenne pepper in a bowl. Use a piece of bacon to wrap each smoked sausage; use a toothpick to secure each. Transfer wrapped sausages into the prepared baking dish and arrange them. Use brown sugar and pack around wrapped sausages to cover about 1/2-inch. Use aluminum foil to cover the pan tightly.
- Place in the preheated oven and bake for 20 minutes. Raise the oven heat to 450°F (230°C). Take off the aluminum foil from the pan.
- Keep on baking in the hot oven for 30-40 minutes until the brown sugar has thickened and melted.

Nutrition Information

- Calories: 242 calories;
- Total Carbohydrate: 22.5 g
- Cholesterol: 33 mg
- Total Fat: 13.7 g
- Protein: 7.7 g
- Sodium: 563 mg

199. Meat Sambusa

"A tasty appetizer originated from the Middle East"
Serving: 15 | Prep: 25m | Ready in: 56m

Ingredients

- 2 tbsps. olive oil, divided
- 2 tbsps. pine nuts
- 1/2 lb. ground beef
- 1 small onion, chopped
- 3/4 tsp. ground cinnamon
- 1/4 tsp. ground allspice
- salt and ground black pepper to taste
- 5 (12-inch) spring roll wrappers
- 5 tbsps. butter, melted

Direction

- Set an oven to 175°C (350°F) and start preheating. Use a parchment paper to line a baking sheet.
- In a large skillet, heat a tbsp. of olive oil on medium heat. Put pine nuts; stir and cook for 2 minutes until they are lightly toasted. Using a slotted spoon, place onto a paper towel-lined plate.
- In the same skillet, heat the remaining 1 tbsp. of olive oil on medium heat. Put in beef; cook and stir to break the clumps for 3-5 minutes until not pink anymore. Add in the onion and stir; stir and cook for 3-5 minutes until tender. Take away from the heat; flavor with pepper, salt, allspice, and cinnamon. Add in pine nuts and stir.
- Slice each spring roll wrapper into three 12x4-inch rectangles. Lightly brush melted butter over each rectangle.
- Arrange a heaping teaspoonful of the beef mixture near the short end of a rectangle. Fold a corner over the filling to enclose and shape into a triangle. Carry on folding until the rectangle has been formed into a triangular packet, seal all the holes to avoid oozing out the filling. Dab the outside of the fold with cold water to seal the sambusa.
- Repeat the process with the beef mixture and the remaining spring roll rectangles. On the lined baking sheet, place the sambusa.
- In the prepared oven, bake for 25 minutes until golden and crisp.

Nutrition Information

- Calories: 94 calories;
- Total Carbohydrate: 2.3 g
- Cholesterol: 20 mg
- Total Fat: 8.1 g
- Protein: 3.2 g
- Sodium: 62 mg

200. Meatballs And Kraut

"A quick and very simple dish to make for family get-togethers."
Serving: 8 | Prep: 10m | Ready in: 1h10m

Ingredients

- 1 (16 oz.) package frozen cooked meatballs, thawed
- 1 (14 oz.) can sauerkraut, drained
- 1 (12 oz.) bottle ketchup-style chili sauce (such as Heinz®)
- 1 cup white sugar
- 1 cup brown sugar
- 1/4 cup hot water
- 2 tbsps. vinegar

Direction

- In a slow cooker, combine vinegar, hot water, brown sugar, white sugar, chili sauce, sauerkraut, and meatballs and stir them to dissolve the sugar. Cook for an hour on High.

Nutrition Information

- Calories: 336 calories;
- Total Carbohydrate: 58.7 g
- Cholesterol: 47 mg
- Total Fat: 7.4 g
- Protein: 10.1 g
- Sodium: 459 mg

201. Meatballs And Sauce

""Marinated meatballs in a savory sauce overnight, then heated again just before serving for your party!""
Serving: 20 | Prep: 8h5m | Ready in: 9h5m

Ingredients

- 5 lbs. Italian meatballs
- 1 (10.75 oz.) can condensed cream of mushroom soup
- 3/4 cup water
- 2 cups sour cream

Direction

- Whisk sour cream, water, mushroom soup, and meatballs. Keep in the refrigerator overnight, covered, so the meatballs can absorb up the flavors.
- Transfer the mixture to a slow cooker and heat until the meatballs are heated through. Serve hot.

Nutrition Information

- Calories: 427 calories;
- Total Carbohydrate: 8.8 g
- Cholesterol: 98 mg
- Total Fat: 35.4 g
- Protein: 17.2 g
- Sodium: 962 mg

202. Men's Dip

"A hot, spicy, and hearty dip that nicely goes with corn chips."
Serving: 8 | Prep: 30m | Ready in: 2h30m

Ingredients

- 1 lb. ground beef
- 3/4 cup chopped onion
- 2 cloves garlic, minced
- 3/4 cup chopped green bell pepper
- 2 jalapeno peppers, seeded and chopped
- 3/4 cup blanched slivered almonds
- 1 (2 oz.) jar pimento peppers, drained and chopped
- 3/4 cup raisins
- 1 (8 oz.) can diced tomatoes, drained
- 1 (6 oz.) can tomato paste
- 2 tbsps. white sugar, or to taste
- 1 tbsp. dried oregano
- 2 tsps. salt

Direction

- Place the crumbled the ground beef into a large skillet on medium heat. Cook and stir to crumble until it begins to brown. Put in jalapeno pepper, bell pepper, garlic, and onion, cook until the meat is not pink anymore. Drain any excess grease. Pour enough water to cover the beef into the pan, put a cover on and bring to a simmer on low heat for half an hour.
- Stir in the sugar, tomato paste, tomatoes, raisins, pimentos, and almonds. Flavor with salt and oregano. Bring to a simmer and stir from time to time for at least an hour on low heat.

Nutrition Information

- Calories: 258 calories;
- Total Carbohydrate: 25.6 g
- Cholesterol: 34 mg
- Total Fat: 12.1 g
- Protein: 13.8 g
- Sodium: 832 mg

203. Mexican Egg Rolls

"Easy and delicious appetizer, or even as a main dish."
Serving: 14 | Prep: 15m | Ready in: 30m

Ingredients

- 1 (14 oz.) package egg roll wrappers
- 1 lb. lean ground beef
- 1 (1.25 oz.) package taco seasoning mix
- 1 (4 oz.) can diced green chilies, drained
- 2 cups shredded pepperjack cheese
- 4 cups oil for frying, or as needed

Direction

- Into a big skillet, break ground beef up over medium-high heat. Let cook till equally browned, and drain off oil. Put the taco seasoning, and allow to cook following packaging instructions. Reserve.
- In a big skillet, heat an-inch of oil, or preheat the deep-fryer to 190 °C or 375 °F.
- Spread out an egg roll wrapper at a time, and in the middle, put a bit more than 1 tbsp. ground beef. Place a small spoonful of green chilies on top, and a small amount of shredded cheese. Roll up following packaging directions, and enclose edges, moistening with water if needed. Redo with the rest of filling and wrappers.
- In hot oil, fry rolls for 5 minutes till golden brown on every side. Take off from oil to drain on paper towels. Serve while hot and fresh.

Nutrition Information

- Calories: 286 calories;
- Total Carbohydrate: 19 g
- Cholesterol: 42 mg
- Total Fat: 17.2 g
- Protein: 12.5 g
- Sodium: 571 mg

204. Mexican Pizza I

""This recipe is so luscious with beef, beans and all the yummy taco toppings you can think of! Slice them into wedges and served as an appetizer or left whole and present as a main dis.""
Serving: 4 | Prep: 17m | Ready in: 50m

Ingredients

- 1 (16 oz.) can refried beans
- 1 lb. ground beef
- 1 (1.25 oz.) package taco seasoning mix
- 1 tbsp. vegetable oil
- 4 (6 inch) corn tortillas
- 8 oz. shredded Cheddar cheese
- 8 tbsps. sour cream
- 2 roma (plum) tomatoes, chopped
- 2 green onion, chopped
- 1 (4 oz.) can diced green chiles, drained
- 1/2 avocado, diced
- 1 tbsp. black olives, sliced

Direction

- Warm the refried beans.
- Place the ground beef into a large skillet and brown. Mix in the seasoning packet.
- Prepare the oven by preheating to 350°F (175°C).
- In large skillet, put a small amount of vegetable oil. Allow the oil to heat, then put one corn tortilla in the skillet. Then turn the tortilla over after 15 seconds and allow to fry for another 15 seconds. Continue this process with the remaining tortillas, allowing them to drain on paper towels when they have been warmed. Once the tortillas have drained, lay them on a cookie sheet.
- On the tortillas, spread a thin layer of beans, next layer the beef and cheese.
- Place the tortillas in the preheated oven and bake for 20 to 30 minutes. Cut the tortillas into wedges and lay them on plates or a serving platter and decorate them with olives, avocado, chiles, green onions, tomatoes and sour cream.

Nutrition Information

- Calories: 770 calories;
- Total Carbohydrate: 42.3 g
- Cholesterol: 150 mg
- Total Fat: 48.1 g
- Protein: 42.1 g
- Sodium: 1542 mg

205. Mexican Pizza II

"This Mexican Pizza recipe calls for Mexican style toppings, two cheeses and ground beef."
Serving: 8 | Prep: 15m | Ready in: 25m

Ingredients

- 1 lb. lean ground beef
- 1 (1 oz.) package taco seasoning mix
- 2/3 cup water
- 2 (16 oz.) cans refried beans
- 4 (10 inch) flour tortillas
- 2 cups shredded Monterey Jack cheese
- 2 cups shredded Cheddar cheese
- 2 tbsps. sour cream
- 1 tomato, diced
- 1 avocado - peeled, pitted and sliced
- 1 (2 oz.) can sliced black olives
- 2 chopped green onions

Direction

- Set the oven at 425°F (200°C) and start preheating.
- Place a large, deep frying pan on medium-high heat; cook in ground beef till evenly brown. Strain; mix in water and taco seasoning mix. Stir in refried beans; keep for later use.
- Evenly distribute the beef mixture on two tortillas. Put a second tortilla on top of each. Top the second tortillas with even amounts of Cheddar cheese and Monterey Jack cheese. Transfer onto a large baking dish.
- Bake for 10 minutes in the preheated oven, till the cheeses are melted.
- Take tortillas out of oven and put green onions, black olives, avocado, tomato and sour cream on top. Slice pizza into 8 wedges and serve while still warm.

Nutrition Information

- Calories: 684 calories;
- Total Carbohydrate: 42.5 g
- Cholesterol: 114 mg
- Total Fat: 41.1 g
- Protein: 35.6 g
- Sodium: 1294 mg

206. Mexican Potato Nachos

"This dish is great to serve at any potluck. You can try pepper-jack cheese instead of Cheddar if you want."
Serving: 8 | Prep: 20m | Ready in: 1h

Ingredients

- 2 tbsps. Vegetable oil

- 2 large baking potatoes, cut into 1/2-inch thick slices
- salt and ground black pepper to taste
- 1 tbsp. vegetable oil
- 1/2 lb. ground beef
- 1 (15 oz.) can black beans, drained
- 2 tbsps. taco seasoning
- 2 tbsps. water
- 8 oz. shredded Cheddar cheese, divided
- 1/4 cup shredded lettuce
- 1 small tomato, chopped
- 1/4 cup sour cream
- 1/4 cup guacamole

Direction

- Start preheating the oven to 450°F (230°C).
- In a big bowl, put 2 tbsps. of vegetable oil; mix potato slices in the oil to blend.
- On a cookie sheet, put 1 layer of the slices and sprinkle black pepper and salt over.
- Put in the preheated oven and bake for 20 minutes until the potato slices turn golden brown.
- As the potato slices bake, in a frying pan, heat 1 tbsp. of vegetable oil over medium heat; add ground beef to the hot oil and brown for 8-10 minutes, crumbling it into small pieces while cooking it. Strain the extra grease.
- Stir black beans into the ground beef, mix in water and taco seasoning. Boil the mixture and lower the heat to medium-low. Simmer for 10 minutes to blend the flavors.
- On a serving dish, put potato slices and sprinkle 1/2 Cheddar cheese over.
- Put the bean and meat mixture on top of the potatoes and sprinkle over nachos with the leftover cheese.
- Spread over the nachos with lettuce, and use dollops of guacamole and sour cream and tomato to garnish.

Nutrition Information

- Calories: 327 calories;
- Total Carbohydrate: 20 g
- Cholesterol: 50 mg
- Total Fat: 20.3 g
- Protein: 16.4 g
- Sodium: 568 mg

207. Mini Philly Cheesesteaks

"Delicious mini Philly cheesesteaks."
Serving: 12 | Prep: 30m | Ready in: 1h20m

Ingredients

- Cheese Sauce:
- 2 tbsps. butter, or as needed
- 2 tbsps. all-purpose flour, or as needed
- 1 cup cold milk
- 2 oz. shredded provolone cheese, or more to taste
- 1 pinch ground nutmeg
- 1 pinch cayenne pepper
- salt to taste
- 1 (12 oz.) skirt steak
- salt and freshly ground black pepper to taste
- 3 tbsps. olive oil, divided, or as needed
- 1/4 cup water
- 1/3 cup diced onion
- 1/3 cup diced sweet peppers
- 2 baguettes, or as needed, cut into 48 1/2-inch thick slices
- 1/4 cup shredded provolone cheese, or as needed

Direction

- Preheat the oven to 200 degrees C/400 degrees F. Line aluminum foil on baking sheets.
- In a skillet, melt butter on medium high heat. In hot butter, whisk flour in. Cook, constantly whisking, for about 1 minute until flour taste cooks off and mixture is pale. Put milk into flour mixture. Cook, constantly whisking, for 3-6 minutes until mixture thickens and is hot. Add salt, cayenne pepper, nutmeg and 2-oz. provolone cheese. Mix until cheese melts completely. Take off from heat.
- Season steak with ground black pepper and salt all over.

- In a skillet, heat 1 tbsp. olive oil on medium high heat. Cook steak in the hot oil, occasionally turning, for 5-7 minutes until meat is pink on the inside and slightly firm. Put meat on a plate.
- Put back skillet on heat. Pour water into skillet. Boil as you scrape browned food bits off the pan's bottom using a wooden spoon. Pour liquid from skillet on steak. Cool the steak to room temperature. Dice the meat. In a big bowl, put meat and the accumulated juices from plate.
- In a skillet, heat 1 tbsp. oil on medium high heat. Sauté peppers and onions in hot oil for about 5 minutes until slightly translucent and softened.
- Mix onions and peppers mixture into the diced meat. Season with pepper and salt.
- On prepped baking sheet, spread bread slices out. Drizzle leftover olive oil on top. Flip slices to make the oiled side face down. On each slice, spread a thick layer of the cheese mixture. Spoon meat mixture on cheese. On top of every slice, sprinkle provolone cheese.
- Bake in preheated oven for 12-15 minutes until cheese melts and it's brown.

Nutrition Information

- Calories: 280 calories;
- Total Carbohydrate: 34.8 g
- Cholesterol: 18 mg
- Total Fat: 9.9 g
- Protein: 12.9 g
- Sodium: 489 mg

208. Mini Reubens

"These are very easy and very yummy appetizers."
Serving: 16 | Prep: 15m | Ready in: 20m

Ingredients

- 1 (1 lb.) loaf cocktail rye bread
- 1 cup thousand island dressing
- 1 1/2 lbs. deli sliced corned beef
- 1 (16 oz.) jar sauerkraut, rinsed and well drained
- 1 lb. sliced Swiss cheese

Direction

- Preheat the oven's broiler.
- On a baking sheet, arrange cocktail rye slices. Place 2 tsps. of thousand island salad dressing on top; after that, fold about 1/2 slice of corned beef to fit the bread, and lay over the dressing. Place over the meat with a small amount of sauerkraut, then lay a slice as big as the bread or 1/4 slice of the Swiss cheese on top.
- Broil until the cheese is melted, for 3 to 5 minutes. Serve warm.

Nutrition Information

- Calories: 242 calories;
- Total Carbohydrate: 6.9 g
- Cholesterol: 59 mg
- Total Fat: 17.1 g
- Protein: 16 g
- Sodium: 994 mg

209. Moroccan Meat Cigars

"A dish best served alongside hummus."
Serving: 4

Ingredients

- 1 tsp. olive oil
- 1/2 lb. lean ground beef
- 1/2 cup canned crushed tomatoes, drained
- 1/4 tsp. ground cinnamon
- 1/4 tsp. ground cumin
- 1/8 tsp. paprika
- 1/8 tsp. ground allspice
- 1 (16 oz.) package phyllo dough
- cooking oil spray

Direction

- Set an oven to preheat at 175°C (350°F). Grease a baking tray lightly.
- In a frypan, heat the olive oil on medium-high heat. Cook the ground beef until it starts to brown and is no longer pink. Drain the fat from the frypan. Put the allspice, paprika, cumin, cinnamon and tomatoes, then turn down the heat to medium and let the mixture simmer for about 10 minutes until it reduces a bit.
- Take 1 phyllo sheet out of the package and keep the remaining covered with clean cloth until time to use. Cut the phyllo sheet into two 14x9-inch rectangles on a flat work surface. Use cooking spray to spritz the first 1/2 sheet, then lay the second half over it and sprits again with oil. Near the narrow end of the dough put 1 tsp of meat mixture liberally. On top of the meat, fold the dough and fold in the sides of the dough, then roll it to a narrow tube shape similar to a cigar. Redo the process until all the meat was rolled up. On prepared baking sheet, lay out the cigars.
- Bake in the oven for about 25 minutes until it turns light brown.

Nutrition Information

- Calories: 460 calories;
- Total Carbohydrate: 60.4 g
- Cholesterol: 37 mg
- Total Fat: 14.9 g
- Protein: 19 g
- Sodium: 620 mg

210. Nacho Dip II

"An easy and quick chili cheese dip to please the crowd."
Serving: 5 | Prep: 5m | Ready in: 35m

Ingredients

- 1 (8 oz.) package cream cheese, softened
- 1 (15 oz.) can chili without beans
- 1 (4 oz.) can diced green chiles, drained
- 8 oz. shredded Monterey Jack cheese
- 1 (14.5 oz.) package corn tortilla chips

Direction

- Preheat the oven to 150°C or 300°F.
- On the bottom of a 9-in. pie plate, spread the cream cheese. Top the cream cheese with layers of chili, green chilis and shredded cheese.
- Bake for 30 minutes at 150°C or 300°F. Serve hot with chips.

Nutrition Information

- Calories: 796 calories;
- Total Carbohydrate: 62.1 g
- Cholesterol: 102 mg
- Total Fat: 50.7 g
- Protein: 27 g
- Sodium: 1152 mg

211.Nacho Dip III

"Serve this delicious cheesy and meaty dip with tortilla chips."
Serving: 64 | Prep: 5m | Ready in: 15m

Ingredients

- 1 lb. lean ground beef
- 1 onion, chopped
- 1 (8 oz.) package processed cheese, cubed
- 1 (10 oz.) can diced tomatoes with green chile peppers, drained

Direction

- In a large deep skillet, place onion and ground beef. Over medium high heat, cook to soften the onions and brown the beef evenly. Drain and put aside.
- Let the cheese melt over low heat in a medium saucepan. Mix in green chili peppers, diced tomatoes, onion and ground beef. Serve warm.

Nutrition Information

- Calories: 32 calories;
- Total Carbohydrate: 0.6 g
- Cholesterol: 8 mg
- Total Fat: 2.4 g
- Protein: 1.9 g
- Sodium: 67 mg

212. New York System Hot Wiener Sauce I

"A tasty wiener sauce best for steamed hotdog buns."
Serving: 12 | Prep: 20m | Ready in: 1h20m

Ingredients

- 3 lbs. ground beef
- 2 tsps. chili powder
- 2 tsps. dry mustard
- 1/2 tsp. ground allspice
- 1/2 tsp. ground nutmeg
- 1/2 tsp. onion salt
- 1/2 tsp. garlic salt
- 1/2 tsp. celery salt
- 1/4 tsp. minced fresh ginger root
- 1 tsp. ground cumin
- 1/2 tsp. Worcestershire sauce
- 1 tsp. soy sauce
- 10 oz. ketchup

Direction

- In a deep, big pan, put the ground beef and cook on medium-high heat until it becomes brown evenly, then drain.
- In the frypan, mix the ketchup, soy sauce, Worcestershire sauce, cumin, ginger root, celery salt, garlic salt, onion salt, nutmeg, allspice, dry mustard and chili powder. Let it simmer for a minimum of 1 hour until it reaches the preferred consistency. Serve it hot.

Nutrition Information

- Calories: 381 calories;
- Total Carbohydrate: 6.6 g
- Cholesterol: 96 mg
- Total Fat: 30.6 g
- Protein: 19.6 g
- Sodium: 582 mg

213. New York System Hot Wiener Sauce II

"Hot meat sauce recipe."
Serving: 28 | Prep: 15m | Ready in: 45m

Ingredients

- 1 lb. ground beef
- 1 1/2 cups chopped onions
- 2 cloves garlic, finely chopped
- 1 (15 oz.) can tomato sauce
- 1 tsp. chili powder
- 1 tbsp. beef bouillon
- 1 tsp. ground cumin
- 1 tsp. white sugar

Direction

- In a big, deep frypan, put the ground beef. Let it cook on medium-high heat until it turns evenly brown. Mix in the garlic and onions. Let it cook and stir until the onions become soft. Stir in white sugar, cumin, beef bouillon, chili powder and tomato sauce. Put cover and lower the heat to a simmer. Let it simmer for 20 minutes prior to serving hot on top of frankfurters.

Nutrition Information

- Calories: 59 calories;
- Total Carbohydrate: 2 g
- Cholesterol: 14 mg
- Total Fat: 4.4 g
- Protein: 3.1 g
- Sodium: 138 mg

214. Painted Chef's Classic Beef Carpaccio

""A recipe with a variation on the Harry's Bar 1950's invention of carpaccio.""
Serving: 4 | Prep: 15m | Ready in: 15m

Ingredients

- 2 eggs
- 1 tbsp. Dijon mustard
- 3 tbsps. fresh lemon juice
- 1/4 cup extra-virgin olive oil
- 1 cup vegetable oil
- 2 dashes hot pepper sauce (e.g. Tabasco™), or to taste
- 3 tbsps. Worcestershire sauce
- salt and pepper to taste
- 8 oz. frozen thinly sliced beef tenderloin carpaccio.
- 1 tbsp. capers, for garnish
- 1 lemon, cut into wedges

Direction

- Combine in the container of a blender a dash of hot sauce, a pinch of salt, lemon juice, Dijon mustard, and eggs. Cover and blend by pulsing to mix. Begin the blender on medium speed and allow to run while adding in the olive oil, then the vegetable oil, in a thin continuous stream until mixture becomes thick enough to cover the back of a metal spoon. Add in the Worcestershire sauce and process for 10 more seconds. Modify taste with salt if needed.
- On a serving plate, pile the frozen beef in a semi-circle. Sprinkle the sauce over the meat. Decorate with freshly ground black pepper and capers and press a bit of lemon juice over the top. Before serving, let it stand for 5 minutes.

Nutrition Information

- Calories: 827 calories;
- Total Carbohydrate: 7.4 g
- Cholesterol: 133 mg
- Total Fat: 84.1 g
- Protein: 13.6 g
- Sodium: 387 mg

215. Party Corned Beef Puffs

"Easy and super tasty."
Serving: 12 | Prep: 15m | Ready in: 45m

Ingredients

- 2 1/2 cups finely chopped deli corned beef
- 2 tbsps. chopped onion
- 2 tbsps. Dijon mustard
- 1 tbsp. mayonnaise
- 1/4 tsp. prepared horseradish
- 1 cup beer
- 1/2 cup butter
- 1 cup flour
- 1/4 tsp. salt
- 4 eggs

Direction

- Mix horseradish, mayonnaise, mustard, onion and corned beef; cover then refrigerate.
- Preheat oven to 230°C/450°F>
- Put butter and beer on rolling boil in big pot; mix salt and flour in till mixture makes a ball. Put dough in big mixing bowl; one by one, beat eggs in with stand mixer/wooden spoon. Stir well after each. By teaspoonfuls, drop on lightly greased baking sheet.
- In preheated oven, bake for 10 minutes; lower temperature to 175°C/350°F. Bake till golden brown for 10 minutes; centers should be dry.
- Split puffs when shells are cool; fill with corned beef mixture. Refrigerate till serving.

Nutrition Information

- Calories: 184 calories;
- Total Carbohydrate: 9.8 g
- Cholesterol: 98 mg
- Total Fat: 12 g
- Protein: 8 g

- Sodium: 515 mg

216. Party Meatballs

"A combination of ingredient apple butter and pork sausage or beef meatballs will definitely satisfy your appetite."
Serving: 8

Ingredients

- 1 cup MUSSELMAN'S® Apple Butter, divided
- 1 tbsp. butter
- 1/2 cup grated red onion
- 1 lb. pork sausage
- 1 lb. ground beef
- 2 cups panko bread crumbs
- 1/4 cup sour cream
- 2 eggs
- 2 tsps. salt
- 1 tsp. black pepper
- 1 tsp. allspice
- 1/2 cup beef broth
- 2 tbsps. honey
- Cayenne pepper

Direction

- Set an oven to 400°F and start preheating, use foil to line a large-rimmed baking sheet.
- In a skillet arranged on medium heat, let the butter melt. Put in the grated onions and sauté until softened, 3-4 minutes once the butter is melted.
- Combine the allspice, pepper, salt, eggs, sour cream, 1/2 cup of apple butter, panko, ground beef, and sausage in a large bowl. When it cools, put the onion. Mix it properly with your hands until blended evenly.
- Measure out the meatballs into 1-oz. portions. Roll to form tight balls and arrange them close together on the baking sheet without touching. You should roll 40-45 meatballs.
- Bake them for 15 minutes. At the same time, combine 1-2 dashes of cayenne pepper, honey, and beef broth with the remaining 1/2 cup of apple butter. Beat them thoroughly.
- Take the meatballs out from the oven after 15 minutes. Place the sauce over the top to cover each meatball, then return to the oven for 5-7 minutes.
- Lightly shake the baking sheet to loosen meatballs when cooked thoroughly, then serve warm.

Nutrition Information

- Calories: 457 calories;
- Total Carbohydrate: 41.8 g
- Cholesterol: 120 mg
- Total Fat: 25.5 g
- Protein: 21.7 g
- Sodium: 1325 mg

217. Philly Cheese Steak Dip

"A simple to prepare hot dip that goes well with your snack table. It's hot, warm and perfect party foods. Also, delicious served cold. Serve with chopped baguette. Bake in two batches to keep it fresh and hot for your guests or bake all at once in a baking dish of 9x13-inch."
Serving: 24 | Prep: 25m | Ready in: 1h23m

Ingredients

- 1 lb. beef top sirloin steaks
- salt and freshly ground black pepper to taste
- 1 tbsp. olive oil
- 1 yellow onion, diced
- 1 tbsp. butter
- 1 red bell pepper
- 1 green bell pepper
- 1/2 cup pepperoncini peppers
- 7 pickled red peppers (such as Peppadew®)
- 3 jalapeno peppers
- 2 (8 oz.) packages cream cheese, softened
- 1/2 lb. provolone cheese
- 1/2 tsp. Worcestershire sauce
- 1 pinch cayenne pepper

Direction

- Cut the steak into thick pieces and then season generously with pepper and salt on each side.
- Over high heat, heat olive oil in a pan until it's smoking. Sear the steak slices for 3 to 4 minutes until the bottoms become brown. Turnover and decrease the heat to medium. Let to cook for 3 to 4 minutes more until juices are seen at the tops. Pour in a bowl to cool.
- Add butter, diced onion, and a big pinch of salt to meat juices in pan. Cook while stirring on medium heat for 5 to 7 minutes while scraping up any browned bits, until the onions begin to soften.
- Dice up pickled red peppers, red bell pepper, jalapenos, green bell pepper, and pepperoncini until you get 1 1/2 to 2 cups. Transfer to the onions and then cook while stirring for about 5 minutes until beginning to soften.
- Preheat an oven to 200 degrees C (400 degrees F).
- Cut the steak into small pieces. Transfer back into bowl with accumulated meat juices. Pour in cream cheese and onion-pepper mixture. Then grate in provolone cheese and save some for topping. Sprinkle with Worcestershire sauce and drizzle with cayenne pepper. Combine the dip well.
- Place half of the dip in a small baking dish and then use a fork to smooth the top. Put the baking dish over a sheet pan. Top with remaining provolone cheese. Reserve the remaining half to bake fresh later for the guests.
- Bake in the preheated oven for about 20 to 25 minutes until heated through and dip is bubbling. Broil for about 1 minute until the top turns brown. Repeat this with the other batch of dip.

Nutrition Information

- Calories: 143 calories;
- Total Carbohydrate: 3.3 g
- Cholesterol: 36 mg
- Total Fat: 11.2 g
- Protein: 7.3 g
- Sodium: 267 mg

218. Philly Cheesesteak Nachos

"This recipe is great any time you want a delicious snack!"
Serving: 4 | Prep: 10m | Ready in: 20m

Ingredients

- 1 tbsp. olive oil
- 1/2 large onion, diced
- 1/2 lb. shaved rib-eye, chopped
- 1 (18 oz.) package restaurant-style tortilla chips
- 1 (8 fl oz) jar processed cheese spread (such as Kraft® Cheez Whiz®)
- 2 fresh jalapeno peppers, sliced

Direction

- Over medium heat, heat olive oil in a skillet and then add onion. Cook while stirring for about 5 to 10 minutes until softened. Place in a bowl. Cook the rib-eye in the same skillet while stirring often for 5 to 10 minutes until it has browned and the juices have evaporated. Mix the onion back into skillet.
- Put a handful of tortilla chips onto each plate. Scoop the rib-eye and onion mixture on top of the chips. Add jalapeno slices and cheese spread on top.

Nutrition Information

- Calories: 884 calories;
- Total Carbohydrate: 89.9 g
- Cholesterol: 62 mg
- Total Fat: 49.9 g
- Protein: 23.1 g
- Sodium: 1464 mg

219. Pickled Pig's Feet I

"Pig's feet recipe."
Serving: 8

Ingredients

- 4 pig's feet
- 2 tbsps. salt
- 2 cups white wine vinegar
- 1 tbsp. whole cloves
- 2 tsps. whole black peppercorns
- 4 whole star anise pods
- 2 tbsps. pickling spice

Direction

- Wash feet thoroughly, using paper towels, pat it dry and put in a big saucepan. Pour in enough water to cover and mix in a tbsp. salt. Boil on high heat; lower the heat to low and let it simmer till meat separate from bones or for 4 to 5 hours.
- Take meat out of the bones and put in a shallow bowl or dish. Put aside. Drain saucepan, keeping 2 cups cooking liquid. Mix together pickling spices, star anise, peppercorns, cloves, vinegar, remaining salt and the reserved cooking liquid in the same saucepan. Let come to a boil and allow to boil for 35 minutes.
- Strain the liquid and reserve. On top of meat, put the reserved liquid. Place on the cover and chill. Refrigerate for a minimum of 10 hours prior to serving.

Nutrition Information

- Calories: 259 calories;
- Total Carbohydrate: 1.4 g
- Cholesterol: 101 mg
- Total Fat: 18 g
- Protein: 21.3 g
- Sodium: 1812 mg

220. Pizza Dip

"It's a great dip for any parties, serve with pita bread chips, crackers, or even a thin sliced baguette."
Serving: 8 | Prep: 10m | Ready in: 35m

Ingredients

- 1 (8 oz.) package cream cheese, softened
- 1 (14 oz.) can pizza sauce
- 1/4 lb. pepperoni sausage, diced
- 1 onion, chopped
- 1 (6 oz.) can black olives, chopped
- 2 cups shredded mozzarella cheese

Direction

- Set the oven to 200°C or 400°F and use nonstick cooking spray to coat a 9-in. pie pan.
- Spread onto the bottom of the pie pan with cream cheese; pour over with pizza sauce and spread it to make an even layer of sauce. Sprinkle with olives, onion and pepperoni. Put mozzarella cheese on top.
- Bake about 20-25 minutes at 200°C or 400°F.

Nutrition Information

- Calories: 305 calories;
- Total Carbohydrate: 8.6 g
- Cholesterol: 68 mg
- Total Fat: 24.5 g
- Protein: 12.6 g
- Sodium: 944 mg

221. Polish Pickles

"A festive-looking dish with white, green and red colors."
Serving: 25 | Prep: 20m | Ready in: 1h20m

Ingredients

- 1 (32 oz.) jar dill pickle spears, drained
- 2 (8 oz.) packages cream cheese, room temperature
- 2 (2.5 oz.) packages thin-sliced beef luncheon meat

Direction

- Remove the excess moisture from the pickles.
- On the 2 slices of lunch meat, spread about 1/4 inch thick of cream cheese, then wrap around a pickle with the meat. Repeat the process with the leftover ingredients.
- Let it chill in the fridge and cut it into rounds.

Nutrition Information

- Calories: 72 calories;
- Total Carbohydrate: 2 g
- Cholesterol: 21 mg
- Total Fat: 6.4 g
- Protein: 2 g
- Sodium: 538 mg

222. Puerto Rican Meat Patties

""The combination of seasonings with meat, wrapped up in wrappers then deep fried into deliciousness. I have to say, this is a genius recipe. I got it from my mother, who got it from her father. Now, you get to try it out too.""
Serving: 8 | Prep: 15m | Ready in: 45m

Ingredients

- 3 tbsps. olive oil
- 1 lb. ground beef
- 1 1/2 cups chopped fresh cilantro
- 1 onion, chopped
- 4 cloves garlic, minced
- 1 green bell pepper, chopped
- 1 (8 oz.) can tomato sauce
- 1 (16 oz.) package egg roll wrappers
- 2 quarts vegetable oil for frying

Direction

- Pour the olive oil into a big, sturdy sauté pan then heat it up at medium heat. Insert the bell pepper, onions and chopped garlic, sautéing until they soften. Insert the meat, cooking and stirring until they start browning. Get rid of the extra fat. Add cilantro and tomato sauce, stirring. Leave it simmering until the cilantro is wilted. Move it away from the heat and leave it cooling until it is easy to handle. Use an egg roll wrapper to start wrapping 2-3 tablespoonful of meat up into a triangular shape. Do the same thing with the rest of the ingredients. Pour in the vegetable oil into a deep frying pan or work then heat it up to 360°F (168°C). Insert the patties, frying until they become a nice golden brown. Move them on paper towel-lined plates. If desired, serve together with guacamole and salsa.

Nutrition Information

- Calories: 522 calories;
- Total Carbohydrate: 36.7 g
- Cholesterol: 40 mg
- Total Fat: 34.7 g
- Protein: 15.9 g
- Sodium: 505 mg

223. Reuben Dip

"A party favorite!"
Serving: 9 | Prep: 5m | Ready in: 30m

Ingredients

- 1/2 cup mayonnaise
- 1/2 cup Thousand Island dressing
- 16 oz. sauerkraut, rinsed and squeezed dry
- 8 oz. shredded corned beef
- 16 oz. shredded Swiss cheese

Direction

- Preheat an oven to 175°C/350°F.
- Mix dressing and mayonnaise in small bowl.
- In 9x13-in. baking dish, spread sauerkraut. Layer mayonnaise-dressing mixture, Swiss cheese and corned beef over sauerkraut.
- Bake it for 20-25 minutes.

Nutrition Information

- Calories: 393 calories;
- Total Carbohydrate: 7.3 g

- Cholesterol: 77 mg
- Total Fat: 31.7 g
- Protein: 20.9 g
- Sodium: 830 mg

224. Reunion Meatballs

"These saucy, flavorful meatballs are ideal for parties, picnics, snack time, and family reunions. Both kids and adults will surely love them."
Serving: 20 | Prep: 15m | Ready in: 25m

Ingredients

- 2 eggs
- 1 envelope onion soup mix
- 1/2 cup seasoned bread crumbs
- 2 tbsps. chopped fresh parsley
- 1 1/2 lbs. lean ground beef
- 1 (16 oz.) can whole berry cranberry sauce
- 3/4 cup ketchup
- 1/2 cup beef broth
- 3 tbsps. brown sugar
- 3 tbsps. finely chopped onion
- 2 tsps. cider vinegar

Direction

- In a large bowl, mix together soup mix, eggs, parsley, and bread crumbs. Crumble beef into the mixture, and mix well; form 1-inch balls from the mixture.
- In a microwave-safe plate, place 12 to 14 beef balls, then cover with waxed paper. Place in the microwave and heat for 3 to 4 minutes on high power, or until they're no longer pink in color. Transfer meatballs to paper towels to drain excess oil. Repeat the procedure with the rest of the meatballs.
- In a microwave-safe dish, mix together cranberry sauce, beef broth, brown sugar, ketchup, vinegar, and onion. Put waxed paper on top and cook in the microwave for 3 to 4 minutes on high power. Serve meatballs with sauce.

Nutrition Information

- Calories: 137 calories;
- Total Carbohydrate: 15.7 g
- Cholesterol: 41 mg
- Total Fat: 4.9 g
- Protein: 7.9 g
- Sodium: 330 mg

225. Ritz Cheesy Meatballs

"With spaghetti sauce, meatballs, mozzarella, and Ritz crackers, you can easily create these tasty pizzas."
Serving: 12 | Prep: 15m | Ready in: 25m

Ingredients

- 12 frozen fully cooked bite-size meatballs
- 3 thin slices mozzarella cheese (0.7 oz. each)
- 24 RITZ Crackers
- 1/4 cup spaghetti sauce, warmed
- 1 tsp. chopped fresh parsley

Direction

- On a microwaveable dish, put one layer of meatballs. Put in the microwave and microwave on high until cooked through, about 45 seconds to 1 minute. Let it cool down slowly.
- In the meantime, slice each cheese slice into 8 slices and put on crackers. Put 1/4 tsp. spaghetti of sauce on top of each.
- Slice meatballs into two; put the meatball halves on the crackers with the cut sides turning down. Put parsley and the rest of the spaghetti sauce on top.

Nutrition Information

- Calories: 115 calories;
- Total Carbohydrate: 6.7 g
- Cholesterol: 28 mg
- Total Fat: 6.5 g
- Protein: 6.9 g
- Sodium: 154 mg

226. Ritz Steakhouse Bites

""Experience the famous classic New York City Steakhouse flavor in this recipe.""
Serving: 6 | Prep: 15m | Ready in: 30m

Ingredients

- Creamed Spinach:
- 2 tsps. olive oil
- 1 (6 oz.) package baby spinach leaves
- 1 tbsp. butter
- 1 tbsp. minced shallots
- 1/2 tsp. nutmeg
- 2 tbsps. heavy cream
- 1/8 tsp. salt
- Pinch of black pepper
- Béarnaise Sauce:
- 1 tbsp. butter
- 2 tbsps. minced shallots
- 1 tbsp. white wine vinegar
- 1 egg yolk
- 1 tbsp. lemon juice
- 1/2 cup melted butter
- 18 RITZ Crackers
- 3 oz. thinly sliced, cooked beef tenderloin, but into bite-sized pieces

Direction

- In a sauté pan, heat olive oil on medium fire. Mix in spinach then place cover, let it steam for 60 seconds. Take off cover then stir spinach until it becomes wilted. Discard spinach then use paper towels to dry and then slice. In the same pan, dissolve butter on medium fire. Sauté shallots for 60 seconds. Mix nutmeg and heavy cream until combined. Mix in sliced spinach until combined. When spinach becomes creamy, take off the heat. Season with pepper and salt. Put aside.
- In another sauté pan, dissolve one tbsp. butter then add white wine vinegar and shallots. For 60 seconds, cook until fluid evaporates. Take out of the pan, put aside, and let it cool.
- In a blender, blend lemon juice and egg yolk then gently blend half a cup of melted butter until mixture becomes creamy and smooth. Drizzle on shallots mixture. Mix sliced fresh tarragon while stirring.
- Now create bites. On top of a RITZ cracker, put 1-1/2 tsp. of creamed spinach. On top of it, place a slice of steak then sprinkle with one and half tsp. béarnaise sauce.

Nutrition Information

- Calories: 301 calories;
- Total Carbohydrate: 8.6 g
- Cholesterol: 104 mg
- Total Fat: 27.6 g
- Protein: 6.2 g
- Sodium: 301 mg

227. Ritz White Pizza Meatball Dip, Created By Lombardi's Pizza

""Inspired by New York City's famous Lombardi's Pizza, this velvety and cheese-filled white pizza meatball is easy to prepare and will be one of your essentials during gatherings.""
Serving: 28 | Prep: 15m | Ready in: 45m

Ingredients

- 1 (8 oz.) package cream cheese, softened
- 1/2 cup mayonnaise
- 2 tbsps. grated Parmesan cheese
- 1 tsp. dried oregano
- 1 cup shredded whole milk mozzarella, divided
- 8 oz. homemade or prepared pre-cooked meatballs, diced
- 3 plum tomatoes, seeded and diced
- 3 pitted black olives, diced
- 3 pitted green olives, diced
- RITZ Crackers for dipping

Direction

- Heat the oven to 350°F.

- Mix in oregano, grated parmesan, mayonnaise and cream cheese.
- Keep one tbsp. of mozzarella cheese. Mix meatballs, tomatoes, olives and the rest of the mozzarella cheese.
- Ladle mixture in one and half quart baking dish then sprinkle the leftover mozzarella cheese on top.
- Let it bake without a cover for 25-30 minutes.
- Serve Ritz crackers with the dip then serve.

Nutrition Information

- Calories: 168 calories;
- Total Carbohydrate: 11.3 g
- Cholesterol: 20 mg
- Total Fat: 11.8 g
- Protein: 4.2 g
- Sodium: 236 mg

228. Roast Beef Dip

"A recipe that can be used as spread for sandwich. Present it chilled and pair with toasted on bread with Swiss cheese or crackers. You can pack the guacamole into a gelatin mold, then rotate and present with the look of pate. Make this recipe 24 hours in advance for best results and to let the flavors enhanced well."

Serving: 12 | Prep: 5m | Ready in: 2h5m

Ingredients

- 1 (13 oz.) can roast beef, drained
- 1 oz. dry onion soup mix
- 1 (8 oz.) package cream cheese, softened
- 1 (8 oz.) container sour cream

Direction

- In a medium-size mixing bowl, put the roast beef. Stir in the sour cream, cream cheese and soup mix. Place inside the refrigerator, covered until serving time.

Nutrition Information

- Calories: 113 calories;
- Total Carbohydrate: 2.8 g
- Cholesterol: 29 mg
- Total Fat: 10.5 g
- Protein: 2.2 g
- Sodium: 253 mg

229. Rouladen Rats

"A delicious German appetizer."

Serving: 6 | Prep: 10m | Ready in: 55m

Ingredients

- 1 1/2 lbs. top round steak
- 1 onion, chopped
- 1 pinch salt
- 1 pinch ground black pepper
- 2 tsps. prepared mustard
- 6 leaves cabbage
- 1 tbsp. butter
- 2 cups water

Direction

- Lay meat, and add pepper and salt to season. Scatter a layer of mustard on top of meat, and a chopped onion layer. In cabbage leaf, roll meat up. Use a toothpick or thread to keep roll together.
- In a medium saucepan, melt margarine or butter, let cabbage rolls fry over medium heat till brown. Put 2 cups of water, and allow to simmer for 35 to 40 minutes.

Nutrition Information

- Calories: 228 calories;
- Total Carbohydrate: 2.7 g
- Cholesterol: 74 mg
- Total Fat: 12.6 g
- Protein: 24.8 g
- Sodium: 74 mg

230. Runzas

"Baked rolls stiffed with onions, cabbage, and beef."
Serving: 16 | Prep: 45m | Ready in: 1h50m

Ingredients

- 4 cups ground beef
- 1 onion, chopped
- 4 cups shredded cabbage
- 1 tsp. salt, or to taste
- 2 cups warm water (100 to 110 degrees F/40 to 45 degrees C)
- 1/3 cup butter, melted
- 2/3 cup instant dry milk powder
- 1/4 cup white sugar
- 1 1/2 tsps. salt
- 1 tsp. active dry yeast
- 1 egg, beaten
- 4 cups all-purpose flour

Direction

- Place a large skillet over medium-high heat. Stir and cook onion and ground beef in the hot skillet until the meat crumbles, is not pink anymore, and browned evenly. Drain excess grease out of the skillet. Stir cabbage in and add 1 tsp. of salt to season. Stir and cook for another 20 minutes, or until the cabbage is tender. Set aside and allow the mixture to cool.
- In a large bowl, mix butter with warm water. In a separate bowl, combine yeast, 1 1/2 tsps. of salt, sugar, and dry milk powder, then stir into the bowl with the butter mixture. Add egg. Stir in 1/2 cup of flour at a time, gradually, until the dough smoothens.
- Lightly dust a work surface with flour and roll out the dough to 1/4-inch thick. Cut 4-inch squares out of the dough. Fill each square with the beef mixture. Pinch the dough's corners together at the top to seal. Transfer, seam side down, to a baking sheet. Repeat process with the rest of the dough and filling. Use a damp cloth to cover the rolls and wait for 20 minutes, or until the dough has risen.
- Preheat oven to 190°C/375°F.
- Bake for 20 minutes, or until golden brown.

Nutrition Information

- Calories: 243 calories;
- Total Carbohydrate: 31.3 g
- Cholesterol: 41 mg
- Total Fat: 8 g
- Protein: 10.9 g
- Sodium: 444 mg

231. Sambousa

"Ground lamb can replace ground beef to add delicious flavor."
Serving: 10

Ingredients

- 1 lb. lean ground beef
- 1/2 carrot, minced
- 1/2 onion, minced
- 1 clove garlic, minced
- 1 tsp. tomato paste
- 1 green onion, chopped
- 1 pinch seasoning salt
- 1 green chile peppers, diced (optional)
- 1 (16 oz.) package egg roll wrappers, cut in half into rectangles
- 1 tbsp. all-purpose flour
- 1 tbsp. water
- 2 cups vegetable oil

Direction

- Brown the meat in a large skillet. Take the meat out from the skillet.
- Sauté green onion, carrot, garlic, and onion in the same skillet used to brown the meat. Put in the seasoning salt and tomato paste when the vegetables become tender. Add in the browned meat and stir.
- Blend the flour with water in a small bowl until forming a watery paste. In the front part of one of the strips, arrange 1 tsp. full of the meat mixture. Beginning from the right front corner, fold over to the left. You've started the triangle shape. Carry on back and forth to

shape into a triangle until there is no wrapper left. Use the water and the flour mixture to seal the wrappers. Repeat the process until there are no ingredients left.
- Taste with oil and fry the triangular packages until they become crisp. Then serve.

Nutrition Information

- Calories: 649 calories;
- Total Carbohydrate: 28.1 g
- Cholesterol: 38 mg
- Total Fat: 54.1 g
- Protein: 12.8 g
- Sodium: 318 mg

232. Sandie's Seven-layer Bean Dip

"A fantastic dish!"
Serving: 24 | Prep: 15m | Ready in: 50m

Ingredients

- 1 (16 oz.) container sour cream
- 1 (8 oz.) package cream cheese, softened
- 1 (1 oz.) package taco seasoning mix
- 1 lb. ground beef
- 1 tsp. ground cumin
- 1 tsp. dried oregano
- 1 tsp. garlic powder
- 1 tsp. salt
- ground black pepper to taste
- 1 (30 oz.) can refried beans
- 1 (16 oz.) jar salsa
- 1 (16 oz.) jar salsa con queso
- 2 cups shredded Mexican cheese blend
- 1 plum tomato, chopped
- 1 (6 oz.) can sliced black olives, drained
- 3 green onions, chopped

Direction

- Preheat an oven to 175°C/350°F.
- Mix taco seasoning mix, cream cheese and sour cream in a bowl.
- Heat a big skillet on medium high heat; mix and cook beef, black pepper, salt, garlic powder, oregano and cumin in the hot skillet for 5-7 minutes till crumbly and browned. Drain; discard grease.
- Spread refried beans in the bottom of a 9x13-inch baking dish. Put a layer of ground beef mixture on refried beans, pressing beef lightly into beans. Put sour cream mixture on top.
- Mix salsa con queso and salsa in a bowl; put over the sour cream mixture layer. In this order, spread Mexican cheese blend, the tomato, the olives then green onions over the sour cream mixture layer.
- In the preheated oven, bake for 30 minutes till bubbly and heated through.

Nutrition Information

- Calories: 229 calories;
- Total Carbohydrate: 12.7 g
- Cholesterol: 45 mg
- Total Fat: 16.2 g
- Protein: 9.8 g
- Sodium: 749 mg

233. Sausage Applesauce Appetizer

"This is absolutely one of the most delicious appetizer."
Serving: 8 | Prep: 10m | Ready in: 55m

Ingredients

- 2 lbs. Italian sausage
- 3/4 cup packed brown sugar
- 1 cup chunky applesauce
- 1 onion, chopped

Direction

- Set the oven to 165°C or 325°F.
- Fry sausage in a big skillet until browned. Drain well, then cut the sausage into bite-sized pieces.

- Mix together onion, applesauce, brown sugar and sausage in a small casserole dish.
- Bake at 165°C or 325°F, about 45 minutes. Serve together with toothpicks for easy nibbling.

Nutrition Information

- Calories: 501 calories;
- Total Carbohydrate: 28.6 g
- Cholesterol: 86 mg
- Total Fat: 35.6 g
- Protein: 16.4 g
- Sodium: 837 mg

234. Sloppy Jo-chos

""I was trying to find a way to use up the leftover sloppy joes. In the end, I found a good and hearty recipe which is perfect for football season.""
Serving: 10 | Prep: 10m | Ready in: 20m

Ingredients

- 1 lb. ground beef
- 1 (15 oz.) can sloppy joe sauce
- 1 (15 oz.) jar nacho cheese dip
- 1 (13.5 oz.) package corn tortilla chips

Direction

- Place a skillet on medium heat, put in the ground beef. Cook while stirring to crumble till no longer pink. Strain fat and blend the sloppy joe sauce into the beef. Melt the nacho cheese dip with a microwave.
- Put the tortilla chips in pile onto a serving platter. Place the ground beef over them; top with the melted cheese dip. Serve immediately.

Nutrition Information

- Calories: 357 calories;
- Total Carbohydrate: 34.9 g
- Cholesterol: 31 mg
- Total Fat: 18.9 g
- Protein: 11.7 g
- Sodium: 782 mg

235. Slow Cooker Reuben Dip

"An easy and creamy hot dip."
Serving: 12 | Prep: 4m | Ready in: 49m

Ingredients

- 1 (16 oz.) jar sauerkraut, drained
- 1 (8 oz.) package cream cheese, softened
- 2 cups shredded Swiss cheese
- 2 cups shredded cooked corned beef
- 1/4 cup thousand island dressing

Direction

- Mix thousand island dressing, corned beef, Swiss cheese, cream cheese and sauerkraut in slow cooker. Cover; cook for 45 minutes on high if you're hungry/low if you're not till cheese melts and it's hot. Occasionally mix while cooking. Use crackers or cocktail rye to serve

Nutrition Information

- Calories: 298 calories;
- Total Carbohydrate: 5.5 g
- Cholesterol: 76 mg
- Total Fat: 22.9 g
- Protein: 17.9 g
- Sodium: 636 mg

236. Spam Musubi

""Spam Musubi is a famous snack in Hawaii. I acquired this one from a friend in Hawaii when I was stationed there.""
Serving: 10 | Prep: 25m | Ready in: 5h25m

Ingredients

- 2 cups uncooked short-grain white rice

- 2 cups water
- 6 tbsps. rice vinegar
- 1/4 cup soy sauce
- 1/4 cup oyster sauce
- 1/2 cup white sugar
- 1 (12 oz.) container fully cooked luncheon meat (e.g. Spam)
- 5 sheets sushi nori (dry seaweed)
- 2 tbsps. vegetable oil

Direction

- Soak rice that is not cooked for 4 hours; stain and wash.
- Place 2 cups water in a saucepan and make it boil. Stir in rice. Lower heat, cover, and simmer for 20 minutes. Mix in rice vinegar then reserve to cool.
- Mix sugar, oyster sauce, and soy sauce in another bowl until the sugar is fully melted. Cut luncheon meat into 10 slices, lengthwise, or to a thickness that you want, then marinate in the sauce for 5 minutes.
- Add oil in a big skillet set on medium-high heat. Then cook slices for 2 minutes each side, or until browned lightly. Slice nori sheets in half then place on a flat work surface. Put a slice of luncheon meat on top, then discard press. Cover nori around the rice mold, securing edges with a bit of water. (You may also form the rice using your hand in the shape of meat slices, 1-inch thick. You may eat musubi chilled or warm.

Nutrition Information

- Calories: 276 calories;
- Total Carbohydrate: 34.7 g
- Cholesterol: 24 mg
- Total Fat: 12 g
- Protein: 6.8 g
- Sodium: 866 mg

237. Spiced Beef On Pita Triangles With Fresh Mango Salsa

"The meat mixture and pita chips can be made in advance for a couple of days."
Serving: 32

Ingredients

- 4 (7-inch) pita breads, split into 2 thin rounds and quartered
- 1 1/2 tsps. ground cumin
- 1 1/2 tsps. ground ginger
- 1/2 tsp. ground cinnamon
- 1/4 tsp. ground cloves
- 1 1/2 lbs. lean ground beef (or ground lamb or turkey)
- 1 large red onion, cut into small dice
- 1 pinch Salt and freshly ground pepper
- 1 (9 oz.) jar Major Grey Chutney
- 1 medium mango, cut into small dice
- 2 tbsps. chopped fresh cilantro

Direction

- Set the oven to 325°. Place the oven rack in the middle position and put on rack with pita triangles. Bake for 10 minutes, until turn golden brown. (Can be stored for a maximum of 7 days in an airtight tin.)
- In a small bowl, combine together cloves, cinnamon, ginger and cumin, then put 1/4 tsp. spice mix in the bowl while sprinkle the leftover over beef. Mix to combine.
- Heat a big skillet (12" in size) on moderately high heat. Put in meat and all but 1/3 cup of onion, then sauté pepper, salt and seasoning while breaking the meat into finely ground texture by stirring often. Stir for 9 minutes, until liquid has evaporated and meat is cooked through. Fold in 1/2 cup chutney and cook for 1 more minute to let flavors blend. (Chill in a covered container for maximum of 5 days.)
- When ready to serve, rewarm beef and create the salsa: Stir spice mix, onion, leftover chutney, cilantro and mango together. On each pita triangle, place a portion of meat and pour

salsa over top to serve. Or, set out salsa, pita chips and meat to allow guests to make their own.

Nutrition Information

- Calories: 96 calories;
- Total Carbohydrate: 9.9 g
- Cholesterol: 15 mg
- Total Fat: 4 g
- Protein: 5.3 g
- Sodium: 139 mg

238. Spicy Beefstick

"A fun and spicy recipe."
Serving: 15 | Prep: 15m | Ready in: 6h15m

Ingredients

- 4 lbs. ground beef
- 1 lb. spicy pork sausage
- 2 1/2 tsps. mustard seed
- 2 1/2 tsps. liquid smoke flavoring
- 1 tbsp. Worcestershire sauce
- 1 tbsp. garlic powder
- 5 tbsps. sugar-based curing mixture (such as Morton® Tender Quick®)
- 1 tbsp. cracked black pepper
- 1 tbsp. caraway seed (optional)
- 2 tsps. cayenne pepper
- 2 tsps. paprika
- 2 tsps. chili powder
- 2 tsps. red pepper flakes

Direction

- Mix red pepper flakes, chili powder, paprika, cayenne pepper, caraway seed, black pepper, curing salt, garlic powder, Worcestershire sauce, liquid smoke, mustard seed, pork sausage and ground beef in big bowl; cover. Refrigerate overnight.
- Knead meat for 5 minutes for the following 3 days; put in fridge. Knead then shape to 6 even logs on 4th day; use aluminum foil to wrap each log. Poke several holes in foil.
- Preheat an oven to 95°C/200°F; put logs on broiler pan to get grease. In preheated oven, bake for 6 hours. Turn oven off; after baking, leave logs in for 3 hours. Refrigerate till chilled; cut then serve.

Nutrition Information

- Calories: 310 calories;
- Total Carbohydrate: 2.3 g
- Cholesterol: 91 mg
- Total Fat: 21.9 g
- Protein: 24.9 g
- Sodium: 2681 mg

239. Spicy Melted Cheese Dip

"Serve this cheesy and spicy dip with tortilla chips on holidays."
Serving: 48 | Prep: 5m | Ready in: 20m

Ingredients

- 1/2 lb. ground beef
- 1/2 lb. ground pork sausage
- 2 lbs. processed cheese food, cubed
- 1 (10 oz.) can diced tomatoes with green chile peppers, with liquid

Direction

- In a large deep skillet, arrange ground pork sausage and ground beef. Cook to brown evenly over medium high heat.
- Let the processed cheese food melt over low heat in a medium saucepan. Meanwhile, add green chilie peppers and diced tomatoes, stir while processed cheese food is melting.
- Drain ground sausage and ground beef. Add into the processed cheese food mixture and mix. Place into a medium dish. Serve warm.

Nutrition Information

- Calories: 98 calories;

- Total Carbohydrate: 1.8 g
- Cholesterol: 19 mg
- Total Fat: 7.8 g
- Protein: 5.1 g
- Sodium: 241 mg

240. Steak And Cheese Egg Rolls

"Gooey cheese and steak in a fried egg roll."
Serving: 16 | Prep: 30m | Ready in: 42m

Ingredients

- 2 lbs. shaved steak
- 6 slices American cheese
- 1 green bell pepper, chopped
- 1 red bell pepper, chopped
- 1 yellow bell pepper, chopped
- salt and ground black pepper to taste
- 1 (16 oz.) package egg roll wrappers
- 2 cups vegetable oil for frying

Direction

- In a big skillet over moderate heat, cook and mix 1/2 of shaved steak for 3 to 5 minutes till browned. Turn onto a plate. Redo with the rest of the steak. Let the juices from steak drain; slice into small portions.
- In a bowl, mix yellow bell pepper, red bell pepper, green bell pepper, American cheese and steak. Add pepper and salt to season.
- On a flat area, spread an egg roll wrapper in form of a diamond. Put a big spoonful of the steak mixture in the middle. Fold the base corner and opposite sides on top of steak mixture; roll up the wrapper heading to the top corner. Redo with the rest of the steak mixture and egg roll wrappers.
- In a big saucepan or deep-fryer, heat the oil. In hot oil, put several egg rolls, seam-side facing down. Fry for 2 to 3 minutes, flipping from time to time, till golden brown. Redo with the rest of rolls.

Nutrition Information

- Calories: 233 calories;
- Total Carbohydrate: 17.2 g
- Cholesterol: 43 mg
- Total Fat: 10.4 g
- Protein: 16.6 g
- Sodium: 344 mg

241. Steak Tartare (thanks To Fredy)

"This is a world-famous recipe."
Serving: 4 | Prep: 15m | Ready in: 15m

Ingredients

- 2 tsps. olive oil
- 2 tbsps. ketchup
- 1 1/2 tbsps. Worcestershire sauce
- 1 tbsp. Dijon mustard
- 2 dashes hot pepper sauce (such as Tabasco®), or more to taste
- 1/4 tsp. curry powder, or to taste
- 1 pinch salt
- 1 pinch ground black pepper
- 4 anchovy fillets
- 2 tbsps. finely chopped onion
- 1 tbsp. finely chopped gherkin
- 1/2 tbsp. capers, roughly chopped
- 10 1/2 oz. beef filet, finely chopped by hand
- 2 egg yolks
- 1/4 cup beer

Direction

- In a serving bowl, put olive oil. Then add ground pepper, salt, curry powder, hot pepper sauce, Dijon mustard, Worcestershire sauce, and ketchup. Mix thoroughly.
- Use 2 forks to crush anchovy fillets on a dish until they are separated finely. Add capers, gherkin, and onion; mix well before scraping into the bowl with the ketchup mixture. Put in the chopped beef; thoroughly mix. Stir in beer and egg yolks.

Nutrition Information

- Calories: 293 calories;
- Total Carbohydrate: 5.5 g
- Cholesterol: 159 mg
- Total Fat: 22.2 g
- Protein: 16 g
- Sodium: 501 mg

242. Stuffed Filet Mignon Bites

"Fans at football games love this quick and easy grilled filet mignon wrapped in bacon with jalapeño cream cheese filling."

Serving: 10 | Prep: 15m | Ready in: 2h23m

Ingredients

- 4 (6 oz.) filet mignon steaks
- 1 (16 oz.) bottle Italian dressing
- 1 (8 oz.) package cream cheese
- 1/4 cup minced jalapeno pepper
- 20 slices thinly sliced bacon

Direction

- Cut steaks into half-inch strips. Beat the steak strips to about 1/2 of their initial thickness; put in a bowl. Pour in Italian dressing and let it marinate for a minimum of two hours.
- In a bowl, combine jalapeño pepper and cream cheese; let it stand.
- Preheat the outdoor grill on high heat. Grease the grate lightly.
- Take the strips out of the marinade and place them on a flat work surface. Slather a tsp. of jalapeño-cheese mixture on every strip. Form a ball by folding the meat around the mixture; use a slice of bacon to wrap each ball. Seal bacon wraps with metal skewers or soaked toothpicks.
- Cook balls on preheated grill for 4 minutes on each side until they are not pink.

Nutrition Information

- Calories: 393 calories;
- Total Carbohydrate: 5.6 g
- Cholesterol: 79 mg
- Total Fat: 32.1 g
- Protein: 20.1 g
- Sodium: 1250 mg

243. Swedish Meatballs III

""If you are searching for a great Swedish meatball recipe, here is the right one! Saltine crackers can be used instead of Swedish crisp bread.""

Serving: 6 | Prep: 30m | Ready in: 1h10m

Ingredients

- 1 tbsp. butter
- 1 onion, finely diced
- 1/2 cup crushed saltine crackers
- 1 1/2 lbs. ground beef
- 1 egg
- 1/4 tsp. ground nutmeg
- 1 pinch ground allspice
- 1/4 tsp. minced garlic
- 1 packet dry white sauce mix
- 4 tbsps. chopped fresh dill
- 1 tsp. sage
- 2 tbsps. all-purpose flour
- 1/4 cup whipping cream

Direction

- Configure oven to 350 deg F (175 deg C) for preheating.
- In a medium frying pan placed over medium heat, melt the butter. Stir in onion and cook for about 5 minutes, until it becomes soft, stirring often. Move to a large bowl. Blend allspice, nutmeg, egg, ground beef, and cracker crumbs with the onion until well combined.
- Cut into meatballs of 4 centimeters (1/2 inch), transfer to a glass baking dish, sprinkle with minced garlic and cover with a foil.
- Bake in oven until it is cooked through, or for 15 minutes. As it cooks, prepare white sauce using the instructions on the packet. Beat in whipping cream, flour, sage and dill. Switch

off the oven, and uncover the meatballs. Spread sauce over meatballs, and place in heated oven for 10 minutes.

Nutrition Information

- Calories: 370 calories;
- Total Carbohydrate: 13 g
- Cholesterol: 126 mg
- Total Fat: 24.6 g
- Protein: 23.6 g
- Sodium: 429 mg

244. Sweet And Sour Meatballs (suan Tien Niu Jou Po Lo La Tzu)

"This family favorite dish can be a wonderful veggie sauce for vegans."

Serving: 6 | Prep: 30m | Ready in: 1h

Ingredients

- 1 lb. ground beef
- 1 egg
- 1 tbsp. cornstarch
- 1 tsp. salt
- 4 tbsps. diced onion
- 1 pinch ground black pepper
- 1 tbsp. vegetable oil
- 1 cup pineapple juice
- 3 tbsps. cornstarch
- 1 tbsp. soy sauce
- 3 tbsps. distilled white vinegar
- 6 tbsps. water
- 1/2 cup granulated sugar
- 4 slices fresh pineapple, cut into pieces
- 1 large green bell pepper, cut into thin strips
- 1/4 carrot, thinly sliced
- 1/3 onion, cut into wedges and separated

Direction

- Blend pepper, diced onion, salt, cornstarch, egg, and the ground beef in a mixing bowl. Shape into about twenty 1-inch balls.
- Brown the meatballs in a large skillet on medium heat; drain the fat and put aside.
- In a large saucepan, heat the oil on low. Add in the pineapple juice and bring to a simmer for a few minutes.
- Blend water, vinegar, soy sauce, and 3 tbsps. of cornstarch in a small bowl. Stir the mixture until smooth and place it into the pineapple juice. Add in the sugar, bring to a simmer and constantly stir until thick.
- Place the onion, carrot, green pepper, pineapple pieces, and meatballs into the sauce mixture. Heat through.

Nutrition Information

- Calories: 341 calories;
- Total Carbohydrate: 37.5 g
- Cholesterol: 77 mg
- Total Fat: 15.1 g
- Protein: 14.6 g
- Sodium: 599 mg

245. Sweet And Sour Meatballs From Heinz

"This meatball recipe full of passion is a crowd-pleaser."

Serving: 8 | Prep: 10m | Ready in: 50m

Ingredients

- 1 lb. lean ground beef
- 1 cup soft, fresh breadcrumbs
- 1 egg, beaten
- 2 tbsps. milk
- 2 tbsps. onion, chopped
- 1 clove garlic, minced
- 1 tsp. salt
- 1/2 tsp. pepper
- 2/3 cup Heinz® Chili Sauce
- 2/3 cup red currant jelly

Direction

- Set an oven to 180°C (350°F) and start preheating. Combine gently the pepper, salt, garlic, onion, milk, egg, breadcrumbs, and beef until blended evenly. Shape into forty bite-sized meatballs.

- On a foil-lined, rimmed baking sheet, arrange the meatballs; bake until cooked thoroughly, or for 20 minutes.
- In a saucepan, blend the jelly and chili sauce on medium heat. Cook and stir for 5 minutes until the jelly is dissolved.
- Drop the cooked meatballs into the sauce; turn down the heat to medium-low and bring to a simmer for 10 minutes. Yields eight servings.

Nutrition Information

- Calories: 234 calories;
- Total Carbohydrate: 28.6 g
- Cholesterol: 61 mg
- Total Fat: 7.8 g
- Protein: 12.2 g
- Sodium: 680 mg

246. Taco Nachos

"My own formula for a kid-friendly nachos."
Serving: 6 | Prep: 15m | Ready in: 25m

Ingredients

- 1 lb. ground beef
- 1 (1 oz.) package taco seasoning mix
- 3/4 cup water
- 3/4 lb. processed cheese, cubed
- 1 tbsp. milk
- 1 (12 oz.) package tortilla chips
- 1 (16 oz.) can refried beans
- 1/2 cup chopped fresh tomato
- 1/3 cup chopped green onions

Direction

- Place a large, deep frying pan on medium-high heat; cook ground beef in till evenly browned. Strain; stir in water and taco seasoning mix. Keep cooking for 5 minutes. Take away from the heat.
- In a small microwave-safe bowl, put milk and processed cheese. Heat in the microwave on high for 1-2 minutes till melted. Stir till well blended and smooth.
- Put tortilla chips onto a large, microwave-safe dish. Sprinkle refried beans over. Pour the beef and the cheese mixtures on top.
- Microwave on high till the cheese is melted into the beef, around 2 minutes. Garnish with green onions and tomato. Serve warm.

Nutrition Information

- Calories: 788 calories;
- Total Carbohydrate: 57.1 g
- Cholesterol: 116 mg
- Total Fat: 48.5 g
- Protein: 31.8 g
- Sodium: 1576 mg

247. Tenderloin Watercress Hors D'oeuvres

"This is an easy and impressive hors d'oeuvre that can be served cold or hot."
Serving: 8 | Prep: 25m | Ready in: 25m

Ingredients

- 1 cup sour cream
- 1 cup mayonnaise
- 1 bunch watercress, divided
- 1/2 tsp. garlic salt
- 1/2 tsp. ground black pepper
- 1 lb. thinly sliced deli roast beef
- 2 French baguettes, thinly sliced

Direction

- In a food processor, combine pepper, garlic salt, 1 cup of watercress, mayonnaise, and sour cream, then pulse until blended well.
- Cut the slices of roast beef in half and loosely roll.
- Arrange slices of the baguette onto serving platters. Place one roast beef roll onto each

baguette slice and drop in 1 teaspoonful of sour cream mixture on top of roast beef. Garnish with a watercress sprig.

Nutrition Information

- Calories: 570 calories;
- Total Carbohydrate: 51 g
- Cholesterol: 50 mg
- Total Fat: 31.2 g
- Protein: 22.7 g
- Sodium: 1413 mg

248. The Best Taco Dip

"This spicy appetizer reheats well."
Serving: 6 | Prep: 15m | Ready in: 45m

Ingredients

- 1 lb. ground beef
- 1 (16 oz.) can refried beans
- 1/2 cup hot taco sauce
- 1 tbsp. chili powder
- 1 tsp. ground cumin
- 1 (16 oz.) container sour cream
- 3/4 cup chopped onion
- 3/4 cup chopped tomatoes
- 3/4 cup black olives, chopped
- 3/4 cup sliced jalapeno peppers

Direction

- Preheat an oven to 175°C/350°F.
- Brown beef in big skillet on medium heat; drain well. Mix cumin, chili powder, taco sauce and beans in; heat till warm.
- Spread bean and meat mixture in 9x13-in. casserole then spread sour cream on bean and beef mixture. Sprinkle peppers, olives, tomatoes and onions. Put cheese on top.
- Bake for 30 minutes at 175°C/350°F. Serve warm.

Nutrition Information

- Calories: 415 calories;
- Total Carbohydrate: 21.6 g
- Cholesterol: 85 mg
- Total Fat: 28.3 g
- Protein: 19.6 g
- Sodium: 811 mg

249. Ultimate Cheese Ball

"This easy cheese ball is great to serve with buttery round crackers that is ideal for any occasion."
Serving: 48 | Prep: 10m | Ready in: 2h10m

Ingredients

- 3 (8 oz.) packages cream cheese, softened
- 1 bunch green onions, finely chopped
- 1 (8 oz.) jar dried beef, chopped
- 1 cup chopped pecans

Direction

- Combine together dried beef, green onions and cream cheese in a moderate sized bowl, then shape the mixture into a ball. Sprinkle with pecans and chill in the fridge for about 2 hours before serving.

Nutrition Information

- Calories: 75 calories;
- Total Carbohydrate: 1.2 g
- Cholesterol: 19 mg
- Total Fat: 6.8 g
- Protein: 2.8 g
- Sodium: 172 mg

250. Veggie Nacho Salad

""This one needs many ingredients but it's worth it and even better with homemade guac.""
Serving: 4 | Prep: 15m | Ready in: 25m

Ingredients

- 1 (10 oz.) bag tortilla chips, or to taste

- 1/2 cup shredded Mexican cheese blend
- 1 tsp. vegetable oil, or as needed
- 1 (12 oz.) can corned beef
- 2 cups shredded lettuce
- 1 1/2 cups shredded purple cabbage
- 1 tomato, diced
- 1/4 cup diced onion (optional)
- 1/2 cup guacamole
- 1 tbsp. sour cream, or to taste
- 1 tbsp. chopped green onions, or to taste
- 1 pinch seasoned salt, or to taste

Direction

- Prepare the oven by preheating to 350°F (175°C). Put tortilla chips on a baking sheet then spread and dust with shredded cheese over chips.
- Place in the preheated oven and bake for about 7 minutes until cheese has melted.
- In the meantime, put oil in a frying pan and heat over medium heat. Put in corned beef and cook for about 5 minutes until heated through.
- Top chips layered with corned beef, lettuce, cabbage, tomato, and onion. Add green onions, sour cream, and guacamole. Dust seasoned salt on top. Toss lightly when at the table.

Nutrition Information

- Calories: 697 calories;
- Total Carbohydrate: 54.6 g
- Cholesterol: 90 mg
- Total Fat: 39.6 g
- Protein: 33.7 g
- Sodium: 1347 mg

251. Waikiki Meatballs

""Use ground ginger to flavor the beef meatballs then leave them in sweet pineapple sauce to simmer.""
Serving: 6 | Prep: 20m | Ready in: 45m

Ingredients

- 1 1/2 lbs. ground beef
- 2/3 cup crushed saltine cracker crumbs
- 1/3 cup minced onion
- 1 egg
- 1/4 cup milk
- 1 1/2 tsps. ground ginger
- 1/2 tsp. salt
- 1 tbsp. olive oil
- 2 tbsps. cornstarch
- 1/2 cup packed brown sugar
- 1 (15 oz.) can pineapple chunks - drained, with juice reserved
- 1/3 cup white vinegar
- 1 tbsp. soy sauce
- 1/3 cup chopped green bell pepper

Direction

- Combine salt, ginger, milk, egg, onion, cracker crumbs and ground beef together in a big bowl; form the mixture into meatballs by the tablespoonful.
- In a big skillet, heat olive oil on medium heat and put the meatballs in. Cook them until the meat is consistently browned throughout and not pink anymore. Drain the excess fat off.
- Mix the soy sauce, vinegar, brown sugar, cornstarch and reserved pineapple juice together in a small bowl until smooth. Pour the mixture into the skillet with the meatballs and cook for 5 minutes until it boils and is thick, stirring regularly. Stir the pineapple chunks and green pepper in and heat thoroughly.

Nutrition Information

- Calories: 442 calories;
- Total Carbohydrate: 39.6 g
- Cholesterol: 102 mg

- Total Fat: 21.9 g
- Protein: 21.6 g
- Sodium: 516 mg

252. Yummylicious Japanese Beef Croquettes

"Delicious Japanese croquettes made with onions, mashed potatoes, and ground beef. They are shaped into patties then coated in panko. These are great as snacks and can be formed into small pieces if you want. Serve them with Tonkatsu sauce."

Serving: 10 | Prep: 10m | Ready in: 30m

Ingredients

- 3 medium russet potatoes, peeled, and chopped
- 1 tbsp. butter
- 1 tbsp. vegetable oil
- 3 onions, chopped
- 3/4 lb. ground beef
- 4 tsps. light soy sauce
- all-purpose flour for coating
- 2 eggs, beaten
- panko bread crumbs
- 1/2 cup oil for frying

Direction

- Boil potatoes in a big pot of salted water; cook for 15 mins, or until tender. Drain the potatoes then move the potatoes to a big bowl. Mix in butter then mash using a potato masher or fork; set aside,
- On medium heat, heat 1 tbsp. oil in a big pan; cook and stir in onions until soft. Mix in soy sauce and beef. Cook while continuously mixing until all the liquid evaporates and the beef is brown. Mix beef with potatoes and onions, then combine well.
- On medium-high heat, heat a half cup oil in a wok or deep pan.
- Form the beef and potato mixture into ten even-sized balls then press into patties; dip in flour. Dip each patty in egg then cover in panko bread crumbs. Put into oil carefully then fry until each side is golden brown.

Nutrition Information

- Calories: 239 calories;
- Total Carbohydrate: 20.4 g
- Cholesterol: 69 mg
- Total Fat: 13.9 g
- Protein: 9.6 g
- Sodium: 196 mg

253. Zesty Porcupine Meatballs

"Serve these meatballs over hot rice."

Serving: 5 | Prep: 20m | Ready in: 40m

Ingredients

- 1 egg
- 2 (10.75 oz.) cans condensed tomato soup
- 1/4 cup instant rice
- 1/4 cup chopped onion
- 1 tbsp. chopped fresh parsley
- 1 tsp. onion salt
- 1/4 tsp. ground black pepper
- 1 lb. lean ground beef
- 1/4 cup Worcestershire sauce

Direction

- Use a fork, lightly beat the egg, then put in a heaping tbsp. of the soup and lightly mix. Mix in rice, pepper, onion salt, parsley, and onion. Stir in the ground beef, mix well with hands. Form the mixture into 1 1/2 inch round meatballs.
- Use cooking spray to coat a large skillet over medium heat. Cook the meatballs and brown on all sides.
- Mix Worcestershire and the remaining soup (decrease or increase the Worcestershire to your desire), stir until smooth, then scoop over the meatballs. Use a lid to cover and simmer for around 20-30 minutes, stirring every few minutes.

Nutrition Information

- Calories: 408 calories;
- Total Carbohydrate: 32.4 g
- Cholesterol: 105 mg
- Total Fat: 21.6 g
- Protein: 20.6 g
- Sodium: 1250 mg

Chapter 6: Chicken Recipes

***

254. Amazing Buffalo Dip

"Got this recipe from someone and now I will never shift to another dips. Deliciously melts in your mouth."
Serving: 10 | Prep: 10m | Ready in: 30m

Ingredients

- 2 cups diced cooked chicken
- 1 (8 oz.) package cream cheese, softened
- 1/2 cup blue cheese salad dressing
- 1/2 cup hot pepper sauce (such as Frank's RedHot®)
- 1/2 cup crumbled blue cheese
- 1/4 cup ranch dressing, or to taste

Direction

- Prepare a slow cooker and put in the blue cheese dressing, ranch dressing, cream cheese, hot pepper sauce, chicken and crumbled blue cheese then mix together.
- Turn on the slow cooker to high temperature for about 20 minutes until cooked and heated through.

Nutrition Information

- Calories: 246 calories;
- Total Carbohydrate: 2.1 g
- Cholesterol: 54 mg
- Total Fat: 21.4 g
- Protein: 11.5 g
- Sodium: 665 mg

255. Asian Style Paper Wrapped Chicken

"This is the paper-wrapped chicken appetizer recipe."
Serving: 6 | Prep: 30m | Ready in: 2h40m

Ingredients

- 2 tbsps. soy sauce
- 1 green onion, finely chopped
- 1 tbsp. hoisin sauce
- 1 tbsp. vegetable oil
- 1 tbsp. white wine
- 1 tbsp. cornstarch
- 1 tsp. white sugar
- 1 tsp. minced fresh ginger
- 1 tsp. chopped garlic
- 1/4 tsp. Chinese five-spice powder
- salt and ground black pepper to taste
- 1 lb. skinless, boneless chicken breast halves, cut into 1-inch cubes
- 1 cup peanut oil for frying, or as needed
- 18 6x6-inch squares of aluminum foil, or as needed

Direction

- In a large bowl, mix soy sauce, black pepper, salt, five-spice powder, garlic, ginger, sugar, cornstarch, white wine, vegetable oil, hoisin sauce, and green onion. Then stir the chicken cubes into the sauce to coat; put in the fridge for 2 hours to marinate.
- On a square of aluminum foil, put 1-2 chicken cubes, then diagonally fold the foil to make a triangle. Tightly fold the edges over several times, about 1/4 inch per time, and pressing

the air out of the packet as much as possible. Repeat the process with the remaining ingredients and foil.

- If needed, pour 1 cup peanut oil to a depth of 1/2 inch into a heavy skillet (for example, a cast-iron pan); heat over medium heat until the oil is shimmering.
- Lay gently the chicken packets into the hot oil, working in batches if needed, cook for about 5 minutes per side, until chicken is no longer pink and the juices run clear (open 1 packet to check). Allow the packets to drain on paper towels. Then directly serve the chicken in foil wrappers and let customers unwrap on their own.

Nutrition Information

- Calories: 150 calories;
- Total Carbohydrate: 4 g
- Cholesterol: 39 mg
- Total Fat: 7.6 g
- Protein: 15.2 g
- Sodium: 376 mg

256. Baked Blazing Hot Wings

"These hot chicken wings are a great substitute for deep-fried ones, which remain juicy rather than crisp."
Serving: 15 | Prep: 10m | Ready in: 1h10m

Ingredients

- 5 lbs. frozen chicken wings
- 2 cups hot pepper sauce (such as Frank's RedHot®)
- 1/2 cup butter
- 2 tbsps. distilled white vinegar
- 1 tbsp. all-purpose flour

Direction

- Set an oven to 200°C (400°F) and start preheating. In a shallow baking dish, place the frozen chicken wings in a single layer.
- In the prepared oven, bake for 25 minutes then turn the wings over. Carry on baking for 20 more minutes until the meat is not pink at the bone anymore and the skin becomes crispy.
- At the same time, in a saucepan, stir and cook vinegar, butter, and hot sauce on medium heat for 5 minutes until the butter melts. Add in flour and beat until the sauce becomes smooth. Carry on cooking for 5 more minutes until the sauce becomes thick.
- Let the grease drain from the chicken wings and allow to stand for 5 minutes. Place the chicken into a large bowl and put in the sauce. Coat the chicken by tossing.

Nutrition Information

- Calories: 169 calories;
- Total Carbohydrate: 0.9 g
- Cholesterol: 48 mg
- Total Fat: 13.6 g
- Protein: 10.4 g
- Sodium: 863 mg

257. Baked Chicken Wings

""Yummy, crispy, and simple. I usually serve with a salad, a vegetable, chicken gravy, or a side of rice.""
Serving: 2 | Prep: 10m | Ready in: 1h10m

Ingredients

- 3 tbsps. olive oil
- 3 cloves garlic, pressed
- 2 tsps. chili powder
- 1 tsp. garlic powder
- salt and ground black pepper to taste
- 10 chicken wings

Direction

- Prepare the oven by preheating to 375°F (190°C).
- Mix the pepper, salt, garlic powder, chili powder, garlic, and olive oil in a large resealable bag; close and shake to mix. Put in the chicken wings; close again and shake to coat. Transfer chicken wings to a baking sheet and arrange them.

- Place the wings in the preheated oven and cook for 1 hour, or until cooked through and crisp.

Nutrition Information

- Calories: 532 calories;
- Total Carbohydrate: 3.9 g
- Cholesterol: 97 mg
- Total Fat: 43.1 g
- Protein: 31.7 g
- Sodium: 123 mg

258. Bat Wings

"Simple basic wing recipe made with only 3 ingredients."
Serving: 6 | Prep: 10m | Ready in: 50m

Ingredients

- 1 cup white sugar
- 1 cup soy sauce
- 1 dash garlic powder
- 2 lbs. chicken wings

Direction

- Set an oven to 190°C (375°F) to preheat, then prepare a 9x13-inch glass baking dish with cooking spray.
- In a medium bowl, whisk together the garlic powder, soy sauce and sugar. In the bottom of the prepped dish, lay out the wings, then evenly pour the soy sauce mixture on top of the wings.
- Bake for 20 minutes in the preheated oven, then use a spatula to flip over the wings and cook for an additional 20 minutes.

Nutrition Information

- Calories: 229 calories;
- Total Carbohydrate: 36.7 g
- Cholesterol: 32 mg
- Total Fat: 3.1 g
- Protein: 14.2 g
- Sodium: 2440 mg

259. Blazing Wings

"This is an extreme kick."
Serving: 15 | Prep: 15m | Ready in: 45m

Ingredients

- 3 cups all-purpose flour
- 2 tbsps. cayenne pepper
- 2 tbsps. paprika
- 2 tsps. salt
- 2 tsps. ground black pepper
- 5 lbs. chicken wings, cut apart at joints, wing tips discarded
- 2 quarts vegetable oil for frying
- 2 cups butter, melted
- 2 (5 oz.) bottles hot pepper sauce (such as Tabasco®)
- 2 (5 oz.) bottles habanero hot sauce
- 5 habanero peppers, seeded and chopped (wear gloves)
- 1 (8 oz.) can crushed pineapple, drained

Direction

- In a large resealable plastic bag, mix the flour, black pepper, salt, paprika, and cayenne pepper.
- Drop into the flour mixture 5-6 wings at a time. Seal the bag and shake to cover the wings with flour.
- In a large saucepan or deep-fryer, heat oil to 175°C (350°F).
- Lower the coated wings gently into the hot oil, deep-fry for 5-10 minutes, or until the coating is golden brown and the center is not pink anymore.
- Strain the wings on paper towels and put aside.
- In the pitcher of a blender, place pineapple, habanero peppers, habanero pepper sauce, hot pepper sauce, and butter. Blend to get a smooth sauce (do not allow the sauce to touch your eyes); then pour the sauce into a large resealable plastic bag.

- Put 5 or 6 fried chicken wings at a time into the bag of sauce, seal the bag, and shake gently to coat the wings in the sauce. Transfer to a platter for serving.

Nutrition Information

- Calories: 541 calories;
- Total Carbohydrate: 23.3 g
- Cholesterol: 97 mg
- Total Fat: 44.3 g
- Protein: 13.5 g
- Sodium: 1504 mg

260. Bombay Chicken Wings

"I made dish for so many years"
Serving: 6 | Prep: 10m | Ready in: 1h35m

Ingredients

- 24 chicken wings
- 2 tbsps. vegetable oil
- 2 tbsps. soy sauce
- 2 tbsps. minced green onion
- 2 cloves garlic, minced
- 1 tsp. curry powder
- 1/2 tsp. ground turmeric
- 1/8 tsp. ground black pepper

Direction

- In the resealable plastic bag, mix the black pepper, turmeric, curry powder, garlic, green onion, soy sauce, vegetable oil and chicken wings. Squeeze out air, seal the bag, and keep in the refrigerator no less than 60 minutes.
- Preheat the oven to 175 degrees C (350 degrees F).
- Spread the chicken wings into the big baking dish.
- Bake in preheated oven approximately 25 minutes till the wings become brown.

Nutrition Information

- Calories: 234 calories;
- Total Carbohydrate: 1.2 g
- Cholesterol: 78 mg
- Total Fat: 12.1 g
- Protein: 28.5 g
- Sodium: 386 mg

261. Bri's Buffalo Chicken Meatballs

"Tasty appetizers accompanied with a spicy ranch sauce."
Serving: 4 | Prep: 15m | Ready in: 30m

Ingredients

- Meatballs:
- 1 lb. ground chicken
- 1/2 cup French-fried onions, slightly crumbled
- 1/4 cup chopped cilantro
- 1/4 cup oats
- 1/2 white onion, grated
- 1/4 bell pepper, grated
- 3 cloves garlic, minced
- 2 tbsps. Worcestershire sauce
- 1/2 tsp. seafood seasoning (such as Old Bay®), or to taste
- 1/4 tsp. garlic salt, or to taste
- 1 pinch ground black pepper to taste
- Dipping Sauce:
- 1/4 cup ranch dressing
- 1/4 cup hot sauce

Direction

- Start preheating the oven to 400°F (200°C). Use aluminum foil to line a cookie sheet.
- In a bowl, combine black pepper, garlic salt, seafood seasoning, Worcestershire sauce, garlic, bell pepper, white onion, oats, cilantro, French-fried onions, and chicken; form into spheres with the size of a golf ball and put on the prepared cookie sheet.
- Put in the preheated oven and bake for 15-18 minutes until the juices run clear and not pink anymore in the middle. When you insert an

instant-read thermometer into the middle, it should display a minimum of 165°F (74°C)

- In a bowl, combine hot sauce and ranch dressing until the color is even. Enjoy with meatballs.

Nutrition Information

- Calories: 436 calories;
- Total Carbohydrate: 21.1 g
- Cholesterol: 73 mg
- Total Fat: 25.8 g
- Protein: 26.8 g
- Sodium: 1081 mg

262. Broccoli Chicken Roli

"Pastries stuffed with veggie and savory chicken."
Serving: 16

Ingredients

- 2 cups chopped, cooked chicken meat
- 2 cups fresh chopped broccoli
- 1/2 cup chopped onion
- 1/2 cup chopped green bell pepper
- 1 1/2 cups shredded Cheddar cheese
- 1/2 cup mayonnaise
- 2 tbsps. Dijon-style prepared mustard
- salt and pepper to taste
- 1 tbsp. minced garlic
- 1 (8 oz.) package refrigerated crescent rolls

Direction

- Mix the garlic, pepper, salt, mustard, mayonnaise, cheese, bell pepper, onions, broccoli and chicken in a big bowl. Combine all together.
- Preheat an oven to 200 °C or 400 °F.
- Using aluminum foil, cover a cookie sheet. In the middle of cookie sheet invert a glass. Unroll the crescent rolls surrounding the bottom of glass, with peak ends away from glass; once done, the pattern should resemble a sun. Onto the thick part of every crescent roll, scoop some of chicken mixture. Fold the peak end of every roll over the top of mixture and tuck it in center. Take off glass from the cookie sheet. The setup of rolls will now be like a crimped tube cake.
- In prepped oven, bake for 25 minutes to half an hour, or till rolls turned golden brown.

Nutrition Information

- Calories: 183 calories;
- Total Carbohydrate: 7.8 g
- Cholesterol: 27 mg
- Total Fat: 12.7 g
- Protein: 8.9 g
- Sodium: 275 mg

263. Buffalo Chicken Fingers From Pretzel Crisps®

"This is a good recipe to go to."
Serving: 6 | Prep: 15m | Ready in: 15m

Ingredients

- 2 cups Buffalo Wing Snack Factory® Pretzel Crisps®
- 1 lb. chicken tenders
- 1 egg
- 1 1/2 cups buffalo wing sauce, divided
- 1/4 cup peanut oil
- 2 tbsps. mayonnaise
- 1 tbsp. sour cream
- 1/4 cup blue cheese crumbles, or to taste
- 1 dash Worcestershire sauce

Direction

- Crush the Pretzel Crisps(R) until fine yet with some texture using a rolling pin. Move to a clean platter. Beat 1 cup of the buffalo wing sauce and the egg in a bowl, then put aside. First, take each chicken tender and dip in the egg mixture, then roll in the crushed pretzels to coat.

- Heat oil in a large skillet over medium-high heat until shimmering. Put in the chicken tenders and cook until golden brown on all sides, flipping frequently (around 6 minutes total). Transfer to paper towels and drain. Combine Worcestershire sauce, blue cheese, sour cream, and mayonnaise in a small bowl. Serve chicken with the remaining 1/2 cup of the reserved wing sauce and blue cheese sauce.

Nutrition Information

- Calories: 414 calories;
- Total Carbohydrate: 32.7 g
- Cholesterol: 84 mg
- Total Fat: 21.5 g
- Protein: 23.3 g
- Sodium: 2358 mg

264. Buffalo Chicken Nacho Bowl

"This dish is tasty yet easy to make. It's perfect to serve at any gatherings. It's a nacho bowl a Buffalo chicken flavor."
Serving: 8 | Prep: 15m | Ready in: 25m

Ingredients

- 1 lb. shredded rotisserie chicken
- 1/4 cup Buffalo wing sauce
- 1 (16 oz.) package tortilla chips
- 1 (15 oz.) can black beans, rinsed and drained
- 1 (8 oz.) package shredded sharp Cheddar cheese
- 1/2 cup sour cream
- 1/4 cup crumbled blue cheese
- 1 tbsp. chopped jalapeno peppers, or to taste
- 1 tbsp. chopped green onion, or to taste

Direction

- Start preheating the oven to 425°F (220°C).
- In a bowl, mix together Buffalo wing sauce and chicken.
- In a baking dish's bottom, put tortilla chips in 1 layer; put 1 layer of Cheddar cheese, black beans, and Buffalo chicken mixture on top. Keep layering with the rest of the Cheddar cheese, black beans, Buffalo chicken mixture, and tortilla chips.
- Put in the preheated oven and bake for 10-15 minutes until the cheese melts. If it's too dark on the top, use aluminum foil to cover the nachos.
- Put green onion, jalapeno peppers, blue cheese, and sour cream on top of the nachos.

Nutrition Information

- Calories: 613 calories;
- Total Carbohydrate: 47.9 g
- Cholesterol: 83 mg
- Total Fat: 34.1 g
- Protein: 30.2 g
- Sodium: 926 mg

265. Buffalo Chicken Wings III

"A great spicy bite."
Serving: 4 | Prep: 20m | Ready in: 1h5m

Ingredients

- 20 chicken wings, split and tips discarded
- 1/2 cup butter, melted
- 1/2 cup red pepper sauce
- 3/4 cup tomato sauce
- 1 1/2 tbsps. chili powder
- 1 tsp. cayenne pepper

Direction

- Set the oven at 190°C (375°F) to preheat.
- In the preheated oven, bake the wings for a half-hour, or until cooked through and crispy.
- In the meantime, combine cayenne pepper, chili powder, tomato sauce, red pepper sauce, and melted butter in a small bowl. Mix them together.
- When the wings are baked, coat them well by dipping in the sauce, then shake the excess off and put the coated wings back into the baking sheet. Then reduce the oven temperature to

120°C (250°F) and continue to bake for 15 minutes longer to set the sauce.

Nutrition Information

- Calories: 406 calories;
- Total Carbohydrate: 4.9 g
- Cholesterol: 112 mg
- Total Fat: 35.7 g
- Protein: 17.9 g
- Sodium: 1224 mg

266. Buffalo Chicken Wontons

"A classic flavor to shine at any party!"
Serving: 9 | Prep: 40m | Ready in: 55m

Ingredients

- 2 tbsps. butter
- 1/2 cup minced celery
- 12 oz. shredded, cooked chicken breast
- 2/3 cup hot pepper sauce (such as Frank's RedHot®)
- 1 cup shredded Cheddar cheese
- salt and pepper to taste
- 1 (16 oz.) package wonton wrappers
- 1 quart oil for frying

Direction

- In a large skillet, let the butter melt on medium heat. Cook the celery in the melted butter for 5 minutes until it becomes soft slightly; place into a large mixing bowl. Place Cheddar cheese, hot sauce, and the chicken into the cooked celery and combine well. Flavor with pepper and salt.
- On your work surface, separately arrange the wonton wrappers. Top the center of each wrapper with approximately a tbsp. of the chicken mixture. Moisten the edges of the wonton wrappers lightly with water using a pastry brush or your finger. Fold one corner over the filling onto the opposite corner of the wrapper to shape into a triangle. Seal by pressing together the edges.
- In a deep pan or deep fryer, heat the oil to 185°C (365°F). Deep fry a few wontons at a time and turn them as necessary until they are lightly browned. Place on paper towels to drain. Serve them hot.

Nutrition Information

- Calories: 353 calories;
- Total Carbohydrate: 29.5 g
- Cholesterol: 43 mg
- Total Fat: 19.2 g
- Protein: 15 g
- Sodium: 840 mg

267. Cheesy Chicken Wraps

"Super easy and quick chicken."
Serving: 8 | Prep: 15m | Ready in: 35m

Ingredients

- 1 lb. skinless, boneless chicken breast halves
- 1 1/2 cups shredded Monterey Jack cheese
- 1 cup shredded Cheddar cheese
- 1 (8 oz.) package cream cheese, softened
- salt and pepper to taste
- 1 (8 oz.) package refrigerated crescent roll dough
- 2 tbsps. melted butter, or as needed

Direction

- Preheat the oven to 175 degrees C (350 degrees F). Use cooking spray or butter to grease a baking sheet.
- In a large pot, place chicken breasts, cover several inches with salted water; bring to a boil. Then reduce the heat to medium and simmer for 15 to 20 minutes, until the center is no longer pink and the juices run clear. Insert an instant-read thermometer into the center, it should display at least 74 degrees C (165 degrees F). Take away the chicken from water and let cool. Use two forks to shred chicken.
- In a bowl, mix thoroughly cream cheese, Cheddar cheese, Monterey Jack cheese,

pepper, and salt together. Blend chicken into the cheese mixture.
- Divide the crescent roll dough, put each part on a flat surface. Spread the chicken-cheese mixture onto each and roll into crescent roll forms. Arrange them on the prepared baking sheet and sweep with melted butter.
- Bake for 20 to 25 minutes in the preheated oven, or until rolls are golden and cheese is melted.

Nutrition Information

- Calories: 432 calories;
- Total Carbohydrate: 12.1 g
- Cholesterol: 104 mg
- Total Fat: 31.1 g
- Protein: 24.6 g
- Sodium: 553 mg

268. Chef John's Chicken Lettuce Wraps

"Very popular chicken lettuce wraps."
Serving: 8 | Prep: 35m | Ready in: 50m

Ingredients

- Chicken Mixture:
- 1 1/2 lbs. skinless, boneless chicken thighs, coarsely chopped
- 1 (8 oz.) can water chestnuts, drained and minced
- 1 cup diced shiitake mushroom caps
- 1/2 cup minced yellow onion
- 1/3 cup chopped green onion
- 1 tbsp. soy sauce
- 1 tbsp. freshly grated ginger
- 2 tsps. brown sugar
- Glaze:
- 1/4 cup chicken stock
- 1/4 cup rice wine vinegar
- 4 cloves garlic, minced
- 1 tbsp. ketchup
- 1 tbsp. soy sauce
- 2 tsps. sesame oil
- 2 tsps. brown sugar
- 1/2 tsp. red pepper flakes
- 1/2 tsp. dry mustard
- 2 tbsps. vegetable oil
- 1 1/2 tbsps. chopped fresh cilantro, or to taste
- 1 1/2 tbsps. chopped fresh basil, or to taste
- 1 1/2 tbsps. chopped green onion, or to taste
- 16 leaves iceberg lettuce, or as needed

Direction

- In a bowl, mix 2 tsps. brown sugar, ginger, 1 tbsp. soy sauce, 1/3 cup green onion, yellow onion, mushrooms, water chestnuts and chicken together. Press the mixture down, put plastic wrap to cover the bowl, and chill till set to use.
- In a bowl, mix dry mustard, red pepper flakes, 2 tsps. brown sugar, sesame oil, 1 tbsp. soy sauce, ketchup, garlic, rice wine vinegar and chicken stock together till glaze is well-combined.
- In a heavy nonstick skillet, heat the vegetable oil on high heat. In hot oil, cook and mix the chicken mixture for 2 minutes till chicken no longer seems raw. Into the chicken mixture, add half of glaze mixture; cook and mix on high heat for 10 to 15 minutes till chicken starts to brown and caramelize.
- Turn the heat to moderately-low, add the rest of the glaze into the chicken mixture, and allow to cook for 3 minutes longer till heated completely and slightly cooked down. Mix in 1 1/2 tbsps. green onion, basil and cilantro. Turn the chicken mixture onto a bowl and serve along with lettuce leaves to wrap.

Nutrition Information

- Calories: 212 calories;
- Total Carbohydrate: 10.8 g
- Cholesterol: 58 mg
- Total Fat: 10.7 g
- Protein: 17.6 g
- Sodium: 332 mg

269. Chicken Caesar Spring Rolls

"There are several magic food products which are just too good to be true."
Serving: 4 | Prep: 25m | Ready in: 25m

Ingredients

- 12 rice wrappers (8.5 inch diameter)
- 1 (5 oz.) package baby romaine lettuce leaves
- 1 cooked boneless chicken breast half, sliced into thin strips
- 1 red bell pepper, sliced
- 1/2 cup Caesar salad dressing

Direction

- Fill a large bowl with room-temperature water. Then soak a rice wrapper in the water for about 15 seconds, until it bends easily.
- Spread the wrapper flat. Place a small handful of lettuce leaves, a few slips of chicken, and a few slices of red bell pepper together in a row across the center, omitting about 2 inches uncovered on each side. Next, fold these uncovered sides inward, and roll the wrapper tightly, starting at the end with the lettuce. After that, repeat the process with the remaining ingredients.
- Slice in half. Enjoy with Caesar dressing for dipping.

Nutrition Information

- Calories: 230 calories;
- Total Carbohydrate: 15.9 g
- Cholesterol: 28 mg
- Total Fat: 13.8 g
- Protein: 9.6 g
- Sodium: 327 mg

270. Chicken Enchilada Dip

"This dip goes great with crackers or chips."
Serving: 30 | Prep: 15m | Ready in: 1h15m

Ingredients

- 1 lb. skinless, boneless chicken breast halves
- 1 (8 oz.) package cream cheese, softened
- 1 (8 oz.) jar mayonnaise
- 1 (8 oz.) package shredded Cheddar cheese
- 1 (4 oz.) can diced green chile peppers
- 1 jalapeno pepper, finely diced

Direction

- Preheat the oven to 175 degrees C/350 degrees F. On a medium baking sheet, put chicken breast halves.
- Bake for 20 minutes in preheated oven until it's not pink. Take off from heat. Cool. Shred.
- In a medium bowl, put shredded chicken. Mix in jalapeno pepper, green chile peppers, cheddar cheese, mayonnaise and cream cheese. Put chicken mixture on a medium baking dish.
- Bake in preheated oven, uncovered, for 30 minutes or until edges become golden brown.

Nutrition Information

- Calories: 128 calories;
- Total Carbohydrate: 0.8 g
- Cholesterol: 28 mg
- Total Fat: 11.5 g
- Protein: 5.7 g
- Sodium: 163 mg

271. Chicken Livers With Bacon

"“Do you like chicken liver? It's a very nice appetizer or just a quick meal for people on-the-go.”"
Serving: 2 | Prep: 10m | Ready in: 40m

Ingredients

- 1 lb. fresh chicken livers

- 1 cup all-purpose flour
- 1 tsp. garlic powder
- salt and pepper to taste
- 4 slices bacon

Direction

- Wash the livers then dry. Put the livers inside a resealable plastic bag. Mix together the flour, salt, garlic powder and pepper in a small bowl then add the mixture to the chicken liver. Seal the bag then shake bag to coat. Set aside.
- Cook the bacon in a large deep frying pan over medium high heat until it becomes evenly brown. Take the bacon out of the pan and leave the bacon fat behind. Set aside.
- Take the coated chicken livers and cook in the bacon fat over medium high heat covered for about 17 to 20 minutes until almost done. Then, add the bacon strips and let it cook together until the chicken is thoroughly cooked and juices run clear.

Nutrition Information

- Calories: 752 calories;
- Total Carbohydrate: 49.1 g
- Cholesterol: 821 mg
- Total Fat: 36.8 g
- Protein: 51.6 g
- Sodium: 629 mg

272. Chicken Livers With Red Wine And Bacon

""You can enjoy this recipe as a light supper or appetizer if you are a fan of chicken livers. This is a family favorite. Enjoy with crusty bread or crackers.""
Serving: 6 | Prep: 15m | Ready in: 35m

Ingredients

- 8 slices bacon, chopped
- 1 sweet onion, finely chopped
- 1 lb. chicken livers, rinsed and trimmed
- 1 1/2 cups Burgundy or other dry red wine
- 1/4 cup chopped pitted green olives

Direction

- In a big skillet on medium heat, sauté the bacon until it is almost crispy. Drain bacon on paper towels. Pour grease from pan, ensuring a thin coating remains on bottom.
- Add onions to the same pan; cook while stirring on medium heat for 5 minutes until soft. Add the chicken livers and stir, quickly brown the outside of livers. Pour the wine in, increase the amount if necessary to cover chicken livers. Mix in olives. Seal and bring to a simmer 20 minutes. Stir in bacon, then serve.

Nutrition Information

- Calories: 214 calories;
- Total Carbohydrate: 4.1 g
- Cholesterol: 287 mg
- Total Fat: 9.1 g
- Protein: 16.8 g
- Sodium: 465 mg

273. Chicken Rangoon

"A great recipe that can use the leftover roasted chicken."
Serving: 6 | Prep: 15m | Ready in: 25m

Ingredients

- 1 (8 oz.) package cream cheese, softened
- 1 pinch onion powder, or to taste
- 1 pinch garlic powder, or to taste
- 1 dash Worcestershire sauce, or to taste
- 1 dash soy sauce, or to taste
- 1 pinch salt, or to taste
- 1 pinch ground black pepper, or to taste
- 1 cup chopped cooked chicken
- 1 (16 oz.) package wonton wrappers
- peanut oil for frying

Direction

- In a large, deep saucepan or a deep fryer, heat the oil to 190°C (375°F).

- In a bowl, stir together the pepper, salt, soy sauce, Worcestershire sauce, garlic powder, onion powder, and cream cheese. Put in the chicken and stir until completely it is incorporated.
- Separately arrange wonton wrappers onto the work surface. Top the center of each wrapper with approximately a tsp. of the cream cheese filling. Lightly moisten the edges of the wonton wrappers with water using a pastry brush or your finger. Fold one corner onto the opposite corner over the filling of the wrapper to shape into a triangle. Seal by pressing together the edges.
- Cook wontons in batches in heated oil for 2-4 minutes until they are lightly browned. Drain on the paper towel-lined plate.

Nutrition Information

- Calories: 498 calories;
- Total Carbohydrate: 44.6 g
- Cholesterol: 66 mg
- Total Fat: 28.1 g
- Protein: 16 g
- Sodium: 563 mg

274. Chicken Salad Pretzel Bites

"An easy and quick appetizer served with crispy pretzels."
Serving: 6 | Prep: 20m | Ready in: 2h20m

Ingredients

- 1 large cooked chicken breast
- 1 stalk celery
- 1/2 small onion
- 2 green onions
- 1/2 cup mayonnaise
- 2 tsps. dried tarragon
- salt and ground black pepper to taste
- 12 thin pretzel crackers (such as Snack Factory® Pretzel Crisps®)
- 3 slices provolone cheese, cut into quarters
- 4 cherry tomatoes, sliced (optional)

Direction

- Pulse chicken breast in a food processor until finely chopped. Transfer to a bowl.
- In the food processor, combine green onions, onion, and celery; pulse until chopped finely. Put into the chicken in the bowl.
- In the bowl with the chicken mixture, stir black pepper, salt, tarragon, and mayonnaise.
- Let the chicken salad chill for at least 2 hours, until the flavors combine.
- Lay a heaping tbsp. of chicken salad and a piece of provolone cheese on top of each pretzel cracker. Decorate with a slice of cherry tomato.

Nutrition Information

- Calories: 497 calories;
- Total Carbohydrate: 50.8 g
- Cholesterol: 41 mg
- Total Fat: 25.4 g
- Protein: 19 g
- Sodium: 1803 mg

275. Chicken Salad-stuffed Tomatoes

""Tofu salad, seafood, or tuna would be a flavorful filling for plum tomatoes too.""
Serving: 4 | Ready in: 15m

Ingredients

- 4 plum tomatoes, halved
- ¼ cup chicken salad
- 2 tsps. sliced fresh chives
- Freshly ground pepper, to taste

Direction

- Use a melon baller to scoop out insides of tomatoes. Stuff with chicken salad. Dust with chives and pepper.

Nutrition Information

- Calories: 49 calories;
- Total Carbohydrate: 4 g
- Cholesterol: 11 mg
- Total Fat: 2 g
- Fiber: 1 g
- Protein: 4 g
- Sodium: 66 mg
- Sugar: 2 g
- Saturated Fat: 0 g

276. Chicken Spring Rolls

"Easy to make spring rolls without fancy sauces, because it is filled with flavorful."
Serving: 10 | Prep: 30m | Ready in: 45m

Ingredients

- 1 quart oil for deep frying
- 2 (10 oz.) cans chunk chicken, drained and flaked
- 1 small onion, grated
- 1/2 cup finely shredded cabbage
- 1 small carrot, grated
- 1/4 cup barbeque sauce
- 1 dash hot pepper sauce
- 1 dash soy sauce
- 1 dash Worcestershire sauce
- 1 (14 oz.) package spring roll wrappers

Direction

- In a big, heavy saucepan or deep-fryer, heat the oil to 190 °C or 375 °F.
- Combine together Worcestershire sauce, soy sauce, hot pepper sauce, barbeque sauce, carrot, cabbage, onion and chicken in a medium bowl.
- In the middle of spring roll wrappers, put about a tbsp. of chicken mixture. With water, dampen the fingers, and moisten edges of wrappers. Roll surrounding the filling. Press seams to enclose.
- Working in small batches, deep fry spring rolls for 3 to 5 minutes, or till golden brown. Allow to drain on paper towels.

Nutrition Information

- Calories: 299 calories;
- Total Carbohydrate: 26.3 g
- Cholesterol: 38 mg
- Total Fat: 13.9 g
- Protein: 16.2 g
- Sodium: 587 mg

277. Chicken Wraps

"This boneless chicken dish was wrapped with pineapple and bacon and dipped in spicy mustard."
Serving: 10 | Prep: 4h5m | Ready in: 4h30m

Ingredients

- 1 lb. skinless, boneless chicken breast halves
- 1/2 lb. bacon
- 1 (20 oz.) can pineapple chunks
- 18 fluid oz. teriyaki sauce

Direction

- Slice the chicken into bite-size pieces and wrap it with approximately 1/3 slice of bacon, thread onto a toothpick and put pineapple chuck on top. Let it marinate for 4 hours or more in teriyaki sauce.
- Set an oven to preheat to 190°C (375°F).
- Put the marinated appetizers onto baking sheets lined with parchment. Let it bake for 20 minutes or until the bacon turns golden brown in color and the chicken is done. Let it drain on paper towels, then serve hot.

Nutrition Information

- Calories: 245 calories;
- Total Carbohydrate: 19 g
- Cholesterol: 42 mg
- Total Fat: 10.8 g
- Protein: 17.2 g

- Sodium: 2703 mg

278. Coxinhas (brazilian Chicken Croquettes)

"This recipe is common in Brazil. Chicken croquettes (coxinhas) are great finger food for occasions and kids' favorite. "

Serving: 20 | Prep: 1h | Ready in: 1h30m

Ingredients

- Filling:
- 2 small skinless, boneless chicken breast halves
- 1 cup chicken broth, or more as needed
- 1 tbsp. olive oil
- 1 onion, chopped
- 2 tbsps. chopped fresh parsley
- 5 chopped green olives, or to taste
- salt and pepper to taste
- Pastry:
- 2 cups chicken broth
- 2 tbsps. butter
- salt to taste
- 1 cup all-purpose flour
- Breading:
- 1 cup all-purpose flour
- 2 eggs, beaten
- 1 cup dry bread crumbs
- oil for frying

Direction

- Over medium heat, mix 1 cup chicken broth and chicken breasts in a pot and bring to boil. Low the heat, cover the pot, and let to simmer for about 20 to 30 minutes until the chicken is cooked through. You should continuously check to make sure there is enough liquid in the pot and add extra stock if need be. Take out from the pot, let to cool a bit. Use 2 forks to shred.
- Over medium heat, heat olive oil in a skillet, add onion and cook for about 5 minutes until soft and translucent. Add in parsley, olives, and shredded chicken. Mix well and then season with pepper and salt. Take out the filling from the heat source and reserve.
- Over medium heat, heat butter and 2 cups of chicken broth in a large saucepan. Season with salt and then bring to a simmer. Pour in flour all at once and mix to create a thick paste. Mix vigorously until mixture becomes smooth and doesn't stick on the bottom of the pan. Take out from the heat source and leave the pastry to cool.
- When the pastry cools enough to handle, place onto an oiled work surface and then knead for 2 to 3 minutes until smooth.
- Pick a portion of the pastry and then fold into a golf ball-sized ball. Oil you finger and then stick at the center of the ball. Press the edges to form a small bowl. Then stuff with two tsps. of the chicken filling and seal the top edges by gathering the top, folding into a teardrop shape. Reserve the croquette and then cover with a damp towel. Repeat this with the remaining filling and pastry.
- Arrange 3 bowls in this order: flour, beaten eggs, breadcrumbs. Fold each croquette in flour, then dunk in the egg and finally cover with breadcrumbs.
- In a deep fryer or large saucepan, heat oil for deep frying and then fry the croquettes in batches, for 7 to 10 minutes until they are golden brown on all sides. Remove from the oil and then drain on paper towels.

Nutrition Information

- Calories: 145 calories;
- Total Carbohydrate: 14.2 g
- Cholesterol: 27 mg
- Total Fat: 7.6 g
- Protein: 4.7 g
- Sodium: 273 mg

279. Creamy Chicken Spread

"This creamy chicken spread is great for parties. It is so tasty that once you have a bite, you won't be able to resist it."

Serving: 5 | Prep: 8h10m | Ready in: 8h10m

Ingredients

- 1 (10.75 oz.) can condensed cream of chicken soup
- 1 envelope (1 tbsp.) unflavored gelatin
- 3 tbsps. water
- 3/4 cup mayonnaise
- 1 (8 oz.) package cream cheese, softened
- 1 onion, chopped
- 1 cup celery, minced
- 1 (5 oz.) can chicken chunks, drained

Direction

- Heat the chicken soup in a small pot.
- Mix water and gelatin in a small bowl and stir the mixture into the heated soup. Stir celery, onion, cream cheese, mayonnaise into the soup mixture. Then put in chicken and continue mixing. Keep in the fridge overnight.

Nutrition Information

- Calories: 512 calories;
- Total Carbohydrate: 9.4 g
- Cholesterol: 84 mg
- Total Fat: 47.7 g
- Protein: 12.9 g
- Sodium: 886 mg

280. Crispy Wings

"Easy, golden, crispy fried chicken wing coated with cornflake crumb, flour, and egg."

Serving: 12 | Prep: 15m | Ready in: 30m

Ingredients

- oil for deep frying
- 1 cup all-purpose flour, divided
- 8 tbsps. garlic powder, divided
- 6 eggs, beaten
- 3 cups crushed cornflake crumbs
- 24 chicken wings
- 1/2 carrot, cut into thick strips

Direction

- Set the oil in a deep fryer or a deep, large skillet and start preheating. Combine 2 tbsps. of garlic powder with 3/4 cup of flour together in a bowl or a shallow dish; blend together 4 tbsps. garlic powder with eggs in a second bowl or shallow dish. Combine together the remaining 2 tbsps. garlic powder, remaining 1/4 cup flour, and cornflake crumbs in a third bowl or shallow dish.
- Plunge each wing into the egg mixture, crumb mixture, flour mixture in reverse order, then go back to the crumb mixture. Put the carrot into the heated oil; put in the wings once it begins to fry. Fry until cooked thoroughly, or for 10 minutes, so that they will have a deep golden color.

Nutrition Information

- Calories: 322 calories;
- Total Carbohydrate: 33.6 g
- Cholesterol: 113 mg
- Total Fat: 15.4 g
- Protein: 13 g
- Sodium: 226 mg

281. Fried Buffalo Wings With Spicy, Sweet, And Umami Sauce

"Boiling the meat before frying truly makes an amazingly crunchy piece of chicken while retaining the meat juicy and tender."

Serving: 6 | Prep: 30m | Ready in: 1h15m

Ingredients

- 1 gallon water

- salt
- 2 tbsps. crushed red pepper flakes
- 2 tbsps. chicken bouillon granules
- 2 lbs. chicken wings, cut apart at joints, wing tips discarded
- 3/4 cup all-purpose flour
- 1/2 cup masa harina flour (Mexican corn masa mix)
- 1 tbsp. paprika
- 1 tbsp. garlic powder
- 3 tbsps. ground cayenne pepper
- salt and ground black pepper to taste
- 2 cups canola oil for frying
- 2 cups lard for frying
- 1/2 cup butter
- 1/2 cup hot pepper sauce
- 1/3 cup molasses
- 1 tbsp. Worcestershire sauce
- 1 tsp. garlic powder

Direction

- In a large stockpot, pour water and stir in the chicken bouillon granules, red pepper flakes, and salt. Bring the mixture to a boil.
- Next, cook the chicken wings in the boiling water for about 10 minutes, until the inside is no more pink and the juices run clear.
- Drain the wings and put aside to cool for about 15 minutes, until easy to handle.
- In a large bowl, whisk together the flour, black pepper, salt, cayenne pepper, 1 tbsp. of garlic powder, paprika, and masa harina. Toss the chicken wings into the seasoned flour until coated lightly; tap to get rid of the excess flour.
- In a large saucepan or deep-fryer, heat lard and canola oil to 175°C (350°F).
- Working in batches of 6 wings at a time, deep-fry for 10-15 minutes, or until deep golden brown. Put the wings aside and drain on paper towels.
- Over low heat, melt the butter in a large saucepan and whisk in 1 tsp. of garlic powder, Worcestershire sauce, molasses, and the hot pepper sauce. Remove the sauce from the heat.
- To serve: Working in batches, stir the wings into the sauce until coated. Transfer the wings to a serving plate to enjoy.

Nutrition Information

- Calories: 519 calories;
- Total Carbohydrate: 39.2 g
- Cholesterol: 80 mg
- Total Fat: 34.5 g
- Protein: 15.7 g
- Sodium: 2231 mg

282. Gluten-free Pesto Chicken Cakes With Spicy Dipping Sauce

"A delicious appetizer filled with great flavor."
Serving: 8 | Prep: 20m | Ready in: 26m

Ingredients

- Dipping Sauce:
- 1/3 cup mayonnaise
- 1/4 cup sour cream
- 1 tbsp. pesto
- 1/2 tsp. hot sauce
- salt and ground black pepper to taste
- Chicken Cakes:
- 1/4 cup low-fat mayonnaise
- 1 egg, beaten
- 2 tbsps. pesto
- 1 clove garlic, minced
- 1 cup gluten-free panko bread crumbs
- 1/3 cup minced red onion
- 3 cups shredded cooked chicken breast
- 1 tbsp. olive oil

Direction

- To make the dipping sauce: In a bowl, mix 1/3 cup mayonnaise, pepper, salt, hot sauce, 1 tbsp. pesto, and sour cream. Put in the fridge.
- In a large bowl, combine garlic, 2 tbsps. pesto, egg, and 1/4 cup mayonnaise. Stir in red onion and bread crumbs. Mix in the chicken

until completely combined. Roll the mixture into balls and press into 1/2-inch cakes.

- Heat oil over medium heat in a nonstick skillet. Put the chicken cakes in a single layer to the oil; cook for about 3 minutes each side, until browned. Transfer to a dish lined with paper towels. Repeat the process with the remaining chicken cakes.
- Serve the chicken cakes with the dipping sauce.

Nutrition Information

- Calories: 309 calories;
- Total Carbohydrate: 10.9 g
- Cholesterol: 73 mg
- Total Fat: 22.4 g
- Protein: 15.6 g
- Sodium: 251 mg

283. Guacamole Chicken

"This is gonna be your entrance to a superfast and satisfying dinner topped with creamy guacamole and melty cheese. A healthy meal that you can pair with Spanish rice."

Serving: 4 | Prep: 30m | Ready in: 40m

Ingredients

- 1 medium avocado
- 2 tsps. chopped pimientos
- 1 tsp. lime juice
- Pinch of salt plus ½ tsp., divided
- Pinch of ground pepper plus ½ tsp., divided
- 2 8-oz. boneless, skinless chicken breasts, halved
- ½ tsp. garlic powder
- 1 tbsp. extra-virgin olive oil
- ½ cup shredded Monterey Jack cheese (1 oz.)
- 2 tbsps. chopped fresh cilantro

Direction

- In a medium bowl, put in avocado; use a fork to crush until becomes smooth with chunks left. Mix in a pinch of pepper, pinch of salt, lime juice and pimientos. Reserve.
- Drizzle chicken with garlic powder, left 1/2 tsp. pepper and left 1/2 tsp. salt. Place a large skillet on the stove and turn on to medium-high heat then put oil to heat. Put the chicken and minimize the heat to medium. Cook for 4 to 6 minutes, rotating once, until each side is cooked enough. Put cheese on top; keep on cooking, covered, for about 2 more minutes until cheese has melted. Then place the chicken to a serving platter and put guacamole on top. Use cilantro to garnish.

Nutrition Information

- Calories: 263 calories;
- Total Carbohydrate: 5 g
- Cholesterol: 69 mg
- Total Fat: 16 g
- Fiber: 4 g
- Protein: 26 g
- Sodium: 428 mg
- Sugar: 0 g
- Saturated Fat: 4 g

284. Honey Sesame Wings

""Try this perfect appetizer as a quick meal with bread and coleslaw or while watching the game.""

Serving: 4 | Prep: 10m | Ready in: 1h10m

Ingredients

- 1/4 cup honey
- 2 tbsps. sesame oil
- 2 tbsps. reduced-sodium soy sauce
- 1 tbsp. chopped fresh ginger
- 2 cloves garlic, minced
- 2 1/2 lbs. chicken wings
- 1 tbsp. toasted sesame seeds
- 3 scallions (green onions), chopped

Direction

- Prepare the oven by preheating to 375°F (190°C). Use aluminum foil to line a baking sheet.
- In a small bowl, mix garlic, ginger, soy sauce, sesame oil and honey together.
- Place chicken wings on the prepared baking sheet.
- Place chicken in the preheated oven and bake for 45 minutes. Use 1/2 of the honey mixture to brush over the wings; bake for 10 minutes. Use the rest of the sauce to brush over wings, dust sesame seeds over the top, and bake wings for about 5 more minutes, until juices run clear and the chicken is not pink at the bone. An instant-read thermometer poked near the bone should register 165°F (74°C). Decorate wings with scallions.

Nutrition Information

- Calories: 354 calories;
- Total Carbohydrate: 20.2 g
- Cholesterol: 59 mg
- Total Fat: 21.7 g
- Protein: 20.2 g
- Sodium: 327 mg

285. Italian Rice Croquettes

"A great recipe to try out on your next party event."
Serving: 40 | Prep: 50m | Ready in: 1h40m

Ingredients

- 2 lbs. chicken giblets
- 1 cup water
- 1/2 tsp. salt
- 4 cups salted water
- 2 cups long grain white rice, uncooked
- 2 cups grated Parmesan cheese
- 1/2 cup marinara sauce
- 1/4 cup dry bread crumbs
- 2 large eggs
- 2 tbsps. chopped fresh parsley
- salt and freshly ground black pepper to taste
- 1 cup dry bread crumbs for coating
- vegetable oil for frying

Direction

- In a pressure cooker, mix 1 cup water, chicken giblets and 1/2 tsp. salt and cook for about 20 minutes.
- Drain giblets. Allow it to cool for about 10 minutes then cut giblets, either by hand or using a food processor; put aside.
- Combine rice and water in a pot over high heat and cook until it starts to boil. Turn heat down to medium-low and simmer, covered, for 20-25 minutes until all the liquid has been absorbed and rice is soft.
- Cool the cooked rice by spreading it onto a baking tray for about 5 minutes. Scoop up rice when cooled onto a large bowl.
- Combine marinara sauce, grated Parmesan cheese, eggs, 1/4 cup bread crumbs, ground pepper, salt, parsley and the giblets. Place plastic wrap to cover and store in the fridge for 1 hour.
- Take rice and giblet mixture from the fridge and form 2-inch football-shaped croquettes.
- Dredge croquettes in bread crumbs and arrange them on a baking tray.
- Heat oil in a big skillet over medium-high temperature. Fry breaded croquettes for about 10 minutes until browned on all sides. Line a plate with paper towels to help absorb excess oil and place fried croquettes onto the plate.

Nutrition Information

- Calories: 99 calories;
- Total Carbohydrate: 10.4 g
- Cholesterol: 60 mg
- Total Fat: 3.2 g
- Protein: 6.9 g
- Sodium: 140 mg

286. Jerry's Wings

""This recipe is great served with ranch dressing or blue cheese.""
Serving: 4 | Prep: 2m | Ready in: 17m

Ingredients

- 1 cup vegetable oil
- 1 lb. chicken wings
- 3/4 cup butter
- 1/4 cup hot pepper sauce

Direction

- Put oil in a deep fryer or large skillet and heat to 375°F (190°C). Put in wings and fry for about 8 minutes. Allow them to drain on paper towels. Transfer the chicken wings to a large mixing bowl.
- Melt butter and hot sauce in a large saucepan. Pour the sauce over the chicken wings and toss until all wings are coated.

Nutrition Information

- Calories: 1047 calories;
- Total Carbohydrate: 0.7 g
- Cholesterol: 179 mg
- Total Fat: 107.7 g
- Protein: 21.3 g
- Sodium: 332 mg

287. Kiki's Favorite Deep-fried Buttermilk Chicken Tenders

"Crispy, lightly and extremely moist deep-fried chicken."
Serving: 4 | Prep: 10m | Ready in: 2h13m

Ingredients

- 1 cup buttermilk
- 2 tbsps. seasoned salt, divided
- 16 chicken breast tenders
- 2 cups panko bread crumbs
- freshly ground black pepper to taste
- 2 cups vegetable oil for frying, or as needed

Direction

- In a bowl, combine 1 tbsp. seasoned salt and buttermilk together. Mix in the chicken tenders. Place cover and chill in the fridge for at least2 hours and up to 6 hours.
- Preheat the oven to 75 °C or 170 °F. With paper towels, line the baking sheet; on a sheet, set a cooling rack and place in the oven.
- In a big, flat bowl, mix pepper, panko bread crumbs and leftover 1 tbsp. seasoned salt together.
- Take tenders off marinade one by one and shake extra buttermilk off. In panko mixture, roll the pieces and put on a big platter.
- In a deep-fryer or big saucepan, heat oil to 190 °C or 370 °F. In hot oil, let the chicken pieces fry 3 or 4 at a time for about 3 minutes till crispy and browned. Put to the cooling rack in the oven to retain warmth as you fry.

Nutrition Information

- Calories: 542 calories;
- Total Carbohydrate: 42.9 g
- Cholesterol: 136 mg
- Total Fat: 20.4 g
- Protein: 57.1 g
- Sodium: 1821 mg

288. Lemon Pepper Chicken Wings

"These wings are fresh, simple, savory and a genuine crowd-pleaser."
Serving: 6 | Prep: 10m | Ready in: 45m

Ingredients

- 6 tbsps. olive oil
- 1/4 cup finely grated lemon zest
- 2 tbsps. coarse sea salt
- 2 tbsps. ground black pepper
- 1 (3 lb.) bag chicken wings

Direction

- Set the oven to 220°C or 425°F. Use parchment paper to line a baking sheet.
- In a bowl, whisk together black pepper, salt, lemon zest and olive oil. Put in wings and toss to coat well. Spread on the prepared baking sheet with coated wings in a single layer.
- In the preheated oven, bake for 35 minutes, until it isn't pink at the bone anymore and juices run clear. An instant-read thermometer tucked near the bone should reach 74°C or 165°F. If you want a crispier skin, bake for longer time.

Nutrition Information

- Calories: 291 calories;
- Total Carbohydrate: 2 g
- Cholesterol: 48 mg
- Total Fat: 24.6 g
- Protein: 15.5 g
- Sodium: 1808 mg

289. Low-carb Chicken Nacho Bites

"These are full of flavor and amazing snack."
Serving: 4 | Prep: 20m | Ready in: 35m

Ingredients

- 1 large cooked chicken breast, shredded
- 1 cup pico de gallo, divided
- 1 cup sour cream, divided
- 1 cup shredded Mexican cheese blend
- 1 tbsp. taco seasoning mix
- cooking spray
- 1 (8 oz.) package mini sweet bell peppers, halved lengthwise and seeded
- 1 (2.25 oz.) can chopped olives

Direction

- Set the oven at 175°C (350°F) to preheat.
- In a large bowl, combine shredded chicken, taco seasoning, 1/2 cup Mexican cheese blend, 1/2 cup sour cream, and 1/2 cup pico de gallo.
- Use cooking spray to spray a baking dish. Fill each pepper with the chicken mixture as much as possible and put in the baking dish. Dust with 1/4 cup Mexican cheese blend over the pepper halves. Cover with the remaining 1/4 cup cheese and olives.
- In the preheated oven, bake for 15-20 minutes, until the peppers have begun to soften and cheese is melted. Lay a dollop of pico de gallo and sour cream on top of each cooked pepper.

Nutrition Information

- Calories: 388 calories;
- Total Carbohydrate: 11.7 g
- Cholesterol: 94 mg
- Total Fat: 26.1 g
- Protein: 23.3 g
- Sodium: 934 mg

290. Marty's Thai Chicken Satay

"My version of chicken satay!"
Serving: 8 | Prep: 20m | Ready in: 1h30m

Ingredients

- 2 tbsps. vegetable oil
- 2 tbsps. soy sauce
- 2 tsps. tamarind paste
- 1 stalk lemon grass, chopped
- 2 cloves garlic, crushed
- 1 tsp. ground cumin
- 1 tsp. ground coriander
- 1 tbsp. lime juice
- 1 tsp. muscovado sugar
- 1/2 tsp. chili powder
- 2 lbs. skinless, boneless chicken breast, cut into strips
- 20 wooden skewers, soaked in water for 30 minutes
- 2 tbsps. crunchy peanut butter
- 2 tbsps. chopped peanuts

- 1 (14 oz.) can coconut milk
- 2 tsps. red Thai curry paste
- 1 tbsp. fish sauce
- 1 tsp. tomato paste
- 1 tbsp. brown sugar

Direction

- In a blender, process chile powder, muscovado sugar, lime juice, coriander, cumin, garlic, lemon grass, tamarind paste, soy sauce, and vegetable oil to make a smooth paste. Toss marinade with chicken strips in a big resealable plastic bag or big bowl. Keep in fridge for an hour.
- Preheat an outdoor grill to medium-high heat. Oil grate lightly.
- Stir and cook brown sugar, tomato paste, fish sauce, curry paste, coconut milk, peanuts and peanut butter in a small saucepan on medium-low heat until it is smooth. Retain warmth.
- On skewers, thread chicken. Grill for 3-5 minutes per side until the center isn't pink anymore. Serve alongside peanut sauce.

Nutrition Information

- Calories: 310 calories;
- Total Carbohydrate: 7.5 g
- Cholesterol: 65 mg
- Total Fat: 20.6 g
- Protein: 27.1 g
- Sodium: 478 mg

291. New Year's Eve Chicken Wings

"You'll go crazy for these chicken wings."
Serving: 20 | Prep: 30m | Ready in: 1h25m

Ingredients

- cooking spray
- 2 quarts vegetable oil for frying
- 5 lbs. chicken wings, separated at joints, tips discarded
- 1 cup hot wing sauce
- 1 lb. carrots, cut into sticks
- 6 ribs celery, cut into sticks
- 2 cups blue cheese salad dressing

Direction

- Set the oven at 375° F (190° C) to preheat. Use cooking spray to grease a baking sheet.
- In a deep fryer or large pot, heat vegetable oil to 190° C (375° F).
- Rinse the wings in a colander and pat with paper towels until very dry. Deep-fry in 5 or 6 batches, for about 10 minutes, or until partially cooked; drain on paper towels and cool slightly. Put the wings back into the hot oil, fry the second time for 6-8 minutes each batch, or until golden brown. Drain on paper towels.
- Transfer to a large mixing bowl and toss to coat with hot wing sauce. Move the wings to the prepared baking sheet in a single layer using tongs. Sweep with any remaining wing sauce.
- Bake in the preheated oven for around 15 minutes, or until wings' surface is nearly dry. Serve on dishes with blue cheese dressing, celery sticks, and carrot sticks.

Nutrition Information

- Calories: 308 calories;
- Total Carbohydrate: 6.6 g
- Cholesterol: 28 mg
- Total Fat: 27.6 g
- Protein: 9.5 g
- Sodium: 654 mg

292. Oven Fried Chicken Wings

""This recipe consist of a cookie sheet, melted butter, garlic powder, Parmesan cheese, and bread crumbs.""
Serving: 20 | Prep: 15m | Ready in: 45m

Ingredients

- cooking spray
- 1 cup grated Parmesan cheese (such as Kraft®)

- 1 cup seasoned bread crumbs
- 1/8 tsp. garlic powder
- 1/8 tsp. onion powder
- 1/8 tsp. ground black pepper
- 1 pinch salt
- 5 lbs. chicken wings, tips discarded
- 1/2 cup melted butter

Direction

- Prepare the oven by preheating to 400°F (200°C). Use aluminum foil to line a baking sheet and generously spray with cooking spray.
- Combine salt, black pepper, onion powder, garlic powder, bread crumbs, and Parmesan cheese in a bowl.
- Dunk chicken wings in melted butter; put into bread crumb mixture and press until well-coated. Put wings on the prepared baking dish and arrange them.
- Place in the preheated oven and bake for about 20 minutes until golden brown. Turn chicken wings over and keep on baking for about 10 more minutes until no pink in the center and evenly browned.

Nutrition Information

- Calories: 163 calories;
- Total Carbohydrate: 4.3 g
- Cholesterol: 40 mg
- Total Fat: 11.6 g
- Protein: 10.1 g
- Sodium: 223 mg

293. Peanut Sesame Chicken Wings

"These tasty chicken wings can be lifted off the pan right away without sticking to it and cleaned up easily"
Serving: 8 | Prep: 30m | Ready in: 50m

Ingredients

- Reynolds Wrap® Non-Stick Foil
- 12 chicken wings
- 1/2 cup creamy peanut butter
- 1/3 cup water
- 2 tbsps. lime juice
- 2 tbsps. reduced-sodium soy sauce
- 1 tbsp. honey
- 1 tsp. toasted sesame oil
- 1/2 tsp. ground ginger
- 1 small clove garlic
- 1 tbsp. fresh cilantro leaves, packed
- 1 tbsp. sesame seeds, toasted

Direction

- Start preheating the broiler. Use Reynolds Wrap® Non-Stick Foil* to line a 15x10x1-inch baking pan. Put the pan aside.
- Slice off tips of the chicken wings and discard. Chop the wings at joints to shape 24 pieces. Place the wing pieces into a large bowl, then put aside.
- In a blender or a food processor, blend the garlic, ginger, sesame oil, honey, soy sauce, lime juice, water, and peanut butter. Put a cover on and blend or process until the mixture becomes smooth. Add 1/3 cup of the sauce to the chicken wings and evenly coat by stirring. In the blender or the food processor, place the cilantro into the remaining sauce and blend or process until it is blended. Put aside. In the prepared pan, place the chicken pieces in a single layer
- Broil the wings 4-5 inches away from the heat for 10 minutes. Turn over the wings. Broil until they turn brown and become tender, or for 10 more minutes. Drain off the fat.
- On a platter, arrange the wings to serve, dust with sesame seeds and serve along with the retained peanut sauce.

Nutrition Information

- Calories: 156 calories;
- Total Carbohydrate: 6.5 g
- Cholesterol: 16 mg
- Total Fat: 10.8 g
- Protein: 10.1 g
- Sodium: 225 mg

294. Peanut-chicken Cabbage Wraps

"This is a healthy and tasty chicken lettuce wrap with delicious low-carb cabbage."
Serving: 4 | Ready in: 30m

Ingredients

- 8 small napa or Savoy cabbage leaves or 4 large, cut in half crosswise
- 1 tbsp. canola oil
- 1 lb. boneless, skinless chicken breast, trimmed and cut into bite-size pieces
- ¼ tsp. salt
- 5 tbsps. prepared peanut sauce
- 1 tbsp. rice vinegar
- 1½ tsps. lime zest
- 1 cup julienned Asian pear
- 1 cup julienned English cucumber
- ¼ cup finely chopped fresh cilantro

Direction

- Rinse the cabbage leaves and dry properly, then remove any tough stems or ribs.
- In a large non-stick skillet, heat the oil on moderately high heat. Add in chicken, flavor with salt, cook and frequently stir for 4-6 minutes until cooked thoroughly.
- At the same time, in a small bowl, beat lime zest, vinegar, and peanut sauce.
- Take the pan away from the heat, add in the sauce mixture and stir to blend. Put cilantro, cucumber, and pear on the chicken and serve in the cabbage leaves.

Nutrition Information

- Calories: 225 calories;
- Total Carbohydrate: 5 g
- Cholesterol: 83 mg
- Total Fat: 10 g
- Fiber: 2 g
- Protein: 28 g
- Sodium: 618 mg
- Sugar: 2 g
- Saturated Fat: 2 g

295. Pixley On A Stick

"A nice appetizer or light meal."
Serving: 30 | Prep: 20m | Ready in: 50m

Ingredients

- 1 lb. sliced bacon
- 5 lbs. boneless skinless chicken breast halves, cut into 2-inch chunks
- 60 wooden toothpicks
- 1 cup white sugar
- 1 (1 oz.) envelope ranch dressing mix

Direction

- Set oven to preheat at 375°F (190°C). Put parchment paper on baking sheets.
- Combine ranch dressing mix and sugar in a shallow bowl.
- Trim bacon slices into two pieces, the short way. Wrap every chicken chunk with half a slice of bacon, keeping it in place using a toothpick. Coat them with sugar-ranch dressing.
- Put these on the baking sheets. Bake in the oven for half an hour, until the crust is brown, the bacon sizzles, and the chicken is well cooked.

Nutrition Information

- Calories: 139 calories;
- Total Carbohydrate: 7.2 g
- Cholesterol: 49 mg
- Total Fat: 3.9 g
- Protein: 17.6 g
- Sodium: 218 mg

296. Popcorn Chicken (taiwanese)

""You'll get addicted to these delicious Taiwanese popcorn chicken bites. The crispy batter is a tasty combination of ginger, soy sauce, and 5-spice flavor. These are quick to make that they are ready in less than 30 minutes.""
Serving: 4 | Prep: 15m | Ready in: 45m

Ingredients

- 1 1/2 lbs. boneless chicken thighs, cut into bite-size pieces
- 1 tbsp. soy sauce
- 1/2 tsp. rice vinegar
- 2 cloves garlic, finely chopped
- 2 tsps. grated ginger
- 1 tsp. Chinese five-spice powder
- 1 tsp. ground white pepper
- 1 tsp. salt
- 1/2 tsp. cayenne pepper
- 1 egg
- 1 cup tempura batter mix, or as needed
- peanut oil for frying
- Garnish:
- 1 bunch Thai basil, chopped
- 2 green onions, chopped
- 1 pinch ground white pepper
- 1 pinch salt

Direction

- In a big bowl, mix together the chicken pieces, rice vinegar, soy sauce, garlic, 5-spice powder, ginger, salt, white pepper, and cayenne pepper. Leave it for 10 minutes to marinate.
- Pour oil in a big cooking pan or a deep-fryer and heat it to 200° C or 400° F.
- Put the egg in a small bowl and beat until it's smooth. In a separate small bowl, pour the tempura batter mix in. Dip the chicken pieces one by one in the egg and then into the tempura batter mix and make sure to shake off the excess. Carefully place the chicken pieces in the hot oil and do it in batches. Fry the chicken for 5-8 minutes until it's golden brown. Move them to a paper towel-lined plate to drain. Do this to the rest of the chicken pieces.
- Sprinkle the chicken pieces with green onions, white pepper, basil leaves, and salt, then serve.

Nutrition Information

- Calories: 524 calories;
- Total Carbohydrate: 14.3 g
- Cholesterol: 163 mg
- Total Fat: 35.5 g
- Protein: 35.8 g
- Sodium: 1057 mg

297. Quick And Easy Baked Buffalo Chicken Dip

""A dip recipe that will definitely please everyone anytime this dish is serve.""
Serving: 8 | Prep: 10m | Ready in: 25m

Ingredients

- 2 (8 oz.) packages cream cheese
- 3/4 cup hot sauce (such as Frank's RedHot ®)
- 1/2 cup shredded pepper Jack cheese
- 1/2 cup blue cheese dressing
- 4 fully cooked chicken breasts, cut into bite-size pieces
- 1/2 cup crumbled blue cheese
- 1/3 cup shredded pepper Jack cheese

Direction

- Preheat the oven to 200 degrees C (400 degrees F). Prepare a baking dish then spread butter on it.
- Mix together blue cheese dressing, hot sauce, 1/2 cup pepper Jack cheese and cream cheese in a large bowl; add in chicken until well coated.
- Transfer the mixture into the greased baking dish and put 1/3 cup pepper Jack cheese and crumbled blue cheese on top of it.
- Place it inside the preheated oven for about 15 to 20 minutes until you see the melting cheese and bubbling up the sides.

Nutrition Information

- Calories: 459 calories;
- Total Carbohydrate: 3.6 g
- Cholesterol: 124 mg
- Total Fat: 39 g
- Protein: 22.4 g
- Sodium: 1099 mg

298. Quick And Easy Chicken Taquitos

"Serve these taquitos on a base of lettuce with sour cream."
Serving: 9 | Prep: 20m | Ready in: 1h

Ingredients

- 3/4 lb. shredded cooked chicken
- 1 (15 oz.) can black beans, drained and rinsed
- 1 (10 oz.) can diced tomatoes with green chile peppers (such as RO*TEL®), drained
- 1 (4 oz.) can diced green chiles, drained
- 1 tsp. ground cumin
- 1/2 tsp. chili powder
- 1/2 tsp. salt
- 1/2 tsp. minced garlic
- 1 cup shredded Mexican cheese blend
- 18 (6 inch) corn tortillas
- cooking spray (such as Pam®)

Direction

- Preheat the oven to 175 degrees C (350 degrees F).
- In a saucepan, combine diced tomatoes, beans, chicken with garlic, salt, chili powder, cumin, diced green chile peppers, and green chile peppers over medium heat; cook and stir for 5-10 minutes, until the filling is heated through. Put the Mexican cheese blend into the filling and stir for 2-3 minutes, until cheese is melted. Take the saucepan away from heat.
- Put corn tortillas on a microwave-safe plate, wrap up with a wet paper towel; heat in the microwave for about 30 seconds, until the tortillas are warmed.
- Scoop 2-3 tbsps. filling into the middle of each tortilla. Tightly roll around the filling, then arrange seam-side down on a baking sheet. Use cooking spray to spray the rolled tortillas.
- Bake for about 30 minutes in the preheated oven, or until crispy and lightly browned.

Nutrition Information

- Calories: 293 calories;
- Total Carbohydrate: 33.5 g
- Cholesterol: 43 mg
- Total Fat: 9.4 g
- Protein: 19.9 g
- Sodium: 745 mg

299. Restaurant-style Buffalo Chicken Wings

"A hot wings recipe I mimicked from a popular restaurant."
Serving: 5 | Prep: 15m | Ready in: 2h

Ingredients

- 1/2 cup all-purpose flour
- 1/4 tsp. paprika
- 1/4 tsp. cayenne pepper
- 1/4 tsp. salt
- 10 chicken wings
- oil for deep frying
- 1/4 cup butter
- 1/4 cup hot sauce
- 1 dash ground black pepper
- 1 dash garlic powder

Direction

- Mix salt, cayenne pepper, paprika and flour in a small bowl. Put chicken wings in big nonporous glass bowl or dish. Sprinkle flour mixture on until coated evenly. Cover bowl or dish. Keep in fridge for 60-90 minutes.
- In a deep fryer, heat oil to 190 degrees C/375 degrees F. Oil should cover entirely wings, around an inch or so deep. In a small saucepan

on low heat, mix garlic powder, pepper, hot sauce and butter. Mix and heat until butter melts and mixture is thoroughly blended. Take off heat. Put aside for serving.

- Fry coated wings for 10-15 minutes in hot oil until wing parts start to brown. Take off heat. Put wings in a serving bowl. Put hot sauce mixture. Mix together then serve.

Nutrition Information

- Calories: 364 calories;
- Total Carbohydrate: 10.7 g
- Cholesterol: 44 mg
- Total Fat: 32.4 g
- Protein: 7.9 g
- Sodium: 497 mg

300. Roasted Red Pepper And Jicama Salsa With Zesty Chunk Guacamole

""A dish that will make your love ones say "Wow" with the taste of different flavors and best serve for parties. Enough to feed a group of people.""
Serving: 12 | Prep: 30m | Ready in: 1h15m

Ingredients

- 1 large red bell pepper
- 1 lb. chicken breast tenders
- 1 tbsp. dried cilantro
- 2 tsps. paprika
- 1/2 tsp. ground black pepper
- 1/2 tsp. monosodium glutamate (MSG)
- 2 tbsps. extra-virgin olive oil
- 1/4 cup extra virgin olive oil
- 1 large yellow onion, minced
- 2 cups matchstick-cut jicama
- 1 tbsp. salt
- 1 tbsp. white sugar
- 3/4 tsp. cayenne pepper
- 1 (10 oz.) can diced tomatoes with green chile peppers, drained and juices reserved.
- 8 oz. sour cream
- 1/4 cup thinly sliced jicama
- salt and ground black pepper to taste
- 1 tbsp. extra-virgin olive oil
- 2 large avocados, peeled, pitted, and diced
- 2 tbsps. lemon juice
- 1 tbsp. dried cilantro
- 1/2 tsp. cayenne pepper
- 1/8 tsp. ground cumin

Direction

- Move an oven rack 6 inches from the heat source and then preheat the oven's broiler.
- Prepare a baking sheet and put the red bell pepper on it.
- Put into the preheated oven until the skin of bell pepper turns to black, 5 minutes each side. The remove it from the oven and let it cool.
- Separate and throw away the blackened skin; chop the pepper and set aside.
- Add paprika, mono sodium glutamate, black pepper and 1 tbsp. cilantro to chicken tenders to season it.
- Place a skillet pan on the stove and turn on to medium heat and put 2 tbsps. of olive oil in the pan. Then put and spread the seasoned chicken tenders in the skillet and lower the heat then cover for about 20 minutes until the chickens pink color fades and is turning into brown on both sides. Once cooked, place the chicken to a plate then set aside to cool down; reserve skillet.
- Place another skillet on the stove in medium heat and put 1/4 cup olive oil then add onion until it turns into dark brown and tender for about 20 minutes.
- Add in 2 cups of jicama, sugar, roasted bell pepper, 1 tbsp. salt and 3/4 cayenne pepper into caramelized onion then stir and cook until jicama begins to soften and remove from heat after 5 more minutes.
- In a pan where chicken was cooked, pour the reserved tomato juices and turn on to medium-high heat for about 5 to 7 minutes until lessen by half and then remove any brown bits in the pan.

- Add sour cream into reduced tomato juice and evenly mixed then remove from heat.
- Add on salt, jimaca slices and pepper to taste.
- Get a clean skillet pan and heat 1 tbsp. olive oil and then put jimaca slices until both sides turns to brown for about 5 to 7 minutes.
- Place avocados, cumin, 1/2 tsp. cayenne pepper, salt, 1 tbsp. cilantro, lemon juice, and tomatoes with green chiles in a bowl to mix together until you reach the slightly creamy guacamole.
- On a large platter, spread out the tomato-sour cream mixture.
- Then put guacamole atop sour cream on top.
- Place the red pepper salsa over guacamole and spread out.
- Slice into chunks the chicken tenders then scatter the jimaca and chunks slices on top of salsa.
- Serve and enjoy.

Nutrition Information

- Calories: 260 calories;
- Total Carbohydrate: 11.5 g
- Cholesterol: 30 mg
- Total Fat: 20 g
- Protein: 10.2 g
- Sodium: 731 mg

301. Saucy Chicken Dip

"It is quick, easy, and tastes terrific."
Serving: 40 | Prep: 20m | Ready in: 45m

Ingredients

- 1 tbsp. vegetable oil
- 3 skinless, boneless chicken breast halves - cubed
- 1 cup shredded mozzarella cheese
- 1 cup shredded Cheddar cheese
- 1 (10.75 oz.) can condensed cream of chicken soup
- 1 hot yellow banana pepper, chopped

Direction

- Set the oven at 350°F (175°C) to preheat.
- Over medium-high heat, heat the oil in a medium skillet. Cook the cubed chicken for 5-10 minutes, or until no more pink.
- Drain chicken and put in a medium saucepan with hot yellow banana pepper, condensed cream of mushroom soup, Cheddar cheese, and mozzarella cheese.
- Uncover and bake for 20-25 minutes in the preheated oven, or until bubbly and lightly browned.

Nutrition Information

- Calories: 38 calories;
- Total Carbohydrate: 0.7 g
- Cholesterol: 11 mg
- Total Fat: 2.3 g
- Protein: 3.6 g
- Sodium: 91 mg

302. Sesame Chicken Strips With Sweet Sauce

"“Flavorful chicken strips especially dipped in the sweet sauce and a hit at summer gatherings.”"
Serving: 11 | Prep: 10m | Ready in: 30m

Ingredients

- 1 cup mayonnaise
- 2 tsps. dried minced onion
- 2 tsps. dry mustard
- 1 cup crushed buttery round cracker crumbs
- 1/2 cup sesame seeds
- 2 lbs. skinless, boneless chicken breast halves
- SAUCE:
- 1 cup mayonnaise
- 2 tbsps. honey

Direction

- Prepare the oven by preheating to 425°F (220°C).

- Mix together mustard, onion, and 1 cup mayonnaise in a shallow bowl or plate. Combine well and reserve. Mix the sesame seeds and cracker crumbs together in another shallow bowl or plate. Slice chicken lengthwise into 1/4-inch strips.
- Dunk chicken strips in mayonnaise mixture, then coat with sesame mixture. Lay coated strips in one layer on a lightly greased cookie sheet.
- Place in the preheated oven and bake for 15 to 18 minutes, or until juices run clear. Combine honey and 1 cup mayonnaise in a small bowl and pair with chicken strips to serve.

Nutrition Information

- Calories: 458 calories;
- Total Carbohydrate: 9.3 g
- Cholesterol: 63 mg
- Total Fat: 37.8 g
- Protein: 21.1 g
- Sodium: 332 mg

303. Slow-cooker Chicken Enchilada Dip

"“Mexican cheese dip!”"
Serving: 12 | Ready in: 3h

Ingredients

- 2 cups chopped fresh tomatoes (about 2 medium)
- 1 cup chopped onion
- 2 cloves garlic
- 1 fresh jalapeño pepper, stemmed
- 1 tbsp. chili powder
- 1 tsp. ground cumin
- ¾ tsp. salt
- 1 lb. boneless, skinless chicken breast
- 8 oz. reduced-fat cream cheese
- 1 15-oz. can black beans, rinsed
- 1 cup corn, fresh or frozen (thawed)
- 1 cup shredded sharp Cheddar cheese
- 2 tbsps. sliced scallions
- 2 tbsps. chopped fresh cilantro

Direction

- In a blender, mix together salt, cumin, chili powder, jalapeno, garlic, onion, and tomatoes. Let puree till gets smooth.
- In a five- to six-quart slow cooker, pour the sauce. In the sauce, nestle chicken. Allow to cook, covered, for 3 hours on High or for 6 hours on Low.
- Take the chicken out and use two forks to shred. Return the chicken back into the slow cooker with the sauce. Add Cheddar, corn, beans, and cream cheese. Stir till combined. Allow to cook, covered, for 10-15 minutes on High till the sauce gets hot and the cheese melts.
- Top with cilantro and scallions and serve!

Nutrition Information

- Calories: 181 calories;
- Total Carbohydrate: 11 g
- Cholesterol: 51 mg
- Total Fat: 9 g
- Fiber: 3 g
- Protein: 15 g
- Sodium: 381 mg
- Sugar: 4 g
- Saturated Fat: 5 g

304. Southern Style Chicken Toast

"Every family loves these dumplings."
Serving: 8 | Prep: 15m | Ready in: 30m

Ingredients

- 1/2 lb. skinless, boneless chicken breast halves - cut into chunks
- 1 carrot, peeled and cut into 1 inch pieces
- 1 egg white
- 2 tsps. cornstarch
- 1/2 tsp. white sugar

- 1/2 tsp. ground ginger
- 1/4 tsp. ground black pepper
- 4 slices white bread
- 2 1/2 tbsps. margarine
- 1/3 cup soy sauce (optional)

Direction

- In a food processor, put black pepper, ginger, sugar, cornstarch, egg white, carrot, and chicken. Pulse until the chicken is well chopped. Slice each bread slice into 4 triangles. Use the chicken mixture to spread each triangle on its side and top.
- In a 12-inch nonstick frying pan, melt half of the margarine over medium heat. Put half of the triangles in the frying pan with the spread side turning down. Cook for 4 minutes until turning golden brown. Use a spatula to turn over and cook for 2 minutes until the other side turns brown. Move to a serving dish and keep warm. Cook the rest of the margarine and triangles in the same way. Enjoy with soy sauce diluted with water to dip.

Nutrition Information

- Calories: 109 calories;
- Total Carbohydrate: 8.9 g
- Cholesterol: 16 mg
- Total Fat: 4.1 g
- Protein: 8.8 g
- Sodium: 756 mg

305. Spicy Buffalo Chicken Bake

"An easy and quick to make recipe that is so flavorful and delicious!"
Serving: 6 | Prep: 10m | Ready in: 30m

Ingredients

- 1 1/2 cups cream cheese, softened
- 2 tbsps. milk
- 1/2 cup Buffalo-style hot pepper sauce
- 1 tbsp. Better Than Bouillon® Roasted Chicken Base
- 2 cups chopped rotisserie chicken
- 1/2 cup cracker crumbs

Direction

- Prepare the oven by preheating to 375 degrees F.
- In a medium size mixing bowl, put in the chicken base, wing sauce, milk and cream cheese together. Mix well. Stir in the chicken.
- Get an 11x7 inch baking dish then scatter the chicken mixture into it. Dash with cracker crumbs on top. Put the baking dish into the preheated oven to cook for 15 to 20 minutes or until cracker crumbs turns into golden brown.
- Slowly get the baking dish then let it cool for 5 minutes.
- Pair with vegetables or crackers and serve right away.

Nutrition Information

- Calories: 389 calories;
- Total Carbohydrate: 14.1 g
- Cholesterol: 99 mg
- Total Fat: 29.3 g
- Protein: 19 g
- Sodium: 1206 mg

306. Sweet And Savory Chicken Puff Pastry Shells

"Puff pastry shells with chicken. Add white wine or apple cider vinegar if apples appear too dry."
Serving: 6 | Prep: 10m | Ready in: 19m

Ingredients

- 6 puff pastry shells
- 1 tbsp. butter
- 2 small apples, peeled and cubed
- 6 slices bacon, diced
- 2 skinless, boneless chicken breast halves, cut into small cubes

Direction

- Preheat oven to 200°C/400°F. Place the pastry shells over a baking sheet.
- Bake for 8 to 10 minutes in preheated oven, or until shells are golden brown.
- Place a saucepan over medium heat and melt the butter. Cook and stir apples in the saucepan for 3 to 5 minutes, or until they are softened slightly. Add bacon and cook for 1 minutes, or until bacon sizzles. Add chicken add cook while stirring for 5 to 7 minutes, or until the chicken is not pink anymore. Evenly split the filling into the 6 baked shells fresh out of the oven.

Nutrition Information

- Calories: 318 calories;
- Total Carbohydrate: 21 g
- Cholesterol: 38 mg
- Total Fat: 19.7 g
- Protein: 15.7 g
- Sodium: 475 mg

307. Teriyaki Chicken Wings With Hot Mango Dipping Sauce

"Baste wings in an orange-soy-ginger mix. Pair with a mango-orange dip for the best experience.""
Serving: 8 | Prep: 50m | Ready in: 1h45m

Ingredients

- Wings:
- 1/2 cup reduced sodium soy sauce
- 1/2 cup reduced sodium chicken broth
- 1/4 cup mirin
- 1/3 cup Stevia In The Raw® Bakers Bag
- 2 tbsps. frozen (thawed) orange juice concentrate
- 2 garlic cloves, sliced lengthwise
- 3/4 inch piece fresh ginger, in 3 slices
- 16 chicken wings
- Sauce:
- 1 cup diced fresh mango
- 2 tbsps. brown mustard
- 2 tbsps. orange marmalade fruit spread
- 2 (1 gram) packets Stevia In The Raw®
- 1 tbsp. fresh lime juice
- 1/8 tsp. cayenne pepper
- 1/2 tsp. salt
- 1/8 tsp. freshly ground pepper
- 2 tbsps. chopped scallions

Direction

- Mix all sauce ingredients together in a small saucepan. Let it boil for 10 minutes over medium-high heat. Let it cool to room temperature. You may remove ginger and garlic if you want. Pour into an airtight container. Chill for maximum 1 day.
- Set oven to preheat at 425°F. Place foil on a 15x11-inch (or larger) baking pan. Spread cooking spray on two 10x10-inch wire racks. Put racks in the pan, making sure they overlap.
- Slice the first joint from the wings, discard. Place wings in the prepared pan in a single layer, with the smooth side up. Bake for 10 minutes.
- Brush sauce on both sides of the chicken wings. Bake for 5 minutes, smooth side up. Brush again, and bake for 5 minutes with the underside up. Brush again, and bake for 5 minutes with the smooth side up. Brush again, baking for 10 minutes with the underside up. Lower oven heat to 400°F. Brush sauce on the surface of the wings. Bake for 10 minutes, topside up.
- Place wings on a platter. Throw out any leftover sauce.
- Mix all sauce ingredients (except scallions) together in a mini-food processor until smooth.
- Place sauce in a bowl. Top with scallions.

Nutrition Information

- Calories: 204 calories;
- Total Carbohydrate: 14.7 g
- Cholesterol: 39 mg
- Total Fat: 9.3 g

- Protein: 14 g
- Sodium: 774 mg

308. Thai Chicken Dip

"Served warm or hot. Try this dip with prawn crackers or papadums."
Serving: 24 | Prep: 10m | Ready in: 20m

Ingredients

- 2 tbsps. vegetable oil
- 1 1/2 lbs. ground chicken
- 2 small red chile peppers
- 2 cloves garlic, crushed
- 1/2 cup chunky peanut butter
- 1/3 cup lime juice
- 1 cup unsweetened coconut cream
- 1 1/2 tbsps. fish sauce
- 1 tbsp. finely chopped Vietnamese mint

Direction

- In a big skillet, heat oil on medium heat. Add chicken. Cool while mixing to crumble until it's not pink. Mix fish sauce, coconut cream, lime juice, peanut butter, garlic and chilies in. boil. Lower heat to low. Simmer for five minutes. Mix mint in. serve hot or warm. Top with a few mint leaves.

Nutrition Information

- Calories: 112 calories;
- Total Carbohydrate: 2.5 g
- Cholesterol: 17 mg
- Total Fat: 8.2 g
- Protein: 8.1 g
- Sodium: 110 mg

309. Thai-style Chicken Wings

"Enjoy this recipe for spicy wings either hot or cold. Plus, they make a perfect appetizer!"
Serving: 6

Ingredients

- 3 lbs. chicken wings
- 1 cup chicken broth
- 1 cup white sugar
- 1/4 cup fish sauce
- 2 tbsps. cider vinegar
- 1 tbsp. cornstarch
- 2 tsps. paprika
- 1 tbsp. vegetable oil
- 1/3 cup minced garlic
- 3 tbsps. minced jalapeno peppers
- 1/4 cup sliced red bell peppers

Direction

- Preheat an oven to 200 degrees C (400 degrees F).
- Mix paprika, cornstarch, vinegar, fish sauce, sugar and broth in a large bowl. Reserve.
- Add chiles, garlic and oil in a hot skillet or wok and then stir fry for about 4 minutes on high heat until garlic is slightly golden. Stir in the broth mixture for about 10 to 15 minutes until it boils and has decreased to about 1 1/4 cups. Keep it warm.
- Put chicken wings into a baking dish of 10x15 inch and then bake with no cover for about 60 to 70 minutes (until crisp and browned). Flip from time to time. Then drain off the fat. Place the wings onto a platter using a slotted spoon and add garlic sauce mixture on top of them, combining thoroughly. If desired, stud with red bell pepper strips.

Nutrition Information

- Calories: 296 calories;
- Total Carbohydrate: 38.4 g
- Cholesterol: 48 mg
- Total Fat: 7.3 g
- Protein: 19.2 g

- Sodium: 911 mg

310. Tiny Chicken Turnovers

"This turnovers dish recipe make a great appetizer."
Serving: 15

Ingredients

- 3 tbsps. chopped onion
- 3 tbsps. butter
- 1 3/4 cups shredded, cooked chicken meat
- 3 tbsps. chicken stock
- 1/4 tsp. garlic salt
- 1/4 tsp. poultry seasoning
- 1/4 tsp. ground black pepper
- 1 (3 oz.) package cream cheese, diced
- 1 1/2 cups all-purpose flour
- 1/2 tsp. salt
- 1/2 tsp. paprika
- 1 cup butter, chilled
- 5 tbsps. cold water

Direction

- Sauté the onion in the butter in a large skillet until tender. Stir in the chicken, cream cheese, pepper, poultry seasoning, garlic salt, and chicken broth. Remove from heat and put aside.
- Set the oven at 190°C (375°F) to preheat.
- Mix flour, paprika, and salt together in a large bowl; cut in butter until the mixture looks like rough crumbs. Add water gradually, using a fork to toss until it forms a ball.
- Roll out the pastry on a floured surface to 1/16 inch thick. Slice with a biscuit cutter or a 2 1/2 inch round cookie. Gather the scraps, reroll and cut into more circles until the pastry is used up.
- On half of each circle, mound a teaspoonful of filling. Use water to moisten the edges; make a half-moon shape by folding the pastry over the filling. Seal the edges by pressing them with a fork. Keep using the fork to prick the tops for steam vents.
- On a baking sheet, arrange the turnovers; in the preheated oven, bake at 190°C (375°F) until golden brown, about 15-20 minutes.

Nutrition Information

- Calories: 220 calories;
- Total Carbohydrate: 10 g
- Cholesterol: 57 mg
- Total Fat: 17.4 g
- Protein: 6.3 g
- Sodium: 237 mg

311.Trisha's Game Day Dip

"It's a spicy dip with the taste of blue cheese and buffalo chicken wings. Serve the dip hot with celery and tortilla chips."
Serving: 40 | Prep: 20m | Ready in: 50m

Ingredients

- 2 cups cubed cooked chicken
- 1 cup chopped celery
- 1 (8 oz.) package cream cheese, softened
- 1 cup hot sauce
- 1 cup blue cheese salad dressing
- 1 cup shredded sharp Cheddar cheese

Direction

- Preheat the oven to 175°C or 350°F.
- In a 2-qt. baking dish, stir blue cheese dressing, hot sauce, cream cheese, celery and chicken together to blend evenly.
- Bake for 30 minutes in the preheated oven till bubbly and hot. To serve, add shredded Cheddar cheese and stir.

Nutrition Information

- Calories: 78 calories;
- Total Carbohydrate: 0.8 g
- Cholesterol: 16 mg
- Total Fat: 6.8 g
- Protein: 3.5 g
- Sodium: 260 mg

312. Val's Hungarian Jewish Chopped Liver

"This dish is basically just chopped liver but enhanced with the traditional Hungarian paprika. Be sure not to add in different kinds of liver and beef since it will ruin the flavor of the liver."
Serving: 8

Ingredients

- 2 tbsps. vegetable oil
- 1 tbsp. unsalted butter (optional)
- 1 large white onion, chopped
- 2 lbs. fresh chicken livers
- 6 hard-cooked eggs
- 1 small white onion, finely chopped
- 1 bunch green onions, chopped
- salt and pepper to taste
- 2 tbsps. paprika
- 2 tbsps. chopped fresh parsley, divided
- 1 head romaine lettuce
- 2 sprigs fresh parsley

Direction

- On medium-high heat, heat butter and oil in a big pan. Cook and stir diced onions until soft. On high heat, sauté chicken liver while stirring frequently. Once the liver is not pink and its juices are clear, transfer the liver with onions to a big mixing bowl.
- Use a potato masher to crush livers. Use your fingers to remove the membranes while mashing. Leave the liver juice in. Crush eggs in another bowl and mix with the liver. Mix in chopped green onions and finely chopped or grated raw onion. The liver mixture should be warm and cook the onions a bit. Sprinkle pepper and salt to taste. Put in at least a tsp. of paprika, add more if desired. Mix in a tbsp. of chopped parsley. Use a large spoon to blend well. Store the mixture in the refrigerator for 1-2 hours.
- Arrange lettuce leaves on plates and the chopped liver on top. Garnish generously with paprika, a tbsp. of fresh chopped parsley, and fresh parsley sprigs to serve.

Nutrition Information

- Calories: 258 calories;
- Total Carbohydrate: 8.5 g
- Cholesterol: 573 mg
- Total Fat: 14.1 g
- Protein: 24.4 g
- Sodium: 116 mg

313. Vegetarian Buffalo Chicken Dip

"Serve this spicy, cheesy and creamy vegetarian dip with wheat tortilla chips."
Serving: 16 | Prep: 10m | Ready in: 1h10m

Ingredients

- 1 (8 oz.) package seasoned chicken-style vegetarian strips (such as Morningstar Farms® Chik'n Strips), diced
- 2 (8 oz.) packages reduced fat cream cheese, softened
- 1 (16 oz.) bottle reduced-fat ranch salad dressing
- 1 (12 fluid oz.) bottle hot buffalo wing sauce (such as Frank's® REDHOT Buffalo Wing Sauce)
- 1 cup Colby-Monterey Jack cheese blend

Direction

- In a slow cooker, place buffalo wing sauce, ranch dressing, cream cheese and diced vegetarian chicken strips. Cook and stir occasionally on Low for 1-2 hours till the dip is hot and cheese is melted. Add shredded cheese, stir to serve.

Nutrition Information

- Calories: 186 calories;
- Total Carbohydrate: 11.7 g
- Cholesterol: 24 mg

- Total Fat: 11.4 g
- Protein: 8.9 g
- Sodium: 1024 mg

Chapter 7: Meatball Appetizer Recipes

***

314. Bacon-wrapped Meatballs

"These generous appetizers are indeed a hit at whatever kind of party I bring them in. The pleasing aroma while you bake it is enticing."
Serving: 4 dozen. | Prep: 35m | Ready in: 50m

Ingredients

- 2 eggs, lightly beaten
- 2 tbsps. milk
- 3/4 cup shredded Parmesan cheese
- 1/4 cup seasoned bread crumbs
- 1/2 tsp. salt
- 1/4 tsp. pepper
- 1 lb. lean ground beef (90% lean)
- 24 bacon strips, cut in half widthwise

Direction

- Combine the milk, eggs, cheese, pepper, bread crumbs, and salt in a big bowl. Crumble the beef on the mixture and stir it well. Form into 1-in. balls.
- Place the bacon in a big skillet and let it cook over medium heat until partly cooked yet not crisp. Transfer to paper towels to remove excess fat and drain. Wrap a piece of bacon around every meatball; seal using a wooden toothpick.
- Arrange the meatballs on an oiled rack in a shallow baking pan. Let it bake for 8 minutes at 375°. Turn to the other side; continuously bake for additional 3-5 minutes or until the bacon is crisp and the meat is no longer pink.

Nutrition Information

- Calories: 42 calories
- Total Carbohydrate: 1 g
- Cholesterol: 19 mg
- Total Fat: 3 g
- Fiber: 0 g
- Protein: 4 g
- Sodium: 135 mg

315. BBQ Cola Meatballs

"Roasted meatballs simmered in barbeque sauce for potlucks that only takes a few minutes to complete."
Serving: 18 | Prep: 15m | Ready in: 4h

Ingredients

- 1 1/2 lbs. lean ground beef
- 1 1/4 cups dry bread crumbs
- 1 egg
- 3 tbsps. grated onion
- 1 (1 oz.) package dry Ranch-style dressing mix
- 1 cup ketchup
- 2 tbsps. apple cider vinegar
- 3/4 cup cola-flavored carbonated beverage
- 1/2 cup chopped onion
- 1/2 cup chopped green bell pepper
- 1 tsp. seasoning salt
- 1/2 tsp. ground black pepper
- 1 tbsp. Worcestershire sauce

Direction

- Set an oven to 190°C (375°F) and start preheating.
- Blend the Ranch dressing mix, grated onion, egg, breadcrumbs, and ground beef together in a large bowl until combined properly. Form into 1-inch meatballs and arrange on a 10x15-

inch jellyroll pan or any baking sheet that has sides that can catch the grease.

- In the prepared oven, bake for half an hour and turning over halfway through. In a slow cooker, combine together the green pepper, chopped onion, cola, cider vinegar, and ketchup while roasting the meatballs. Flavor with Worcestershire sauce, pepper, and seasoning salt.
- Take the meatballs away from the baking sheet and drop them into the sauce in the slow cooker. Put a cover on and cook for 3 hours on Low, then before serving, take the lid away and cook for 15 more minutes.

Nutrition Information

- Calories: 136 calories;
- Total Carbohydrate: 11.8 g
- Cholesterol: 36 mg
- Total Fat: 5.5 g
- Protein: 9.4 g
- Sodium: 396 mg

316. BBQ Meatballs With Pepper And Cheese Animal Cut-outs

"A great snack after a tiring day to serve with cold milk and BBQ sauce."

Serving: 6 | Prep: 45m | Ready in: 1h15m

Ingredients

- 2 slices bread, crusts removed, torn into pieces
- 1/2 cup whole milk
- 1 egg, beaten
- 1 tbsp. dried parsley
- 1/2 tsp. salt
- 1/8 tsp. garlic powder
- 1/8 tsp. onion powder
- 1/2 tsp. dried Italian herb seasoning
- 1/4 tsp. sugar
- 1 tbsp. freshly grated Parmesan cheese
- 1 lb. ground beef
- 1/4 cup grated sweet onion
- 1 cup barbecue sauce, plus additional for serving
- Animal Cut-Outs:
- 1 green bell pepper
- 1 orange bell pepper
- 1 red bell pepper
- 4 (1/4-inch) slices Colby-Monterey Jack cheese
- 4 (1/4-inch) slices mild Cheddar cheese
- Animal vegetable cutters
- 25 4-inch toothpicks

Direction

- Set an oven to 175°C (350°F) and start preheating.
- In a bowl, immerse pieces of torn bread in the milk for 5 minutes. Twist gently to squeeze the milk out. Place the beaten egg into the immersed bread and combine properly.
- In a small bowl, mix together Parmesan cheese, sugar, Italian herb seasoning, salt, parsley, onion, powder, and garlic powder. Put into the egg-bread mixture.
- In the mixing bowl, arrange the ground beef. Put onions and the seasoning mixture; using a fork, combine together. Put in up to 1 tbsp. of milk if the mixture becomes too dry. Roll to form 25 meatballs and place them on a rimmed baking sheet.
- In the prepared oven, bake for 18 minutes until they are browned and cooked thoroughly.
- Place the meatballs on a paper towel to drain. Take the grease out from the baking sheet. Place the meatballs back onto the baking sheet. Pour over the meatballs with a cup of BBQ sauce.
- Put the sheet into the oven, bake for 12 minutes more.
- Create animals out of red, orange, and green peppers with a small animal vegetable cutter. Slice the animals out of mild Cheddar and Colby Jack cheese.
- Place the meatballs on a paper towel to drain and if desired, put in more BBQ sauce. Put the cheese animal cut out and then pepper animal

cut out to the toothpicks. Do quickly to insert a toothpick into each meatball.

Nutrition Information

- Calories: 413 calories;
- Total Carbohydrate: 25.5 g
- Cholesterol: 113 mg
- Total Fat: 24 g
- Protein: 23.3 g
- Sodium: 1011 mg

317. Bone-crunching Meatballs

"Unique meatball recipe."
Serving: 5 dozen. | Prep: 30m | Ready in: 40m

Ingredients

- 1 can (8 oz.) sliced water chestnuts, drained
- 1 large egg, lightly beaten
- 3 tbsps. reduced-sodium soy sauce
- 1/2 cup chopped green onions (green part only)
- 1/4 cup dry bread crumbs
- 2 tbsps. minced fresh cilantro
- 1-1/2 tsps. grated lime zest
- 1-1/2 tsps. minced fresh gingerroot
- 1 garlic clove, minced
- 1/4 tsp. salt
- 1/4 tsp. pepper
- 1-1/2 lbs. lean ground turkey
- 2 tbsps. canola oil
- Plum sauce

Direction

- Halve water chestnut slices to get 60 pieces; put aside. Keep leftover water chestnut slices for later.
- Mix initial 10 ingredients in big bowl. Crumble turkey on mixture; stir well. Divide to 60 portions; form each portion around water chestnut piece.
- Preheat an oven to 350°. Sauté meatballs in oil in big nonstick skillet for 5 minutes or till browned in batches. Put in 13x9-in. baking dish.
- Cover. Bake till meat isn't pink anymore or for 10-15 minutes; drain. Serve it with plum sauce.

Nutrition Information

- Calories: 27 calories
- Total Carbohydrate: 1 g
- Cholesterol: 12 mg
- Total Fat: 2 g
- Fiber: 0 g
- Protein: 2 g
- Sodium: 71 mg

318. Boudin Balls

""Impressive taste with textural contrast between moist, savory inside and crispy outside that is a beauty to indulge.""
Serving: 12 | Prep: 45m | Ready in: 6h25m

Ingredients

- 1 3/4 lbs. boneless pork shoulder, cut into 1-inch cubes
- 6 oz. chicken livers, rinsed and trimmed
- 1 yellow onion, diced
- 2 stalks celery, diced
- 1/2 cup diced poblano pepper
- 1/2 cup seeded and diced jalapeno pepper
- 6 cloves garlic, minced
- 3 tbsps. kosher salt
- 1 1/2 tbsps. ground black pepper
- 1 tsp. chili powder
- 1 tsp. cayenne pepper
- 4 cups cooked white rice, or more to taste
- 1/2 cup chopped fresh parsley
- 1/2 cup chopped green onion
- 1 cup all-purpose flour
- 1 pinch cayenne pepper, or to taste
- salt and ground black pepper to taste
- 1 cup dry bread crumbs
- 2 eggs, beaten
- 2 cups oil for frying, or as needed

Direction

- Mix 1 tsp. cayenne pepper, chili powder, 1 1/2 tbsps. ground black pepper, kosher salt, garlic, jalapeno pepper, poblano pepper, celery, onion, livers, and pork shoulders in a large pot. Use a lid to cover the pot and chill in the refrigerator for 2 hours or overnight until flavors combine.
- Cover the pork mixture with 2-inches of water; bring to a boil, adjust the heat to low, and simmer for about 1 1/2 hours until the meat is tender. Take away from the heat. Pour mixture through a strainer, reserving meat and strained liquid separately.
- Put drained meat mixture to a cutting board and finely chop.
- Mix green onion, parsley, rice, and chopped meat in a bowl. Slowly add reserved cooking liquid to meat mixture, 1 spoonful at a time, stirring until fully incorporated between each addition, until the mixture has a consistency similar to paste. Use plastic wrap to cover the bowl and chill in the refrigerator for at least 2 hours to overnight until chilled.
- Put oil in a large saucepan or a deep-fryer and heat to 350°F (175°C).
- Form chilled meat mixture into 1-inch balls.
- Combine black pepper, salt, 1 pinch cayenne pepper, and flour in a shallow bowl. Pour breadcrumbs into another shallow bowl. Whisk eggs in another shallow bowl.
- Press 1 ball into flour mixture gently to coat; shake off the excess flour. Dunk ball into the beaten egg; press ball into bread crumbs. Transfer breaded ball onto a plate and repeat the breading method with the rest of meatballs.
- Cook boudin balls in preheated oil, working in batches, flipping once, until hot on the inside and crispy on the outside, 3-4 minutes.

Nutrition Information

- Calories: 301 calories;
- Total Carbohydrate: 32.7 g
- Cholesterol: 108 mg
- Total Fat: 12.2 g
- Protein: 14.3 g
- Sodium: 1569 mg

319. Buffalo Chicken Meatballs

"A simple, flavorful, and healthy meatballs to serve along with blue or ranch cheese dressing."

Serving: 6 | Prep: 15m | Ready in: 25m

Ingredients

- oil for frying
- 1 (6 oz.) package chicken-flavored stuffing mix
- 1 lb. ground chicken
- 1/3 cup hot sauce (such as Frank's RedHot ®)
- 2 eggs
- 1 tsp. hot sauce (such as Frank's RedHot ®), or to taste

Direction

- Heat the oil in a large saucepan or deep fryer to 175°C (350°F).
- Put the stuffing mix into a plastic resealable bag and crush it with a rolling pin into fine crumbs. In a large bowl, use a potato masher to mash eggs, 1/3 cup of hot sauce, chicken, and the crushed stuffing mix until just blended. Shape the mixture into 1-inch meatballs.
- In the heated oil, fry the meatballs for 10-15 minutes until they are browned and cooked thoroughly. An instant-read thermometer should register at least 165°F (74°C) when inserted into the center. Use approximately a tsp. of hot sauce to drizzle the meatballs.

Nutrition Information

- Calories: 358 calories;
- Total Carbohydrate: 21.3 g
- Cholesterol: 109 mg
- Total Fat: 19.9 g
- Protein: 22.7 g
- Sodium: 846 mg

320. Buffalo Meatballs

"Serve these with blue cheese dressing, hot sauce, and celery sticks."

Serving: 75 | Prep: 15m | Ready in: 35m

Ingredients

- 2 tbsps. olive oil
- 3/4 cup hot pepper sauce (such as Frank's RedHot®)
- 1/2 cup butter
- 2 lbs. ground chicken
- 1 2/3 cups dry bread crumbs
- 2 stalks celery, minced
- 2 large eggs
- 2 tbsps. hot pepper sauce (such as Frank's RedHot®), or to taste

Direction

- Set the oven at 230°C (450°F) to preheat. Use olive oil to coat a large rimmed baking sheet.
- Heat butter and 3/4 cup hot sauce over low heat in a saucepan, whisking constantly, until the butter is melted and fully incorporated. Cool to room temperature.
- In a bowl, stir chicken, eggs, celery, hot sauce mixture, and bread crumbs until mixed evenly; form into 1-inch balls and put on the prepared baking sheet.
- In the preheated oven, bake for about 15 minutes, or until cooked through. Check by inserting an instant-read thermometer into the center and it should state at least 74°C (165°F). Cool for 5 minutes on the baking sheet. Transfer the meatballs to a platter and drizzle with 2 tbsps. hot sauce.

Nutrition Information

- Calories: 41 calories;
- Total Carbohydrate: 1.9 g
- Cholesterol: 16 mg
- Total Fat: 2.2 g
- Protein: 3.2 g
- Sodium: 104 mg

321. Carla's Sausage Cheese Balls

"Cheesy, meaty, and delicious."

Serving: 12 | Prep: 20m | Ready in: 40m

Ingredients

- 1 (16 oz.) package bulk mild pork sausage
- 1 (16 oz.) package bulk hot pork sausage
- 1 (8 oz.) package shredded sharp Cheddar cheese
- 2 cups biscuit baking mix (such as Bisquick®)

Direction

- Set the oven at 200°C (400°F) to preheat.
- Use aluminum foil to line a baking sheet.
- In a large bowl, mix hot sausage and mild sausage until combined evenly.
- Add Cheddar cheese into the sausage mixture and stir.
- Put into the sausage mixture with the biscuit baking mix, about 1/2 cup at a time, blend until the baking mix is moistened.
- Next, shape the meat mixture into 1 1/4 to 1 1/2-inch ball.
- Place on the prepared baking sheet.
- In the preheated oven, bake for about 20 minutes until the cheese is browned and the center of the meatballs is not pink anymore.

Nutrition Information

- Calories: 349 calories;
- Total Carbohydrate: 13.1 g
- Cholesterol: 63 mg
- Total Fat: 25.5 g
- Protein: 16.3 g
- Sodium: 1043 mg

322. Cheese Meatballs

"These rich, cheesy meatballs are good complements for party appetizers."
Serving: about 4 dozen. | Prep: 20m | Ready in: 35m

Ingredients

- 3 cups (12 oz.) finely shredded cheddar cheese
- 1 cup biscuit/baking mix
- 1/2 tsp. salt
- 1/4 tsp. pepper
- 1/4 tsp. garlic powder
- 1 lb. lean ground beef (90% lean)

Direction

- Combine the first 5 ingredients in a large bowl. Crumble the beef over the mixture and mix well. Next, roll into 1-in. balls. On a greased rack in a shallow baking pan, place these meatballs.
- Bake for 12-15 minutes at 400°, or until the meat is no more pink; drain.

Nutrition Information

- Calories: 148 calories
- Total Carbohydrate: 5 g
- Cholesterol: 36 mg
- Total Fat: 9 g
- Fiber: 0 g
- Protein: 10 g
- Sodium: 314 mg

323. Cheesy Meatballs

"“My cheese, sausage, and beef recipes are always a hit.”"
Serving: about 9 dozen. | Prep: 60m | Ready in: 05h00m

Ingredients

- 1 large egg
- 1/2 cup 2% milk
- 2 tbsps. dried minced onion
- 4 tbsps. chili powder, divided
- 1 tsp. salt
- 1 tsp. pepper
- 1-1/2 cups crushed Ritz crackers (about 1 sleeve)
- 2 lbs. ground beef
- 1 lb. Jones No Sugar Pork Sausage Roll sausage
- 2 cups shredded process cheese (Velveeta)
- 1 can (26 oz.) condensed tomato soup, undiluted
- 2-1/2 cups water
- 1 cup packed brown sugar

Direction

- Prepare the oven by preheating to 400 degrees. Whisk pepper, salt, 2 tbsps. chili powder, minced onion, milk, and egg in a large bowl; mix in crushed crackers. Put in cheese, sausage, and beef; whisk lightly but thoroughly.
- Form the mixture into 1-inch balls. Transfer meatballs to greased racks in 15x10x1-inch baking pans. Bake for 15-18 minutes or until browned.
- In the meantime, mix the leftover chili powder, brown sugar, water, and soup in a 5 or 6-1t slow cooker. Mix in meatballs gently. Cook for 4 to 5 hours on low, covered, or until meatballs are cooked through.

Nutrition Information

- Calories: 51 calories
- Total Carbohydrate: 4 g
- Cholesterol: 11 mg
- Total Fat: 3 g
- Fiber: 0 g
- Protein: 2 g
- Sodium: 104 mg

324. Chicken Parmesan Meatball Sliders

"A wonderful recipe for ground chicken meatballs that are served over the toasted slider rolls with the Ragu® Old World Style® Traditional Sauce."
Serving: 4 | Prep: 15m | Ready in: 40m

Ingredients

- 1 lb. ground chicken
- 1/4 cup panko bread crumbs
- 2 cloves garlic, minced
- 1 tsp. dried oregano
- 1/2 tsp. kosher salt
- 1 egg, beaten
- 1 cup shredded Parmesan cheese
- 1 cup Ragu® Old World Style® Traditional Pasta Sauce
- 12 slider rolls, halved horizontally

Direction

- Set an oven to 190°C (375°F) and start preheating.
- In a bowl, blend together mozzarella cheese, egg, salt, oregano, garlic, breadcrumbs, and chicken. Combine thoroughly and roll the mixture into twelve 1 1/2-inch meatballs.
- In an oven-proof skillet, arrange the meatballs. Bake for 20-25 minutes until the meatballs are cooked thoroughly.
- Heat Ragu® Old World Style® Pasta Sauce until it is warmed thoroughly. Then toast the rolls. Scoop the sauce on the bottom of a slider bun to create a slider. Put the top of bun and meatball on top. Then serve.

Nutrition Information

- Calories: 544 calories;
- Total Carbohydrate: 486.6 g
- Cholesterol: 130 mg
- Total Fat: 16.4 g
- Protein: 42.3 g
- Sodium: 1068 mg

325. Chicken Wing Dings

"Delicious meatballs made from the sauce Buffalo chicken wings."
Serving: 2-1/2 dozen meatballs (1-1/2 cups dip). | Prep: 25m | Ready in: 35m

Ingredients

- 1/4 cup finely chopped celery
- 1/4 cup finely chopped onion
- 1/4 cup finely chopped carrot
- 1 envelope ranch salad dressing mix
- 1 large egg, lightly beaten
- 1 lb. ground chicken
- 2 cups crushed potato chips
- 2 tbsps. canola oil
- 1 container (8 oz.) spreadable cream cheese
- 3/4 cup crumbled blue cheese
- 2 tbsps. whole milk
- 2 garlic cloves, minced
- 1/2 cup buffalo wing sauce

Direction

- Blend the first 5 ingredients. Place the crumbled chicken over the mixture and combine properly. Form into 1-inch balls and roll them in the potato chips. Heat the oil in a large skillet on medium heat. Working in batches, cook the meatballs until they are not pink anymore; let drain. For the dip: Blend garlic, milk, blue cheese, and cream cheese spread. Drizzle the wing sauce over the meatballs; serve along with the dip.

326. Chinese Meatballs

"“You can use 5 tbsps. of chopped crystallized ginger instead of the fresh one if desired.”"
Serving: about 6 dozen. | Prep: 35m | Ready in: 03h35m

Ingredients

- 2 large eggs, lightly beaten
- 2 tbsps. soy sauce
- 1 tsp. salt

- 6 green onions, sliced
- 2 lbs. lean ground pork
- 2 cans (8 oz. each) sliced water chestnuts, drained and chopped
- 1 cup dry bread crumbs
- SAUCE:
- 1/4 cup cornstarch
- 1 cup pineapple juice
- 1/3 cup sugar
- 4 tsps. minced fresh gingerroot
- 1 can (10-1/2 oz.) condensed beef consomme, undiluted
- 1/2 cup white vinegar

Direction

- Prepare the oven by preheating to 400 degrees. Mix the first four ingredients in a large bowl. Put in bread crumbs, water chestnuts, pork; stir lightly but thoroughly. Form the mixture into 1-inch balls. Put in a 15x10x1-inch pan that is greased. Bake for 15 minutes.
- Combine juice and cornstarch in a 5- or 6-qt slow cooker until smooth. Mix in the rest of the ingredients. Put in meatballs; gently mix to coat. Cook for 3-4 hours on low, covered until the sauce is thickened and meatballs are cooked through. Freeze option: Place cooled meatball mixture in freezer containers and freeze. To use, keep in the refrigerator overnight to partially thaw. Put in a covered saucepan to heat through, stirring gently and putting a little broth if needed.

Nutrition Information

- Calories: 41 calories
- Total Carbohydrate: 4 g
- Cholesterol: 12 mg
- Total Fat: 2 g
- Fiber: 0 g
- Protein: 3 g
- Sodium: 109 mg

327. Cocktail Meatballs III

"These are easy and yummy."
Serving: 18 | Prep: 25m | Ready in: 35m

Ingredients

- 3 lbs. ground beef
- 2 (1 oz.) packages dry onion soup mix
- 3 slices white bread
- 2 tbsps. half-and-half
- 1 (28 oz.) bottle ketchup
- 1 cup packed dark brown sugar
- 2 tbsps. Worcestershire sauce

Direction

- Set the oven at 350°F (175°C) to preheat.
- Remove the crusts from the white bread, and shred into small bread crumbs. Combine half-and-half cream, white bread crumbs, the soup mix, and beef in a medium-size mixing bowl. Roll into 1-inch balls and place in 9x13 inch baking dishes (bake the meatballs in batches or as many baking dishes as it takes).
- Bake until browned, around 10-15 minutes.
- Set a slow cooker to high temperature, mix Worcestershire sauce, brown sugar, and ketchup together. Cook until the mixture boils, then lower the temperature to low, continue to cook until you are ready to present the meatballs.
- Put the meatballs in the sauce and enjoy.

Nutrition Information

- Calories: 346 calories;
- Total Carbohydrate: 27.4 g
- Cholesterol: 65 mg
- Total Fat: 20.6 g
- Protein: 13.9 g
- Sodium: 863 mg

328. Cocktail Meatballs IV

"An incredibly simple appetizer to make."
Serving: 6 | Prep: 30m | Ready in: 1h

Ingredients

- 2 lbs. ground beef
- 10 oz. grape jelly
- 1/4 cup chili sauce
- 2 tbsps. prepared mustard

Direction

- Set an oven to 175°C (350°F) and start preheating. Use aluminum foil to line a large roasting pan.
- Form the ground beef into golf-size balls. On the lined roasting pan, arrange them until finished, 20-25 minutes.
- At the same time, in a 2-quart Dutch oven, heat together the mustard, chili sauce, and jelly. Drain the meatballs and place into the Dutch oven. Put a cover on and bring to a simmer on low for 30 minutes. Then serve hot with toothpicks in a chaffing dish.

Nutrition Information

- Calories: 601 calories;
- Total Carbohydrate: 33.4 g
- Cholesterol: 129 mg
- Total Fat: 40.4 g
- Protein: 25.7 g
- Sodium: 313 mg

329. Cranberry Appetizer Meatballs

"Savory meatballs with tangy sauce to serve as a party snack."
Serving: about 7 dozen. | Prep: 25m | Ready in: 35m

Ingredients

- 2 large eggs, lightly beaten
- 1 cup dry bread crumbs
- 1/3 cup minced fresh parsley
- 1/3 cup ketchup
- 2 tbsps. finely chopped onion
- 2 tbsps. soy sauce
- 2 garlic cloves, minced
- 1/2 tsp. salt
- 1/4 tsp. pepper
- 2 lbs. ground beef
- CRANBERRY SAUCE:
- 1 can (14 oz.) whole-berry cranberry sauce
- 1 bottle (12 oz.) chili sauce
- 1 tbsp. brown sugar
- 1 tbsp. prepared mustard
- 1 tbsp. lemon juice
- 2 garlic cloves, minced

Direction

- Set an oven to 400 degrees and start preheating. Blend the first 9 ingredients. Put the crumbled beef over the mixture and combine thoroughly. Form into 1-inch balls.
- In a shallow baking pan, arrange the meatballs on a rack. Bake for 15 minutes until they are not pink anymore. Place into a 3-quart chafing dish or slow cooker.
- At the same time, blend all the sauce ingredients in a large saucepan; bring to a simmer and stir from time to time for 10 minutes. Spread over the meatballs. Then serve them warm.

Nutrition Information

- Calories: 39 calories
- Total Carbohydrate: 4 g
- Cholesterol: 11 mg
- Total Fat: 1 g
- Fiber: 0 g
- Protein: 2 g
- Sodium: 124 mg

330. Crock Pot® Party Meatballs

"The best part of this recipe is that they are very easy to make."
Serving: 8 | Prep: 5m | Ready in: 3h5m

Ingredients

- 1 (2 lb.) bag frozen cooked meatballs
- 1 (14.5 oz.) can whole berry cranberry sauce
- 1 (12 oz.) bottle tomato-based chili sauce
- 1/2 lemon, juiced
- 2 drops hot sauce (such as Tabasco®), or more to taste

Direction

- In a slow cooker, put frozen meatballs. Add the hot sauce, lemon juice, chili sauce, and cranberry sauce. Stir to evenly distribute the sauce over meatballs.
- Cook on High for about 3 hours, or until the meatballs are completely defrosted and hot.

Nutrition Information

- Calories: 320 calories;
- Total Carbohydrate: 27.3 g
- Cholesterol: 94 mg
- Total Fat: 14.6 g
- Protein: 19.1 g
- Sodium: 210 mg

331. Curried Chicken Balls Appetizer

"The savory recipe goes well for any occasion."
Serving: about 5 dozen appetizers. | Prep: 20m | Ready in: 20m

Ingredients

- 6 oz. cream cheese, softened
- 2 tbsps. orange marmalade
- 2 tsps. curry powder
- 3/4 tsp. salt
- 1/4 tsp. pepper
- 3 cups finely chopped cooked chicken
- 3 tbsps. finely chopped green onion
- 3 tbsps. finely chopped celery
- 1 cup finely chopped almonds, toasted

Direction

- Beat the first 5 ingredients in a large bowl until well combined. Stir in the celery, onion, and chicken.
- Form into 1-in. balls, then roll in almonds. Wrap up and chill until firm (it can be chilled up to 2 days).

Nutrition Information

- Calories: 98 calories
- Total Carbohydrate: 3 g
- Cholesterol: 23 mg
- Total Fat: 6 g
- Fiber: 1 g
- Protein: 8 g
- Sodium: 122 mg

332. Easy Sauerkraut And Sausage Balls

""A must have recipe for New Year's Eve with your family!""
Serving: 10 | Prep: 20m | Ready in: 50m

Ingredients

- 1 (20 oz.) can sauerkraut
- 1 lb. bulk pork sausage

Direction

- Prepare the oven by preheating to 350°F (175°C). Use aluminum foil to line a baking sheet. Put a wire rack on top of the aluminum foil.
- Put sauerkraut in a colander in the sink and use the back of a large spoon to squeeze all the liquid out. Flake sauerkraut into a large bowl and put in the sausage; stir well. Roll sausage mixture into quarter-size balls and transfer to

the rack on the prepared baking sheets and arrange them.

- Place in the preheated oven and bake for 30 to 40 minutes until browned and cooked through.
- An instant-read thermometer poked into the center should register at least 160°F (70°C).

Nutrition Information

- Calories: 126 calories;
- Total Carbohydrate: 2.7 g
- Cholesterol: 26 mg
- Total Fat: 9.8 g
- Protein: 6.7 g
- Sodium: 775 mg

333. Easy Sausage Cheese Balls

"These are really great for appetizers or for breakfast with the make-ahead sausage cheese balls."
Serving: 36 | Prep: 10m | Ready in: 25m

Ingredients

- 1 lb. sausage
- 4 cups shredded Cheddar cheese
- 3 cups baking mix

Direction

- Set the oven to 200°C or 400°F.
- Mix together dry baking mix, cheese and sausage in a medium size bowl, then shape the mixture into walnut-sized balls. Put on a cookie sheet lined with foil
- Bake for 12-15 minutes. Serve hot.

Nutrition Information

- Calories: 137 calories;
- Total Carbohydrate: 7.5 g
- Cholesterol: 22 mg
- Total Fat: 9.4 g
- Protein: 5.5 g
- Sodium: 354 mg

334. Enchilada Meatballs

"These will be a hit at parties."
Serving: 6

Ingredients

- 2 cups crumbled cornbread
- 1 (10 oz.) can enchilada sauce, divided
- 1/2 tsp. salt
- 1 1/2 lbs. ground beef chuck
- 1 (10 oz.) can tomato sauce
- 1 cup shredded Mexican cheese blend, divided

Direction

- Preheat the oven to 175° C (350° F).
- Combine salt, 1/2 of the cheese, 1/2 of the enchilada sauce, and cornbread in a large bowl. Crumble the beef into the mixture, and use your hands to blend well. Roll into 1-inch meatballs, and arrange on any cookie sheet with sides to catch the drippings, or on a 10x15 inch jellyroll pan.
- Bake until the meat is cooked through in the preheated oven, about 18-22 minutes.
- During the cooking time of the meatballs, in a saucepan, make the tomato sauce and the remaining enchilada sauce warm up. Then use a slotted spoon to take the meatballs out of the pan, and put in a serving dish. Pour over the meatballs with the heated sauce, then dust on top with the rest of the cheese. Use toothpicks for serving.

Nutrition Information

- Calories: 398 calories;
- Total Carbohydrate: 15.4 g
- Cholesterol: 100 mg
- Total Fat: 28.1 g
- Protein: 21.2 g
- Sodium: 812 mg

335. Flavorful Turkey Meatballs

"Low-fat and low-calorie meatballs!"
Serving: 2 servings. | Prep: 15m | Ready in: 35m

Ingredients

- 2 tbsps. dry bread crumbs
- 2 tbsps. chopped green pepper
- 1 egg white
- 1 garlic clove, minced
- 2 drops Louisiana-style hot sauce
- 1/3 lb. lean ground turkey
- 1 tsp. canola oil
- SAUCE:
- 1/4 cup ketchup
- 2 tbsps. water
- 4 tsps. lemon juice
- 4 tsps. red wine vinegar
- 2 tsps. brown sugar
- 2 tsps. molasses
- 1/2 tsp. ground mustard
- 1/4 to 1/2 tsp. chili powder
- 1/8 to 1/4 tsp. cayenne pepper
- 1/8 tsp. pepper

Direction

- Mix hot sauce, garlic, egg white, green pepper and breadcrumbs in big bowl. Crumble turkey on mixture; stir well. Form to 1-inch balls. Brown meatballs in oil in small nonstick skillet; drain.
- Mix sauce ingredients; put on meatballs. Boil. Lower heat. Cover. Simmer till heated through for 10 minutes.

Nutrition Information

- Calories: 63 calories
- Total Carbohydrate: 6 g
- Cholesterol: 15 mg
- Total Fat: 2 g
- Fiber: 0 g
- Protein: 4 g
- Sodium: 134 mg

336. Glazed Sausage Bites Appetizer

"These zesty meatballs have a different flavor."
Serving: 2 dozen. | Prep: 15m | Ready in: 40m

Ingredients

- 1 lb. Jones No Sugar Pork Sausage Roll sausage
- 1 egg
- 1/2 cup saltine or butter-flavored cracker crumbs
- 2 tbsps. milk
- 1/2 tsp. rubbed sage
- 1/2 cup water
- 1/4 cup ketchup
- 2 tbsps. brown sugar
- 1 tbsp. soy sauce
- 1 tbsp. vinegar

Direction

- Combine the sausage, sage, milk, crumbs, and egg in a bowl; mix well. Roll into 1-in. balls. Brown the meatballs over medium heat in a skillet; drain. Combine and mix well the remaining ingredients. Put into the skillet; bring to a boil. Lower the heat; simmer, covered, until the meatballs' centers are no more pink, for 15-20 minutes.

337. Grandma's Cocktail Meatballs

"Tasty and easy recipe for meatballs to make for family events or holiday meals."
Serving: 8 | Prep: 15m | Ready in: 45m

Ingredients

- 2 lbs. ground beef
- 1/4 cup crushed saltine crackers
- 1 egg
- 1 (1 oz.) package dry onion soup mix
- 2 tbsps. vegetable oil
- 14 oz. apple jelly
- 13 oz. ketchup

- 1/2 cup red wine

Direction

- In a bowl, combine the onion soup mix, egg, crackers, and beef together; form into around fifty 1-inch balls.
- In a nonstick skillet, heat the oil on medium-high heat. In the heated oil, brown the meatballs for 2 minutes on each side.
- In a large pot, stir together ketchup and apple jelly on medium-high heat; stir and cook until the mixture becomes smooth and the jelly is melted. Pour the wine into the jelly mixture and stir, drop the meatballs, turn down the heat to medium-low and then cook at a simmer for 25 minutes until the meatballs are cooked thoroughly.

Nutrition Information

- Calories: 442 calories;
- Total Carbohydrate: 47.5 g
- Cholesterol: 94 mg
- Total Fat: 18.2 g
- Protein: 21.1 g
- Sodium: 914 mg

338. Ham Balls With Brown Sugar Glaze

"Sweet smoky meatballs to impress your guests."
Serving: about 6 dozen. | Prep: 30m | Ready in: 60m

Ingredients

- 1 lb. fully cooked ham, cubed
- 1 lb. ground pork
- 1 cup whole milk
- 1 cup crushed cornflakes
- 1 large egg, lightly beaten
- 1/4 cup packed brown sugar
- 1 tbsp. ground mustard
- 1/2 tsp. salt
- GLAZE:
- 1 cup packed brown sugar
- 1/4 cup vinegar
- 1 tbsp. ground mustard

Direction

- Set an oven to 350 degrees and start preheating. In a food processor, working in batches, pulse the ham until ground finely. Blend the next 7 ingredients until they are just combined. Form into 1-inch balls; on greased 15x10-inch rimmed baking pans, arrange them in a single layer.
- For the glaze: In a small saucepan, stir and cook all the ingredients on medium heat until the sugar has dissolved. Spread over the ham balls. Bake for 30-35 minutes until the ham balls just starts to brown, rotate the pans and stir carefully halfway through. Toss them gently in the glaze. Then serve warm.

Nutrition Information

- Calories: 52 calories
- Total Carbohydrate: 5 g
- Cholesterol: 11 mg
- Total Fat: 2 g
- Fiber: 0 g
- Protein: 3 g
- Sodium: 113 mg

339. Ham Ballz

"A tasty mustard sauce baked with balls of ham."
Serving: 18 | Prep: 30m | Ready in: 3h50m

Ingredients

- 3 lbs. ground ham
- 1 1/2 lbs. ground pork
- 1/2 lb. ground beef
- 1 1/2 cups cracker crumbs
- 3 eggs
- 1 1/2 cups milk
- 1/2 cup chopped onion (optional)
- 1/2 cup all-purpose flour for coating
- 1 3/4 cups brown sugar

- 1 1/2 cups water
- 2/3 cup vinegar
- 2 tbsps. dry mustard

Direction

- Combine the onion, milk, eggs, cracker crumbs, beef and pork, and ground ham in a large bowl. Shape 1/2 cupfuls of meat into balls and roll them in the flour. Arrange in a baking dish, then put in the fridge for 2 hours or overnight.
- Set an oven to 175°C (350°F) and start preheating. In a saucepan, combine the mustard, vinegar, water, and brown sugar. Mix them thoroughly, and boil. Before baking, place over the ham balls.
- In the prepared oven, bake and baste with the drippings from time to time for an hour and 20 minutes.

Nutrition Information

- Calories: 499 calories;
- Total Carbohydrate: 29.1 g
- Cholesterol: 136 mg
- Total Fat: 27.1 g
- Protein: 32.7 g
- Sodium: 268 mg

340. Hearty Party Meatballs

"A filling, flavorful appetizer."
Serving: 2 dozen. | Prep: 45m | Ready in: 01h25m

Ingredients

- 4 bacon strips, diced
- 2 tsps. beef bouillon granules
- 2 cups boiling water
- 1 egg
- 1/4 cup dry bread crumbs
- 3/4 tsp. salt, divided
- Dash pepper
- 1 lb. lean ground beef
- 2 medium onions, sliced and separated into rings
- 1/4 cup all-purpose flour
- 1 can (12 oz.) beer or 1-1/2 cups beef broth
- 2 tsps. brown sugar
- 2 tsps. white vinegar
- 1/2 tsp. dried thyme
- 1/4 to 1/2 tsp. browning sauce, optional

Direction

- Cook bacon in a small skillet over medium heat until crisp; then remove to paper towels. Drain and reserve the drippings. Dissolve bouillon in boiling water in a small bowl. Combine 1/4 cup of bouillon, egg, pepper, 1/4 tsp. salt, and bread crumbs in a large bowl. Crumble the beef over the mixture and mix well. Form into 1-in. balls.
- In a large skillet, put in 1 tbsp. of the reserved bacon drippings and brown the meatballs; drain. Transfer to a greased 11x7-in. baking dish using a slotted spoon. Sauté onions in the same skillet until softened; drain. Put over the meatballs.
- Mix 2 tbsps. of reserved drippings and flour in a saucepan until smooth. Stir gradually in the remaining bouillon and beer or broth. Add the remaining salt, thyme, vinegar, and brown sugar. Bring to a boil; then cook and stir until thickened, for 2 minutes. If desired, stir in the browning sauce. Next, pour over the meatballs. Bake at 350°, covered, until meat is no more pink, for 40-45 minutes. Dust with bacon.

Nutrition Information

- Calories: 225 calories
- Total Carbohydrate: 12 g
- Cholesterol: 69 mg
- Total Fat: 12 g
- Fiber: 1 g
- Protein: 14 g
- Sodium: 566 mg

341. Hoisin Meatballs

"You can use beef broth instead of wine to make the hoisin sauce."

Serving: about 2 dozen. | Prep: 15m | Ready in: 02h45m

Ingredients

- 1 cup dry red wine or beef broth
- 3 tbsps. hoisin sauce
- 2 tbsps. soy sauce
- 1 large egg
- 4 green onions, chopped
- 1/4 cup finely chopped onion
- 1/4 cup minced fresh cilantro
- 2 garlic cloves, minced
- 1/2 tsp. salt
- 1/2 tsp. pepper
- 1 lb. ground beef
- 1 lb. ground pork
- Sesame seeds

Direction

- Start preheating the broiler. Beat the soy sauce, hoisin sauce, and wine together in a 3-quart slow cooker. Put a cover on and cook on high for half an hour. At the same time, blend the next 7 ingredients. Put in pork and beef; combine lightly yet thoroughly. Form them into 1 1/2-inch meatballs; in a broiler pan, arrange them on a rack. Broil 3-4 inches away from the heat for 3-4 minutes until they are browned.
- Drop the meatballs into the slow cooker. Put a cover on, cook and stir halfway through on low for 2-3 hours until the meatballs are cooked thoroughly. Dust with the sesame seeds. Freeze option: Put the cooled meatball mixture in the freezer containers to freeze. Put in the fridge overnight to thaw partially to use. Put a cover on, microwave on high and stir gently halfway through for approximately 8 minutes until heated thoroughly.

Nutrition Information

- Calories: 73 calories
- Total Carbohydrate: 1 g
- Cholesterol: 28 mg
- Total Fat: 5 g
- Fiber: 0 g
- Protein: 6 g
- Sodium: 156 mg

342. Italian Turkey Meatballs

"These meatballs are packed with the Italy flavors."

Serving: 8

Ingredients

- 1 1/2 lbs. ground lean turkey
- 1/4 cup shredded Parmesan cheese
- 2/3 cup dry Italian bread crumbs
- 1/3 cup chopped fresh parsley
- 3 tbsps. chopped fresh oregano
- 2 tsps. chopped fresh rosemary
- 1 tsp. dry mustard
- 1/4 cup tomato sauce
- 1/4 tsp. salt
- 1/2 tsp. crushed red pepper
- 3 garlic cloves, minced
- 2 tsps. Melt® Organic Buttery Spread, softened

Direction

- Set the oven at 400° to preheat.
- In a bowl, mix all the ingredients except for the Melt(R); stir well. Roll out around 30 balls of the mixture. Use the melted Melt to coat a broiler pan, then put the balls on. Bake until the inside of a cut meatball is not pink anymore, for around 15 minutes. Server with sauce and pasta or place on a sandwich.

Nutrition Information

- Calories: 188 calories;
- Total Carbohydrate: 8.1 g
- Cholesterol: 65 mg
- Total Fat: 8.6 g
- Protein: 19.6 g

- Sodium: 351 mg

343. Joe's B.b.q Barbecue Meatballs

"It'll be a great game-day snack."
Serving: about 3-1/2 dozen. | Prep: 30m | Ready in: 40m

Ingredients

- 2 eggs, lightly beaten
- 1/2 cup dry bread crumbs
- 1/4 cup barbecue sauce
- 2 tbsps. dried minced onion
- 1 tbsp. brown sugar
- 1 tbsp. ketchup
- 2 garlic cloves, minced
- 1 lb. Johnsonville® Ground Mild Italian sausage
- 3/4 lb. ground beef
- SAUCE:
- 1 tbsp. canola oil
- 1 cup chopped sweet onion
- 1 can (15 oz.) tomato sauce
- 1/4 cup packed brown sugar
- 1/4 cup barbecue sauce
- 1 tbsp. Italian seasoning
- 1 tbsp. Dijon mustard
- 1 cup shredded part-skim mozzarella cheese, optional

Direction

- Set the oven at 400°F to preheat. Combine the first 7 ingredients in a large bowl. Add beef and sausage; lightly mix but thoroughly. Roll into 1-1/4-in. balls. In a shallow baking pan, place the balls on a greased rack. Bake until cooked through, about 10-12 minutes.
- In the meantime, to make the sauce: Over medium-high heat, heat oil in a Dutch oven. Add onion; cook and stir until softened. Next, stir in mustard, Italian seasoning, barbecue sauce, brown sugar, and tomato sauce; bring to a boil. Lower the heat, uncover and simmer until slightly thickened, about 6-8 minutes, occasionally stirring.
- Put in the meatballs and gently stir to coat. Sprinkle with cheese if desired, cover and allow to stand for 5 minutes.

344. Meatballs In Cherry Sauce

"These tasty home-cooked meatballs with a cherry glaze that are a great dish for Christmas gathering."
Serving: about 3-1/2 dozen. | Prep: 30m | Ready in: 45m

Ingredients

- 1 cup seasoned bread crumbs
- 1 small onion, chopped
- 1 egg, lightly beaten
- 3 garlic cloves, minced
- 1 tsp. salt
- 1/2 tsp. pepper
- 1 lb. lean ground beef (90% lean)
- 1 lb. ground pork
- SAUCE:
- 1 can (21 oz.) cherry pie filling
- 1/3 cup sherry or chicken broth
- 1/3 cup cider vinegar
- 1/4 cup steak sauce
- 2 tbsps. brown sugar
- 2 tbsps. reduced-sodium soy sauce
- 1 tsp. honey

Direction

- Set an oven to 400 degrees and start preheating. Blend the first 6 ingredients in a large bowl. Add in pork and beef; combine lightly yet thoroughly. Form into 1-inch balls. In a shallow baking pan, arrange on a greased rack. Bake till cooked completely or for 11-13 minutes. Place on paper towels to drain.
- Blend the sauce ingredients in a large saucepan. Boil and constantly stir on medium heat. Turn down the heat; remove the cover and bring to a simmer until thick, or for 2-3 minutes. Drop in the meatballs, heat thoroughly and gently stir.

Nutrition Information

- Calories: 76 calories
- Total Carbohydrate: 7 g
- Cholesterol: 19 mg
- Total Fat: 3 g
- Fiber: 0 g
- Protein: 5 g
- Sodium: 169 mg

345. Mexican Style Meatballs

"Delicious mini meatballs in chipotle tomato sauce."
Serving: 20 | Prep: 25m | Ready in: 1h10m

Ingredients

- 1 1/2 lbs. ground beef
- 1 1/2 lbs. ground pork
- 2 eggs
- 1 1/2 cups plain dried bread crumbs
- 1 tsp. salt
- 1 tsp. ground black pepper
- 2 cloves garlic, minced
- 1/2 cup water
- 2 (28 oz.) cans diced tomatoes with juice
- 3 chipotle peppers in adobo sauce
- 4 tsps. vegetable oil
- 2 small onions, minced
- 4 cloves garlic, minced
- 2 tsps. ground cumin
- 2 cups chicken broth
- 1 tsp. salt
- 1/2 cup chopped fresh cilantro, for garnish (optional)

Direction

- With your hands, combine together the water, 2 cloves of minced garlic, pepper, 1 tsp. of salt, bread crumbs, eggs and ground beef and pork in a big bowl. Shape into an-inch meatballs, and reserve on a waxed paper piece.
- Into a blender container, put the diced tomatoes together with chipotle peppers. Process till velvety, and reserve.
- In a big Dutch oven, heat oil over medium heat. Put onion; cook and mix till soft. Mix in cumin and the rest of garlic, and allow to cook for several minutes to let the fragrance out. Add in chicken broth and tomato mixture. Put the leftover tsp. of salt to season, and combine thoroughly. Boil, then while browning the meatballs, allow to simmer over low heat.
- Over medium-high heat, heat a big skillet. Coat with cooking spray. Put meatballs, but ensure not to overcrowd them. If needed, fry them in 2 batches. Let cook, mixing from time to time till outside is browned. Take off from skillet, and put into pot of simmering sauce. Allow the meatballs to simmer in sauce for approximately half an hour. Or longer if preferred.
- For special events, put the meatballs in a chafing dish with sauce, and garnish with cilantro, serve.

Nutrition Information

- Calories: 245 calories;
- Total Carbohydrate: 9.8 g
- Cholesterol: 70 mg
- Total Fat: 15.9 g
- Protein: 14.3 g
- Sodium: 473 mg

346. One-bite Tamales

"A wonderful meatballs dish for a holiday meal."
Serving: about 5-1/2 dozen. | Prep: 40m | Ready in: 04h00m

Ingredients

- 1-1/4 cups cornmeal
- 1/2 cup all-purpose flour
- 5-3/4 cups V8 juice, divided
- 4 tsps. chili powder, divided
- 4 tsps. ground cumin, divided
- 2 tsps. salt, divided
- 1 tsp. garlic powder
- 1/2 to 1 tsp. cayenne pepper

- 1 lb. bulk spicy pork sausage
- Tortilla chip scoops

Direction

- Set an oven to 350 degrees and start preheating. Combine the cayenne, garlic powder, a tsp. of salt, 2 tsps. of cumin, 2 tsps. of chili powder, 3/4 cup of V8 juice, flour, and cornmeal. Put in sausage; stir lightly yet thoroughly. Form into 1-inch balls.
- On a greased rack in a 15x10-inch pan, arrange the meatballs. Bake for 20-25 minutes until cooked thoroughly.
- At the same time, combine salt, cumin, chili powder, and the remaining V8 juice in a 4-quart slow cooker. Stir in the meatballs gently. Put a cover on and cook on low for 3-4 hours until heated thoroughly. Serve together with tortilla chip scoops.

Nutrition Information

- Calories: 37 calories
- Total Carbohydrate: 4 g
- Cholesterol: 4 mg
- Total Fat: 2 g
- Fiber: 0 g
- Protein: 1 g
- Sodium: 172 mg

347. Party Appetizer Meatballs

"What makes these meatballs taste so delicious is the sauce."

Serving: 8 dozen. | Prep: 15m | Ready in: 55m

Ingredients

- 2 lbs. lean ground beef
- 2 large eggs, lightly beaten
- 1 cup shredded part-skim mozzarella cheese
- 1/2 cup dry bread crumbs
- 1/4 cup finely chopped onion
- 2 tbsps. grated Parmesan cheese
- 1 tbsp. ketchup
- 2 tsps. Worcestershire sauce
- 1 tsp. Italian seasoning
- 1 tsp. dried basil
- 1 tsp. salt
- 1/4 tsp. pepper
- SAUCE:
- 1 bottle (14 oz.) hot or regular ketchup
- 2 tbsps. cornstarch
- 1 jar (12 oz.) apple jelly
- 1 jar (12 oz.) currant jelly

Direction

- Combine the first 12 ingredients in a bowl. Roll into 1-in. balls. In a shallow baking pan, arrange the meatballs on a greased rack.
- Bake for 10-15 minutes at 350°; drain. In a roasting pan, combine cornstarch and ketchup. Stir in jellies, put in the meatballs. Cover and continue to bake for another 30 minutes.

Nutrition Information

- Calories: 133 calories
- Total Carbohydrate: 19 g
- Cholesterol: 34 mg
- Total Fat: 3 g
- Fiber: 0 g
- Protein: 7 g
- Sodium: 271 mg

348. Passover Meatballs

"These nice and moist meatballs are great for the spring holiday season."

Serving: 6 dozen. | Prep: 30m | Ready in: 01h20m

Ingredients

- 2 eggs, lightly beaten
- 1 cup water, divided
- 1-1/2 cups finely chopped onion, divided
- 1/2 cup matzo meal
- 1 tsp. salt
- 1/4 tsp. pepper
- 2 lbs. ground beef
- 1 can (8 oz.) tomato sauce

- 1 cup sugar
- 1/2 cup lemon juice

Direction

- Combine the eggs, pepper, salt, matzo meal, 1/2 cup onion, and 1/2 cup water in a large bowl. Crumble the beef over the mixture and blend well. Roll into 1-in. balls.
- Combine the remaining water and onion, lemon juice, sugar, and tomato sauce in a Dutch oven. Add meatballs and boil. Reduce the heat; simmer, covered, until the meat is no longer pink, for 45 minutes. Use a slotted spoon to serve with.

Nutrition Information

- Calories: 74 calories
- Total Carbohydrate: 8 g
- Cholesterol: 24 mg
- Total Fat: 3 g
- Fiber: 0 g
- Protein: 5 g
- Sodium: 115 mg

349. Peppered Meatballs

"These saucy meatballs are so hearty with plenty of ground pepper."

Serving: 1-1/2 dozen. | Prep: 35m | Ready in: 02h35m

Ingredients

- 1/2 cup sour cream
- 2 tsps. grated Parmesan or Romano cheese
- 2 to 3 tsps. pepper
- 1 tsp. salt
- 1 tsp. dry bread crumbs
- 1/2 tsp. garlic powder
- 1-1/2 lbs. ground beef
- SAUCE:
- 1 can (10-3/4 oz.) condensed cream of mushroom soup, undiluted
- 1 cup (8 oz.) sour cream
- 2 tsps. dill weed
- 1/2 tsp. sugar
- 1/2 tsp. pepper
- 1/4 tsp. garlic powder

Direction

- Combine cheese and sour cream in a large bowl. Add garlic powder, bread crumbs, salt, and pepper. Crumble the meat over the mixture and mix well. Roll into 1-in. balls.
- In a shallow baking pan, place the meatballs on a greased rack. Bake at 350° until no more pink, for 20-25 minutes; drain.
- Transfer the meatballs to a 1-1/2-qt. slow cooker. Mix the sauce ingredients, then pour over the meatballs. Cook on high, covered, until heated through, for 2-3 hours.

Nutrition Information

- Calories: 259 calories
- Total Carbohydrate: 5 g
- Cholesterol: 77 mg
- Total Fat: 18 g
- Fiber: 0 g
- Protein: 17 g
- Sodium: 565 mg

350. Piquant Meatballs

"“Meatballs baked in a well-seasoned sauce are on the menu all the time for our casual Christmas gatherings. Easy to reheat leftovers in a slow cooker-if there's any.”"

Serving: 4 dozen. | Prep: 20m | Ready in: 60m

Ingredients

- 1 can (14 oz.) jellied cranberry sauce
- 1 bottle (12 oz.) chili sauce
- 1 tbsp. lemon juice
- 2 eggs, lightly beaten
- 1 cup crushed cornflakes
- 1/3 cup ketchup
- 1/3 cup dried parsley flakes
- 3 tbsps. soy sauce
- 2 tbsps. dried minced onion

- 3/4 tsp. salt
- 1/2 tsp. pepper
- 1/4 tsp. garlic powder
- 2 lbs. lean ground beef (90% lean)

Direction

- Mix lemon juice, chili sauce, and cranberry sauce in a saucepan. Bring to a boil over medium heat; stir and cook until smooth. Put aside.
- Mix the next nine ingredients in a bowl; put in the beef and stir well. Form into 1-inch balls. Transfer to a greased 13x9-inch baking dish. Pour sauce over meatballs.
- Bake without a cover for 40 to 50 minutes at 350 degrees or until the sauce is bubbly meatballs are not pink.

Nutrition Information

- Calories: 183 calories
- Total Carbohydrate: 22 g
- Cholesterol: 54 mg
- Total Fat: 5 g
- Fiber: 1 g
- Protein: 13 g
- Sodium: 722 mg

351. Pistachio-turkey Meatballs In Orange Sauce

"Mini meatballs that everyone loves."
Serving: 4-1/2 dozen. | Prep: 25m | Ready in: 45m

Ingredients

- 2/3 cup chopped pistachios
- 2 green onions, finely chopped
- 1/4 cup dry bread crumbs
- 1 large egg, lightly beaten
- 1 tsp. grated orange zest
- 1/2 tsp. salt
- 1/8 tsp. pepper
- 1 lb. ground turkey
- 1 Johnsonville® Mild Italian Sausage Links (4 oz.), casing removed
- SAUCE:
- 3 tbsps. butter
- 1 tbsp. olive oil
- 1/4 cup finely chopped sweet red pepper
- 1/8 tsp. crushed red pepper flakes
- 2 tbsps. white wine
- 4 tsps. cornstarch
- 1 cup orange juice
- 1/2 cup reduced-sodium chicken broth
- 1 tbsp. honey
- 1/2 tsp. grated orange zest
- 1 tbsp. minced fresh basil
- 2 tbsps. chopped pistachios

Direction

- Preheat an oven to 375°. Mix initial 7 ingredients in big bowl. Add sausage and turkey; lightly but thoroughly mix. Form to 1-in. balls.
- On greased racks inside shallow baking pans, put meatballs. Bake till cooked through or for 18-22 minutes.
- Heat oil and butter on medium heat in big skillet. Add pepper flakes and red pepper; mix and cook till red pepper is tender or for 2-3 minutes. Add wine and cook for 1 minute more.
- Whisk orange zest, honey, broth, orange juice and cornstarch till blended in small bowl. Mix into pan; boil. Mix and cook till thickened or for 1-2 minutes. Mix meatballs and basil in. Sprinkle pistachios on.

Nutrition Information

- Calories: 49 calories
- Total Carbohydrate: 2 g
- Cholesterol: 12 mg
- Total Fat: 4 g
- Fiber: 0 g
- Protein: 2 g
- Sodium: 66 mg

352. Potluck Meatballs

""A hearty mini meatballs that you can't miss and make a good main dish over noodles too.""
Serving: 2-1/2 dozen. | Prep: 25m | Ready in: 60m

Ingredients

- 1 egg, lightly beaten
- 2/3 cup soft bread crumbs
- 1/2 cup grated onion
- 1 tsp. salt
- 1/2 tsp. ground allspice
- 1/4 tsp. pepper
- 1 lb. ground beef
- 1 tbsp. cornstarch
- 1 can (10-1/2 oz.) condensed beef consomme, undiluted

Direction

- Mix the first six ingredients in a large bowl; break beef into pieces over mixture and stir well. Form into 1-1/4-inch balls. Brown meatballs in batches in a large skillet; drain.
- Bring to a 1-1/2-qt baking dish that is greased. Mix consomme and cornstarch until smooth; add into the skillet. Bring to a boil, whisking to loosen browned bits from the pan. Boil for 2 minutes or until thickened.
- Pour over the meatballs. Bake for 35 to 40 minutes at 350 degrees, uncovered, or until not pink anymore.

Nutrition Information

- Calories: 117 calories
- Total Carbohydrate: 4 g
- Cholesterol: 53 mg
- Total Fat: 6 g
- Fiber: 0 g
- Protein: 11 g
- Sodium: 477 mg

353. Rosemary Sausage Meatballs

"A wonderful recipe to make a great starter of a meal or a tasty appetizer."
Serving: about 2 dozen. | Prep: 20m | Ready in: 45m

Ingredients

- 2 tbsps. olive oil
- 4 garlic cloves, minced
- 1 tsp. curry powder
- 1 large egg, lightly beaten
- 1 jar (4 oz.) diced pimientos, drained
- 1/4 cup dry bread crumbs
- 1/4 cup minced fresh parsley
- 2 tbsps. minced fresh rosemary
- 2 lbs. Jones No Sugar Pork Sausage Roll sausage
- Pretzel sticks or toothpicks, optional

Direction

- Set an oven to 350 degrees and start preheating. Heat the oil in a small skillet on medium; sauté the garlic together with the curry powder for 1-2 minutes until it becomes tender. Allow to slightly cool.
- Blend the garlic mixture, rosemary, parsley, breadcrumbs, pimentos, and egg in a bowl. Put in the sausage; combine lightly yet thoroughly.
- Form into 1 1/4-inch balls. In a 15x10x1-inch pan, arrange them on a greased rack. Bake for 25-30 minutes until they are cooked thoroughly. Serve together with pretzels if desired.

354. Saucy Sweet And Sour Meatballs

"These saucy meatballs fastly disappear."
Serving: About 3 dozen. | Prep: 20m | Ready in: 50m

Ingredients

- 1 bottle (12 oz.) chili sauce
- 1 jar (10 oz.) sweet-and-sour sauce

- 1 cup pineapple chunks
- 2 tbsps. brown sugar
- 1 egg, lightly beaten
- 2 tbsps. crushed saltines
- 1/2 tsp. ground allspice
- 1/4 tsp. ground nutmeg
- 1 lb. Jones No Sugar Pork Sausage Roll sausage
- 1 large green pepper, cut into 1-inch pieces

Direction

- Combine brown sugar, pineapple, sweet-and-sour sauce, and chili sauce in a large saucepan; bring to a boil. Lower the heat; simmer, covered, for 15 minutes.
- In the meantime, combine nutmeg, allspice, cracker crumbs, and egg in a large bowl. Crumble the sausage over the mixture and blend well. Roll into 1-in. balls.
- Broil the meatballs 4-5 in. from the heat until a thermometer states 160°, about 6-8 minutes; drain. Put the meatballs and green pepper into the sauce. Uncover and simmer until heated through, about 10 minutes.

Nutrition Information

- Calories: 165 calories
- Total Carbohydrate: 22 g
- Cholesterol: 31 mg
- Total Fat: 8 g
- Fiber: 0 g
- Protein: 3 g
- Sodium: 762 mg

355. Sausage Cheese Bites Snack

"A delicious sack to serve for a warm a family gathering or evening meal."

Serving: 16 servings. | Prep: 15m | Ready in: 30m

Ingredients

- 1 lb. mild Jones No Sugar Pork Sausage Roll
- 4 cups biscuit/baking mix
- 2 cups shredded cheddar cheese
- 1 cup water

Direction

- Cook the sausage in a skillet on medium heat until it is not pink anymore; drain off the sausage.
- Blend the cheese and baking mix in a large bowl. Put in the sausage and stir until combined thoroughly. Pour in water and stir until just blended. Form into 1 1/2-inch balls.
- Arrange them on the greased baking sheets. Bake at 375 degrees until golden brown, or for 15 minutes.

Nutrition Information

- Calories: 230 calories
- Total Carbohydrate: 19 g
- Cholesterol: 25 mg
- Total Fat: 14 g
- Fiber: 1 g
- Protein: 7 g
- Sodium: 579 mg

356. Sausage-cheese Balls

"A great recipe to make a tasty appetizer that should be shared with others"

Serving: 24 | Prep: 20m | Ready in: 45m

Ingredients

- 3 cups Original Bisquick® mix
- 1 lb. uncooked bulk pork sausage
- 4 cups shredded Cheddar cheese
- 1/2 cup grated Parmesan cheese
- 1/2 cup milk
- 1/2 tsp. dried rosemary leaves, crushed
- 1 1/2 tsps. chopped fresh parsley
- Barbecue sauce or chili sauce, if desired

Direction

- Heat the oven to 350°F. Lightly grease the sides and bottom of a 15 1/2x10 1/2x2x1-inch jelly roll pan.
- Stir all the ingredients together with spoon or hands. Form the mixture into 1-inch balls. Arrange them in the greased pan.
- Bake until brown, or for 20-25 minutes. Take out from the pan right away. Serve warm together with the sauce for dipping.

Nutrition Information

- Calories: 220 calories;
- Total Carbohydrate: 11.9 g
- Cholesterol: 37 mg
- Total Fat: 14.6 g
- Protein: 10.2 g
- Sodium: 586 mg

357. Slow Cooker Sweet And Sour Meatballs

"This amazing recipe for meatballs can be applied for both spring and winter meals."

Serving: 3 dozen. | Prep: 30m | Ready in: 03h30m

Ingredients

- 2 large eggs, lightly beaten
- 1/4 cup panko (Japanese) bread crumbs
- 2 garlic cloves, minced
- 2 tsps. salt-free garlic herb seasoning blend
- 1/2 tsp. salt
- 1/4 tsp. pepper
- 2 lbs. ground beef
- 1 can (15 oz.) tomato sauce
- 1 cup chicken broth
- 1 bottle (12 oz.) chili sauce
- 1/2 cup packed brown sugar
- 1/2 cup cider or white vinegar
- 1 green onion, thinly sliced

Direction

- Set an oven to 375 degrees and start preheating. Blend the first 6 ingredients in a large bowl. Put in the beef; combine lightly yet thoroughly. Form into 1 1/2 inch meatballs. In a 15x10x1-inch baking pan, arrange the meatballs on a greased rack. Bake until they are lightly browned, or for 15-20 minutes.
- Blend the vinegar, brown sugar, chili sauce, broth, and tomato sauce in a large bowl. Place the meatballs into a 5-quart slow cooker. Place the sauce over the top. Put a cover on and cook on low heat until the meatballs are cooked thoroughly, or for 3-4 hours. Dust with green onion to serve.

Nutrition Information

- Calories: 77 calories
- Total Carbohydrate: 7 g
- Cholesterol: 26 mg
- Total Fat: 3 g
- Fiber: 0 g
- Protein: 5 g
- Sodium: 292 mg

358. Spicy Pineapple Sauce

"This ginger spiced pineapple and maple syrup sauce is perfect to go with meatballs."

Serving: 24 | Prep: 20m | Ready in: 45m

Ingredients

- 1 (20 oz.) can crushed pineapple in heavy syrup, drained with syrup reserved
- 1 tbsp. cornstarch
- 1 tsp. ground ginger
- 3/4 cup orange juice
- 2 tbsps. maple syrup

Direction

- Combine together ground ginger, cornstarch and crushed pineapple in a medium-sized bowl, then stir in sufficient reserved pineapple juice, gradually, to make the mixture smooth.

- Blend together maple syrup with orange juice in a medium saucepan on medium heat, then cook and stir until thickened and clear, about 5 minutes. Blend in the pineapple mixture and keep on cooking and stirring for 15 minutes, until thick and well-blended.

Nutrition Information

- Calories: 28 calories;
- Total Carbohydrate: 7.1 g
- Cholesterol: 0 mg
- Total Fat: 0 g
- Protein: 0.1 g
- Sodium: < 1 mg

359. Swedish Meatballs II

" "Swedish meatballs recipe; old and classic. Serve with fresh bread and sautéed vegetables." "
Serving: 4 | Prep: 25m | Ready in: 55m

Ingredients

- 6 tbsps. butter, divided
- 1 onion, chopped
- 1 cup dried bread crumbs
- 1 cup evaporated milk, divided
- 1 1/2 lbs. ground beef
- 1 egg, beaten
- 1 tsp. salt
- 1/4 tsp. ground black pepper
- 1 pinch dried parsley
- 1 1/2 tsps. all-purpose flour
- 1 tbsp. tomato sauce
- ground nutmeg to taste

Direction

- In a large skillet placed over medium heat, melt 3 tbsps. of butter. Sauté the onion for 5 to 10 minutes, or until soft.
- Mix the bread crumbs with 2 tbsps. of evaporated milk in a separate bowl. Stir to ensure the milk is absorbed by the crumbs. Add the egg, salt, ground beef, parsley, ground black pepper and onion to taste. Combine well and shape into meatballs of a golf ball size.
- Melt the rest of the butter in the same skillet over medium- to medium-high heat and mix in the meatballs. Turn the meatballs by carefully shaking the skillet, as needed. Sauté until meatballs are browned on all sides, or for 10 to 15 minutes. Put the meatballs in a serving platter, leave the liquid in the skillet. Stir flour into the skillet until it becomes smooth. Slowly add the nutmeg, evaporated milk and tomato sauce to taste, stirring until the mixture is smooth, creamy and warmed. Strain over meatballs.

Nutrition Information

- Calories: 906 calories;
- Total Carbohydrate: 29.6 g
- Cholesterol: 255 mg
- Total Fat: 70 g
- Protein: 38.5 g
- Sodium: 1124 mg

360. Sweet And Sour Meatballs

" "Slow-cooked meatballs in a sweet and sour sauce." "
Serving: 12 | Prep: 20m | Ready in: 1h50m

Ingredients

- 1 (12 fluid oz.) can or bottle chile sauce
- 2 tsps. lemon juice
- 9 oz. grape jelly
- 1 lb. lean ground beef
- 1 egg, beaten
- 1 large onion, grated
- salt to taste

Direction

- Mix grape jelly, lemon juice, and chili sauce. Pour into the slow cooker and simmer on low heat until warm.

- Mix salt, onion, egg, and ground beef. Stir well and roll into 1 inch balls. Put into the sauce and simmer for 1 1/2 hours.

Nutrition Information

- Calories: 152 calories;
- Total Carbohydrate: 17.4 g
- Cholesterol: 38 mg
- Total Fat: 5.6 g
- Protein: 8.3 g
- Sodium: 22 mg

361. Sweet And Sour Meatballs I

"Well-heated meatballs dipped in a sour and sweet sauce."
Serving: 7 | Prep: 10m | Ready in: 5h10m

Ingredients

- 2 lbs. ground beef
- 1 egg
- 1 onion, chopped
- 1 pinch salt
- 1 (12 fluid oz.) can or bottle chili sauce
- 2 tsps. lemon juice
- 1 cup grape jelly

Direction

- Place the salt, onion, egg, and beef in a large bowl. Combine them together, form into little balls.
- Blend the grape jelly, lemon juice, and chili sauce in a slow cooker. Add in the meatballs and stir, cook for 4-5 hours on high.

Nutrition Information

- Calories: 562 calories;
- Total Carbohydrate: 37.5 g
- Cholesterol: 137 mg
- Total Fat: 35.2 g
- Protein: 24 g
- Sodium: 99 mg

362. Taco Meatballs

"These meatballs makes really a big difference from what you have imagined."
Serving: 3-1/2 dozen. | Prep: 45m | Ready in: 60m

Ingredients

- 1 cup biscuit/baking mix
- 1 envelope taco seasoning
- 1 cup shredded cheddar cheese
- 1/2 cup water
- 1 lb. lean ground beef (90% lean)
- Salsa and taco sauce

Direction

- Mix the first 4 ingredients together in a big bowl. Crumble the beef over the mixture and combine well. Form into balls with 1 inch size.
- On a greased rack in a shallow baking pan, position meat balls. Bake at 350° without a cover until balls are not pink anymore, for 15 to 20 minutes. Drain, then serve together with taco sauce and salsa.

Nutrition Information

- Calories: 120 calories
- Total Carbohydrate: 8 g
- Cholesterol: 24 mg
- Total Fat: 6 g
- Fiber: 0 g
- Protein: 9 g
- Sodium: 407 mg

363. Tangy And Sweet Meatballs

""I often present these savory meatballs for our guests and everybody enjoys the special sauce and surprised to know that it's made with gingersnaps.""
Serving: 8 servings. | Prep: 30m | Ready in: 01h10m

Ingredients

- 3 large eggs
- 1 medium onion, chopped

- 1-1/2 cups dry bread crumbs
- 1 tsp. salt
- 2 lbs. ground beef
- 2 tbsps. canola oil
- SAUCE:
- 3-1/2 cups tomato juice
- 1 cup packed brown sugar
- 10 gingersnaps, finely crushed
- 1/4 cup white vinegar
- 1 tsp. onion salt

Direction

- Mix the salt, bread crumbs, onion, and eggs in a large bowl. Crumble beef over the mixture and stir well. Form into 1-1/2-inch balls.
- Brown meatballs in batches in oil in a large skillet. Transfer to a 13x9-inch baking dish that is greased.
- Mix the sauce ingredients in a large saucepan. Bring to a boil over medium heat, stirring until cookie crumbs are dissolved. Pour over meatballs.
- Bake without a cover for 40-45 minutes at 350 degrees or until the meat is not pink anymore.

Nutrition Information

- Calories: 526 calories
- Total Carbohydrate: 55 g
- Cholesterol: 155 mg
- Total Fat: 21 g
- Fiber: 1 g
- Protein: 29 g
- Sodium: 1226 mg

364. Tangy Pork Meatballs

"A delicious recipe with barbecue sauce."
Serving: 7-1/2 dozen. | Prep: 15m | Ready in: 30m

Ingredients

- 2 eggs, lightly beaten
- 2/3 cup dry bread crumbs
- 2 tbsps. dried minced onion
- 2 tsps. seasoned salt
- 2 lbs. ground pork
- SAUCE:
- 1-1/2 cups ketchup
- 1 can (8 oz.) tomato sauce
- 3 tbsps. Worcestershire sauce
- 2 to 3 tbsps. cider vinegar
- 2 tsps. liquid smoke, optional

Direction

- Combine the eggs, salt, onion, and bread crumbs in a large bowl. Crumble the pork over the mixture and blend well. Roll into 3/4-in. balls.
- In a shallow baking pan, put the meatballs on the greased rack. Bake at 400° until a thermometer reads 160°, for 15 minutes; drain.
- In the meantime, combine the sauce ingredients in a large saucepan. Uncover and simmer for 10 minutes, stirring sometimes. Put in the meatballs. Serve in a chafing dish or 5-qt. slow cooker.

Nutrition Information

- Calories: 95 calories
- Total Carbohydrate: 6 g
- Cholesterol: 34 mg
- Total Fat: 5 g
- Fiber: 0 g
- Protein: 7 g
- Sodium: 336 mg

365. The Best Sweet And Sour Meatballs

"Pleasant served with rice."
Serving: 4 | Prep: 20m | Ready in: 1h

Ingredients

- 1 lb. ground beef
- 1 egg
- 1/4 cup dry bread crumbs
- 1 onion, diced

- 1 cup packed brown sugar
- 3 tbsps. all-purpose flour
- 1 1/2 cups water
- 1/4 cup distilled white vinegar
- 3 tbsps. soy sauce

Direction

- Combine onion, bread crumbs, egg, and ground beef in a medium bowl. Thoroughly mix and roll into golf ball-sized balls.
- Over medium heat, gently brown the meatballs in a large skillet, then put aside.
- Combine soy sauce, white vinegar, water, flour, and brown sugar in a large saucepan. Mix thoroughly. Place in the meatballs and bring to a boil. Lower the heat and simmer for 30 minutes, stirring regularly.

Nutrition Information

- Calories: 516 calories;
- Total Carbohydrate: 67.1 g
- Cholesterol: 122 mg
- Total Fat: 16.8 g
- Protein: 24.5 g
- Sodium: 815 mg

Index

A

B

C

D

E

F

G

H

I

J

K

L

M

N

O

P

Q

R

S

T

Conclusion

Thank you again for downloading this book!

I hope you enjoyed reading about my book!

If you enjoyed this book, please take the time to share your thoughts and post a review on Amazon. It'd be greatly appreciated!

Write me an honest review about the book – I truly value your opinion and thoughts and I will incorporate them into my next book, which is already underway.

Thank you!

If you have any questions, **feel free to contact at:** *mrappetizer@mrandmscooking.com*

Mr. Appetizer

www.MrandMsCooking.com

Made in the USA
Monee, IL
20 September 2025